Rural and Small Town Planning

D1714781

Prepared for:
Old West Regional Commission
Billings, Montana

Prepared by:
American Planning Association
Washington, D.C.
Chicago, Illinois

Judith Getzels and Charles Thurow, Editors

Planners Press, Chicago 60637

This book is the result of tax-supported research and as such is not subject to copyright. Portions of the book may be freely reprinted with customary credit to the source, except where material is specifically covered by prior copyright, as noted herein.

ISBN 0–918286–19–0

Library of Congress Catalog Card Number 79-93345

Table of Contents

Foreword

Rural America is changing. New growth is coming from energy development, from increased agricultural demands and from recreational and second home developments. Along with this change comes a greater need for planning.

Rural planning is different from urban planning. The problems are different, the solutions are different, and the available resources to get the job done are different. Most important, the people are different. They have different attitudes toward the land, different institutions, and different traditions. Of course, there are many similarities too, but the differences have received too little attention.

This book is about planning in rural areas. It is written for the young professional new to the task of rural planning. It focuses on the Old West Region—Nebraska, South Dakota, North Dakota, Montana, and Wyoming—because it is the result of a manual prepared by APA's research division for the Old West Regional Commission. Because the American Planning Association's Planners' Press felt it would be useful to rural planners in many other states as well, we sought and received the kind permission of the Commission and the U.S. Department of Commerce, funder of the work, to distribute the book throughout the nation. The book covers general plan preparation, implementation tools such as subdivision regulations, zoning and development permitting, as well as planning techniques for infrastructure, transportation, housing, and community services.

The rural planner must be resourceful, and be a skilled technician tackling a wide range of problems with limited resources. Just as important, the planning must be politically astute, responsive to the needs of the people the planner serves. In rural planning the trick is to do what works best—to innovate, to improvise, to rely on common sense. This book is designed to give the planner some tools to use to discover what will work.

12/79

Acknowledgments

The editors wish to express their appreciation for the assistance given by many agencies and individuals in writing this report.

We would particularly like to thank the individuals who served as advisors to this project. They not only provided their time and energy in reviewing drafts, but also provided ideas and suggestions on individual chapters. Their contributions added significantly to the content and style of the book. These advisors were: Senator Douglas Bereuter, Lincoln, Nebraska; Cal Cumin and Associates, Billings, Montana; Robert Kuzelka, Comprehensive Planning Coordinator, Nebraska Office of Planning and Programming, Lincoln, Nebraska; Joseph Racine, Planning Director, Gillette, Wyoming; Lowell Richards, Director, First Planning and Development District, Watertown, South Dakota; Newell Sorensen, Planning Director, Big Horn and Park Counties, Basin, Wyoming; Russell Staiger, Planning Administrator, North Dakota State Planning Division, Bismarck, North Dakota; Stan Steadman, Assistant Project Director, Western Coal Project, Missouri River Basin Commission, Billings, Montana; and Earl Stewart, Chairman, Department of Community and Regional Planning, North Dakota State University, Fargo, North Dakota.

We wish to thank Professor Paula Watson, City Planning and Landscape Architecture Librarian, University of Illinois at Urbana-Champaign, for the many publications she brought to our attention for use in Chapter 8. Randy Suko conducted the research on housing and wrote the first draft of that section of the same chapter.

In addition, we would like to give general thanks to the

members of the American Planning Association and other individuals who sent us materials and responded to our telephone inquiries. Among these individuals, we would specifically like to thank Jan Blickenstaff, Glendive, Montana, and Mark Hinthorne, Yakima, Washington, who gave Mr. Toner assistance on his chapter.

Finally, we wish to thank the Old West Regional Commission, especially David Gaarder and Jeannette Studer. Both served as project officers for this report.

While the material in this report was reviewed in draft by the staff of the Old West Regional Commission, the contents do not necessarily reflect the official views or policies of the Commission. The report was prepared under Contract No. 10670212 to the Old West Regional Commission and reflects the views of the contractor, the American Planning Association, which is solely responsible for the facts and accuracy of the information provided herein. Work was completed July, 1978.

The APA Research Program is an independent research activity supported by grants and contracts and devoted to advancing public agency planning practice. Individual research reports are not reviewed for approval by the Board of Directors or by the membership of the Association. Israel Stollman is the Executive Director, David Mosena is Director of Research.

Chapter I
Getting to Know the
People and the Place

Introduction

Suppose this is your first rural planning job and you have
become planning director of a rural county such as Perkins
County, South Dakota. In Perkins County there are a few small
towns, Lemmon (the largest) and Bison, Lodgepole, and Prairie
City to name some more. There are not too many people, and
most of them are ranchers or farmers. Growth would be something new to Perkins County, since the county has been losing
population since the turn of the century. Many of the people
have been on this land from homesteading days, the land
having passed from father to son.

If you were to ask the people of Perkins County about their
problems, they might talk about the bad weather, or they
might talk about getting a couple of roads paved. A few would
be concerned about the continued out-migration of young
people, but most citizens of Perkins County have taken this for
granted. It's not a problem anymore, it's just something that
happens. For many people housing would be a problem, but
this too would not generate tremendous concern. It's been a
problem for too long.

All of these things would be on the surface, evident to
nearly anyone with eyes or to anyone who would ask. There is
planning work to be done here, and planning could help the
people. And, right around the corner are coal companies who
are beginning to pay close attention to the lignite, and that
would change things (considerably). So it is an interesting,
challenging job—a typical one facing a new rural planner.

But where does one begin? People don't know you, and you don't know them. You haven't a planning commission to work with, and no county commissioner has even mentioned a plan or land-use regulations. In fact, you've almost been convinced that "planning" is a poor word here, something which generates a certain cold stare or frown. There are no other planners around, no one to talk to, and here you are in Perkins County. Where do you begin?

How does a novice rural planner begin work? What do you do first? Should you follow the textbook? Is there a textbook? Should you wait for something specific to do, or should you just do something, anything, to show that you can? Chances are that the county commissioners don't know exactly what it is they want you to do, but they do know that they don't want you telling them anything until they feel confident about you. So how do you perform in those uneasy first months?

Rural planners indicate that in general there are three major phases in the development of an effective rural planning program. By working through these phases, the new rural planner can meet the minimum standards necessary to good planning practice.

The first phase is "Getting to know the people and getting to know the place." While this is a continual responsibility for any conscientious planner, it is especially important in rural areas. A new planner should be spending most of the first months on the job working at this task. To accomplish this, there are a variety of useful techniques which will be discussed later.

The second phase is "Picking a problem and solving it— quickly and effectively." This means what it says—that the novice planner needs to identify a key problem which can be solved quickly and easily. The objective in this phase is to demonstrate to the rural clientele that a planner can do something—that given a specific problem, the planner can generate the resources to solve it. Obviously, this will rarely be a major problem since solving such a problem would take considerable time and resources. Instead, in this phase the planner selects a smaller, more manageable one.

In the third phase, "Selling planning," the novice planner begins to move in more traditional planning areas. Having laid the essential groundwork in the first two phases, the novice planner begins to work toward the preparation of plans and the eventual adoption of land-use regulations.

Novice planners should be cautioned that one never really completes any single phase. The nature of effective planning requires a planner to know more and more about the people and the place; it requires the planner to achieve continual success at a variety of problems; and it requires the planner to sell planning again and again through the planning process. Thus, each phase is continually repeated.

The degree of emphasis given to these phases in the first several months of work is important to the novice planner. It is in the early months that the reputation of the planner will be established, and it is at that time that the planner's success or failure will be assured. By following the experience of established rural planners, novice rural planners can avoid major mistakes and establish a successful rural planning practice.

But before taking a first rural planning job, the rural planner should consider the basic requirements for the job and the status of planning in rural areas. In almost all cases, a rural planner must be a generalist—someone versed in several areas of planning—since the work will require problem-solving skills throughout the planning spectrum and beyond. In many cases, the rural planner will be the single staff member of a local government. Thus, he or she must know something about city management, finance, transportation, capital improvements, water and sewer, fire and police—virtually every aspect of local government.

The most important skill of all for local planners is the ability to work with people. This is something which is not given much attention in traditional planning education. But for the rural planner who will be spending virtually all of the time working with local people, this skill is essential.

Finally, a rural planner must be willing to work in a professional void. As there will be little contact with fellow planners or even with other bureaucrats, there may not be any opportunity to discuss problems or alternative approaches with other planners. Most assistance, if it comes at all, will come through telephone discussions or by the few trips made outside the jurisdiction.

The People and the Place

While basic approaches to rural planning vary from planner to planner, almost all rural planners agree that to be effective, a new planner must know the people he works with. Planners can tell story after story of new rural planners who leaped into their jobs without knowing or understanding the people they were working for. In most cases, this abrupt entry damaged the planner's credibility and set effective planning back for months if not years to come.

The first step in getting to know the people and the place is to get rid of any assumptions you might have about "rural people" or "the rural way of life" or how rural people look at their jobs or what it is that rural people find important. About the only assumption that can be made is that rural people and rural areas are all different. There is no "rural consensus." What is important in one area will not be important in other areas. Although agriculture, for example, may be the dominant economic force in many rural places, it will not be the dominant force in all places. Likewise, economic and social forces in rural areas change, sometimes very quickly. Thus, what was important one or three or five years past may not be important today.

There are a variety of techniques that rural planners can use to increase their knowledge of their jurisdiction and the region in which the jurisdiction lies. A good way to begin is to try to understand local geography. The executive director of a Wyoming county planning department suggested, "Become totally familiar with the area—drive it, walk it, get your maps out, know the place names so that when you talk with people, they know that you know."

At a minimum the novice planner should become familiar with United States Geological Survey Topographic Maps (Scale 1:24,000) which are available for most of the country. Aerial photographs, often available from state planning offices or from state highway offices or from the Soil Conservation Service, are also useful. The planner should examine local topography, geology, hydrology, and soils, as well as roads, highways, and the names and locations of all cities and towns and unincorporated places. The best method is to walk and drive and bicycle the area until it becomes second nature.

During the same period, the planner should examine written materials that describe the social, economic, political and environmental structure of the area. Local libraries, historical societies, chambers of commerce, colleges and universities, soil conservation offices, and other local organizations house important materials. The planner should examine base data such as the Census of Population, the Census of Agriculture and the Census of Business and Industry.

Past issues of the local newspaper are excellent sources of information and will often generate insights on key local issues and the local political power structure. Books and magazine articles pertaining to the economic and social history of the area are also useful. Careful attention should be paid to the development of the local economy, and planners should note how the local economy has changed over the years.

After spending a little time on local geography, history, social and political structure and the local economy, it is important to begin to talk with the people, not in a formal interview, but just to ask questions—questions about their work, about their history, about the local economy. The objective here is to reach a loose cross-section of people who represent the basic political and social system of the area.

The key word in this task is "listen." As one planner puts it, "You visit with people, you listen, you don't explain things or try to tell them what you can do." The director of a South Dakota planning and development district makes the same point: "It really helps to listen, really listen. When you start off with all the answers, people turn you off. They can't really trust you until you have shown that you can listen and that you understand what they are talking about."

Novice planners must also take care to attend every meeting they can. One Montana state planner advises: "Go to every meeting you can—city councils, county commissions, chambers of commerce, special districts, school boards. But attend on a low-key basis, and listen more than you talk."

At these meetings it is likely that many people will be curious about you and about what you plan on doing. Planners find that they are asked to respond to specific questions or proposals. Since most planners at this stage are not sufficiently knowledgeable about the area, its people, or their elected officials, experienced planners suggest that your responses reflect only those things that you know for certain, and not those you speculate about. Also, note the experienced planners, don't be afraid of saying "I don't know"; people will respect that. In particular, people will appreciate an "I don't know" followed by "but I'll find out and let you know."

Public meetings generate important information on just about every important aspect of rural planning work. In attending the meeting, for example, the planner often discovers that many of the same people appear over and over again. Oftentimes, these are key decision makers—the local power structure—whose opinions carry considerable weight in the community.

Some of these decision makers may not even be associated with traditional planning bodies. For example, the planner might discover that a key decision maker appears on the governing board of the conservation district, the school district, and the local chamber of commerce. But this same person is not on the county commission or town council, the traditional sources of planning authority. In future planning work, it would be important for the planner to involve these key people in the planning process.

In addition to identifying key decision makers, attendance at meetings also generates information on important local issues. These issues often transcend any single organization so that the major topic of discussion remains the same in many different meetings sponsored and conducted by many different organizations. Thus, by attending a variety of meetings, new planners can discover at least some critical issues.

Another advantage in meeting attendance is that at meetings new planners might identify minor problems that would make good candidates for early, effective solutions, an important success factor for the new planner.

Having researched the area, talked to people, and observed and listened at a variety of meetings, the new planner is now prepared to talk informally with local elected officials. One planner suggests, "Get to know local public officials. Make one-to-one contact with elected officials, find out what their feelings are towards planning, what they do for a living, what their interests are, and the things that they want you to be aware of. If you can't catch the official after a meeting, put your boots on and go to see him. If it's a farmer, don't get him in the field, get him after lunch or after dinner."

Another rural planner adds: "You don't sit down and talk zoning. You sit down and talk the key issues of interest to everyone—whether it's a little wet or a little dry this year and if that's causing trouble—so that the person realizes that you know something about what makes him tick." This planner emphasizes the low-key, soft-sell approach: "You always chew the fat a bit before you give the hard sell. So many people forget this basic thing, the social relationships—planning schools especially—you can't come in as Eddie Expert or Peter Professional. You have to prove that you are human and that at least you understand or care a little bit about them."

Informal discussions with local elected officials, after meetings, at their homes or places of business, over coffee, on the streets, or over a beer, will complete a necessary first phase in getting to know the people and getting to know the place. At this point, information has been gathered by the planner concerning local history, social structure, power structure, economic structure and processes, and, most significantly, a set of important local issues. This collection of facts, attitudes, and concerns sets the new planner on an effective planning course.

Governmental Units To begin planning work, the novice planner should have some appreciation of key state legislation and important planning authorities.

All states share enabling legislation which permits counties, cities, and sometimes townships to prepare plans and adopt land- use regulations. This legislation also sets forth the procedural steps that must be followed in embarking on any local planning activity—setting up a planning commission, preparing a plan, adopting regulations and so forth.

In addition to the enabling legislation, local planners should be aware of the critical decision-making authority. In many states, this is the county commission. The commissioners, three or more officials, usually elected at large in the county, are the principal decision-making authority in rural areas. Although city councils, city commissions, and town councils are also important, the county commissioners are essential to most rural planning activities. For example, most rural planners are not hired by small towns, they are hired by counties or by regional councils. Even at the regional council level, the county commissioners, serving on the regional council board, are key decision makers.

State enabling legislation also provides for the establishment of planning commissions, zoning commissions, joint planning boards, or planning and zoning commissions to prepare plans and to administer zoning regulations. In general, planning boards or commissions must be established to prepare plans. Once the plan is prepared, a planning commission or zoning commission may then prepare land-use regulations. These same commissions are charged with administering zoning ordinances. Most legislation also provides for zoning boards of adjustment or appeals to deal with appeals from the decision of a zoning administrator. In almost all cases, the local elected officials—county commissioners, city commissioners, city councils, or town councils, have final authority in making planning and zoning decisions. The decisions by the other commissions are purely advisory.

Most states also provide legislation on extraterritorial powers for cities. This enables cities to participate in county decisions on planning questions, especially new subdivisions, within a short radius of city limits (usually one to three miles). To complement extraterritorial powers, most states also provide joint powers for cities, counties, and special districts. Under this provision, cities, counties, and special districts may join together to provide for the planning, financing, and provision of a range of public services.

For new rural planners, there are two important sources of information on governmental powers, responsibilities, enabling legislation and other important legislation. The first are the various state offices of planning or community affairs and the second are the regional councils which are located in many states. Between the state offices and the regional councils, new rural planners can gather all the information needed to learn the basic division of powers, the procedural steps necessary to begin planning, and the requirements of various state laws.

Problems with annexation often plague rural planners. While the exact character of the law varies from state to state, the laws do share common features. First, parcels under consideration must be "contiguous or adjacent" to the annexing jurisdiction. Second, the process may be initiated by either the governing body of the annexing jurisdiction or by a majority of landowners or voters in the parcel.

Many laws are vague in terms of the specific criteria to be applied by the annexing jurisdiction. Using such terms as "orderly growth," "efficient delivery of services" and "path of natural expansion," the laws generally leave annexing jurisdictions great discretion. In several states, the annexation law is being examined and revised by various special study groups.

As an indication of some of the special problems that might arise, consider, for example, that in Nebraska, there are six sections of the state code devoted to annexation by four classes of cities. Many more sections are devoted to various sub-classifications of the cities. In North Dakota, 75 percent of landowners or voters in an area must support an annexation petition if it is to be considered by the annexing jurisdiction. Conversely, if 20 percent of the landowner/voters oppose, the annexation will fail. In Montana, a city must have a comprehensive plan in order to complete any annexation. Likewise, the city must also prepare a five-year public facilities/service plan for the area to be annexed. But no annexation may occur if the area is within a fire district which is ten years (or more) old, and if the area is not withdrawn from this fire district. In Montana, needless to say, it is difficult to deannex from an established fire district. Thus, the rate of annexation is slowed from what it would otherwise be.

Because of the peculiarities in annexation laws from state to state, planners are advised to review the key statutes and consult with regional agencies and members of state planning offices.

Although the states do share common planning provisions, there are important differences. In the Appendix at the end of this chapter, some of the fine points are identified for the states comprising the Old West Region.

Pick a Problem and Solve it—Quickly and Effectively

A key objective for any new rural planner is to establish credibility with his clientele, the elected and appointed officials. The quicker one's credibility is established, the easier it will be for the planner to do planning work. The trouble is that in the beginning, rural people are not impressed by the technical excellence or imagination reflected in a traditional planning product. Rural people will not show overwhelming gratitude for a good new policy plan or a fine set of performance controls.

For the most part, the people you work with will be project- or problem-oriented. Problems are not perceived in a grand scheme—the "systems view" just isn't there. Problems are viewed independently. The problems that people want solved are those that affect people in the most direct and immediate ways—dust flying from unpaved roads, sewer backup, a run-down school bus and so forth. As one planner put it, "People are project-oriented—they want results, not 'planning', from the work."

The first job, then, is to select a problem which can be solved quickly and effectively. The planner must also insure that this is a problem in the minds of his clients. A deputy director of a Nebraska state planning office said: "Planning without a problem to solve is not too effective. It may be mobile homes, truck junkyards, or floodplain development, but you have to go in and identify the problems and make sure the people want to solve them. New planners must take a careful approach and look for key opportunities to solve a real planning problem and not create a problem that they can solve. Usually when a guy gets fired, it was because he was not meeting immediate needs and was manufacturing problems to solve."

In addition to the selection of a small, manageable problem to solve, novice planners must also avoid embarking, at this point, on any major planning exercise. Aside from the resource commitment that would have to be made for such a project, the planner would be gambling that a major project could be successfully completed without having his or her credibility established. In this situation, there just isn't any room for the slightest error, political or technical, since the planner has nothing to fall back on. And given the relative inexperience of most new rural planners, the odds in favor of such an error are unacceptable. Thus, in this phase, planners must hold off major planning works.

In most cases, the type of problem to be solved will have very little to do with conventional planning practice. As a North Dakota planner says: "You have to be willing to help with anything. It may have nothing to do with planning, yet it may be important to the community. For example, a road right-of-way might need some research. That might take a few minutes of work, and the commissioners would be impressed that you could act quickly. Or a small town might want to purchase a garbage truck, and you would have to identify grants and make the application. There are many, many things that you could do, but you would have to insure that it is something that the people really wanted solved."

This type of problem solving, which most planners call technical assistance, is usually highly personalized. That is, the planner is generally responding to a key concern of a single official. As a North Dakota official said: "You establish technical assistance capability by helping the mayor of this town or the county commissioner of that county to solve a specific problem. Once they see that you are interested in their problems, and that you can solve one or two, then they'll be willing to listen a bit more about broader planning issues."

If much of the work in this phase is technical assistance, much of the work of technical assistance is accomplished through one's ability to search out available financial assistance. While many planners tend to reject this type of work in favor of traditional planning work, a rural planner must demonstrate considerable skills in "grantsmanship." In many cases, the elected officials view grantsmanship as the primary reason for a planner's existence. In case after case, a planner is evaluated according to the number or size of the grants obtained—"Well, the planner's doing good work—he's got us a lot of money."

There are four important sources of written material on federal grants which should be at the disposal of the rural planner. The first is the *Catalogue of Federal Domestic Assistance*—a listing of all grants available, all categories, dollars available, application criteria and so forth. The second source is the Commerce Clearing House publication, *Urban Affairs Reporter,* which can keep the planner posted on the latest information concerning grants—new grants, changes in old grants, etc. The third source is the *Federal Reporter,* which outlines application requirements for new grants and establishes rules and regulations on a variety of federal laws. The fourth source is a program sponsored by the Soil Conservation Service of the U.S. Department of Agriculture, entitled the Federal Assistance Program Retrieval System. In this program, a community may discover grant eligibility for a number of categories simply by providing the program officers with a simple listing of economic, population, and social data about the jurisdiction. With this information, the program generates a list of grants in a number of areas for which the jurisdiction may be eligible. (See bibliography.)

In addition to consulting written material, planners should also contact: (1) staff of his regional planning council; (2) staff of the planning division of the state; (3) federal regional staff; and, (4) federal staff located in Washington. With the information provided by the written materials coupled with that obtained in personal visits or by telephone, the planner is able to evaluate the possibilities for grants in a number of areas. The objective here is to minimize the search process and focus on those areas which would make highly probable candidates for approval.

A planner's work in searching out and obtaining grants has immediate and powerful returns. "Elected officials," comments a South Dakota planner, "know that the same person who got them a lot of money is also the same one with the community plans and regulations. You can't separate the one from the other." Elected officials are far more likely to listen to a new planner about broader planning issues when that planner has demonstrated that he can do things for them in a number of other areas. Thus, grantsmanship is extremely important, perhaps the single most important part of this phase.

The objective of achieving a quick and early success is only achieved when the elected officials perceive the planner as doing good work. But, when a planner solves a problem he or she must remember that the solution and any credit for the solution goes to the elected officials. As one planner said, "We try to find successful projects but we want to be behind the elected official, not in front of him." Consequently, the planner must work hard to insure that his or her elected officials receive the credit for solving the problem.

Selling Planning

There is a saying in rural planning circles that "planning may not be O.K. but a planner may be O.K." This means that the work of a rural planner is highly personalized—there is no separating the person from the work. Thus, a community may object strenuously to the concept of planning, but the same community may give great license to one of its own, a planner, to do his work—although he is a planner, says the community, he's our planner.

To be effective, a new rural planner must sell himself first and planning second. To do good work, a planner needs to be a member of the community before he can hope to influence the planning in that community. Consequently, after the planner is an accepted member of the community, he can then begin to think about selling planning to the community.

In many of the more successful programs, planners build upon their early success in problem-solving—planning becomes a simple extension of previous good works. Thus, if the planner arranged a grant for a new garbage truck, the next job is to examine the solid waste disposal system, or to demonstrate how a new subdivision might make another such truck necessary. Since the planner has demonstrated the ability to solve a minor problem, officials are more willing to listen to the planner on the solution of major problems.

Another effective technique is to build upon existing institutional arrangements. For example, in many rural areas farmers and ranchers have been cooperating for years on weed and pest control and planned irrigation systems. In this instance, local elected officials are very familiar with the benefits of cooperative planning. Consequently, a new planner would do well to capitalize on this history, to demonstrate that his proposals represent nothing more than a simple extension and improvement over past practice.

Another useful approach is to make clear how planning could have helped solve specific past problems. For example, in one small North Dakota community without a zoning ordinance, a fertilizer plant was located right in the middle of the town. The plant, needless to say, was a continual source of irritation to community members who objected to the odors. The plant was also a serious threat to the public safety due to the explosive character of many of its products and processes. By pointing up how a zoning ordinance could have protected the community from such a plant, a planner can demonstrate the value of planning.

One rural planner in Colorado reported that local commissioners were impressed with a discussion of the ways in which planning could have prevented a premature subdivision which had disastrous effects on the county service load. The next time the commissioners were faced with a new subdivision, they called in the planner. The planner evaluated the subdivision and determined that as it was to be built on steep, unstable slopes, it would damage the floodplain, and that it could force the county to pay for improvements that should have been completed by the developer. The conclusions impressed the commissioners and the recommendations were adopted because the planner demonstrated to the commissioners how planning could have prevented one mistake and how it could prevent mistakes in the future.

In Montana, a planning director used a similar tactic in discussing a new subdivision with continual sewer problems. The planner told the commission that the problem stemmed from a sewer design capacity that was much too small for the load. Preplanning could have prevented this. A house numbering problem was used to the same effect. (In this case, a simple change in the numbering system provided valuable assistance to the local fire department in making it easier for them to locate residences.) With minimal attention to the subdivision, the planner pointed out, problems could be prevented.

In many of these examples, the planners noted that their most convincing arguments for planning stemmed from the use of planning for "the protection of private property rights." In rural communities, this is an extremely important and effective argument. When people see planning as acting in their own best interests—as protecting their property rights, as protecting their governmental services, and as protecting them from tax increases—the work of selling planning is almost complete. People then see planning as something which gives them more control over their own lives.

A South Dakota planner used a different technique to the same end: "We use a sampling technique to figure out what the governing board thinks hurts the most. We do it annually and ask, 'What hurts the most?' in various subject areas. The answers give us a feeling for what people think is most important. And then we use our overall work program to address those concerns so that we are working in at least some priority areas as seen by the governing board. We need to make sure that we are not working on any areas that are not considered important by our board."

In other cases, the planners have taken a sampling technique and applied it on a community scale. In Springfield, Oregon, for example, planners prepared a random sampling (10 percent) of the town's population and distributed questionnaires on key issues. The responses were then tabulated and categorized, translated into issue statements, and returned to the same sample. The people were asked to put the issues into order of priority and return the material. Using the submissions, the planners then asked members of the sample group to participate in a planning process to solve these problems. Since the people had first identified the key issues and then had put them into priority order, most were willing to give their time to serve on citizen committees to solve these problems. The cost of this program was said to be minimal.

The advantage of a community-wide approach such as this is that it exposes a broad segment of the community to the planning process. It insures that members of the community are involved from the first in the work of planning. This means that key community concerns are the central focus of all planning work, and that the agenda of all planning work is set by the citizens. In this process, the planner is assured that the problems addressed are really those shared by the entire community.

One of the most difficult problems faced by rural planners is that, in many areas, there are no widely held opinions about the worth or validity of planning. As a result, novice planners often make recommendations based on their own assumptions about the validity of planning that are simply not shared by local officials. In many urban or suburban areas, for example, very few people question the need for a community plan or land-use regulations—the people assume the value of such plans and regulations. But in many rural areas, the opposite is true; people question the validity of planning and do not automatically assume that "community plans and land-use regulations" are worthwhile.

A planning director in Wyoming comments: "Every planning decision or recommendation requires an answer. There is no planning history, no planning bureaucracy, no tradition or culture of planning to fall back on. The burden of proof is on the planners to show that their decisions are right. Every conclusion must be justified."

While the methods and techniques suggested previously can be useful in overcoming objections, another useful device is to educate the local officials in the planning process. But the language of planning cannot be allowed to become a stumbling block for elected officials. The problem with language is one that is often overlooked by rural planners. With several years of planning education behind them, rural planners often assume that code words such as "HUD", "OWRC," "EDA," and "701" have meaning to almost everyone. The specific technical language of planning, "work programs," "comprehensive plans," "policy plans," "planning programs," "work flows," "growth management" and so forth is equally confusing. Phrases like "We'd use 'HUD's 701' to implement our 'growth management strategy'" leave many rural officials befuddled.

If it takes six months or a year for planners simply to explain the language of planning, rural planners are in for a difficult time. This is particularly true for regional councils whose membership might meet only four or six times per year. In a survey of members of North Dakota's regional councils, sponsored by the state planning division, most members responded that it took them at least two to five meetings to understand the language. That's too long.

To combat this problem and to instill an appreciation for the basic values of planning, many rural planners sponsor special training sessions for their elected and appointed officials. A planning and development district in South Dakota sponsors one- to two-day training sessions per year on local planning and zoning. "We try to get county commissioners and planning commissioners to come in and get a feeling for what planning and zoning administration is all about."

In Illinois, the state sponsors a two-day seminar for local officials on planning and zoning. Experts are brought in from around the state to lecture on various aspects of planning and zoning. Local officials, in turn, are encouraged to discuss their problems with both the experts and with other officials around the state. Such programs make excellent sense for elected and appointed officials with little or no planning experience.

In other states, colleges and universities sponsor "Planning Certificate" programs for both officials and novice planners. These programs rely on extension courses and correspondence courses to complete the requirements for a planning certificate. Although these programs are not as beneficial to elected officials as are the planning and zoning seminars, they provide a good substitute.

Perhaps the most effective education for local officials stems from their actual work in preparing local plans and land-use regulations. Instead of preparing plans and regulations, some rural planners guide the officials through the process so that the plans and regulations are structured from the very beginning by those same officials. This has the distinct advantage of educating local officials in the planning process, and it also has the advantage of producing plans and regulations which are thoroughly understood by local officials. Generally speaking, such plans and regulations are much more effective than those prepared by consultants or by rural planners themselves.

Appendix

Planning Provisions in the Old West Region

Nebraska

Nebraska has no state law mandating planning activity in the rural areas. As in all states, however, they do have the enabling legislation which permits counties and cities to adopt plans and regulations.

While regional councils cover about two-thirds of Nebraska, very few are involved in local planning assistance. Many regional councils limit their roles to grantsmanship.

At the local level, new planners are likely to be working for counties. This is due to the small size and limited budgets of most rural towns. However, many planners find that their time is split between the county, their principal employer, and one or more small towns within the county who seek part-time planning assistance.

Nebraska state law does require the preparation of a plan to support a zoning ordinance. Thus, before adopting a zoning ordinance, the community must prepare a plan. To prepare such a plan, the community must establish a planning commission. Once the plan and zoning ordinance are adopted, the community must file an annual report to the state on how they are performing their planning work.

Although a community must establish a planning commission to prepare a plan which must be completed before a zoning ordinance can be adopted, there is no law which mandates the preparation of plans and land-use regulations.

This is strictly a voluntary exercise. Only about one-third of the counties have adopted a zoning ordinance. Thus, only one-third have prepared plans and have established planning commissions and are currently at work on local plans or land-use regulations.

As in many states, Nebraska has an Extraterritoriality Jurisdiction Act and an Inter-Local Cooperation Act. In the Extraterritoriality Act, cities are allowed to exercise zoning authority (presuming they have adopted a zoning ordinance) over areas outside of their city limits. Depending upon the size of the city, this can run from one to three miles. The Inter-Local Cooperation Act permits cities, counties and special districts to join together to perform a variety of services. This law would permit, for example, several counties to join together to do planning work. But in practice, the law has meant that a single county might join with several of its villages to establish one planning commission and one zoning administrator for the county area.

Although most water and sewer services are controlled by the counties or cities, there are three special districts which deserve mention. The first, sanitary improvement districts, can be used by large property owners to incorporate their lands and to sell bonds for water, sewer, roads, and other public facilities. In addition, these special districts may also apply for federal funds to provide facilities. Thus the sanitary improvement district may be used in rural areas to set the essential groundwork for urban development.

The second, rural water districts, are important since they may provide water to rural areas which heretofore required individual wells. In so doing, the rural water district established a necessary condition for future urban development.

The third, natural resource districts, are unique to Nebraska. The natural resource districts blanket the state and often cover more than one county. These districts have taxing powers and land-use authority over erosion, sedimentation, drainage and soils. But to exercise these land-use powers, the districts must have the approval of 75 percent of the electorate, the landowners, and thus far no district has established land-use controls.

North Dakota

As in Nebraska and South Dakota, North Dakota has no law which mandates local planning. But as in all states, North Dakota does have the enabling legislation which permits local units (counties, cities, and townships) to adopt plans and land-use regulations.

Regional councils are extremely active in North Dakota. The state has border to border coverage by these councils and they are involved in both grants and local technical assistance. Regional councils are extremely important sources of information and assistance to county or city planners. Many have prepared local plans and local land-use regulations. Others have prepared model plans and regulations. Most councils have an excellent grasp of local planning issues and a good relationship with local elected officials.

The critical planning work occurs at the county level since most cities and townships in the rural areas cannot support continuous planning activities. While county budgets are thin, they are larger than those of cities and townships. Thus, planners, if they are not working for a regional council, would most likely be working for a county in the rural areas.

In 1974, most counties had established planning commissions. Although eighteen counties (out of fifty-three) had completed comprehensive plans, only seven counties had adopted their plans, and another nine counties were working on their comprehensive plans. Most of the larger cities, such as Fargo, Bismarck, Grand Forks, and Williston, were also active in planning activities.

The preparation and adoption of zoning ordinances has kept pace with the work on comprehensive plans. In 1974, twenty counties had adopted zoning ordinances and another eight counties were in the process of preparing land-use regulations. However, only twelve counties have adopted subdivision regulations.

One interesting provision of North Dakota state law requires a zoning ordinance to be in conformance with a comprehensive plan. While the law does not require the preparation of such plans, North Dakota planners have interpreted this law to mean that any zoning ordinance must be backed up by a comprehensive plan. Thus, if a community desires to establish a zoning ordinance, they must also prepare a comprehensive plan to guide the ordinance.

There are two special districts of importance to planning work. The soil conservation districts, which cover the entire state, have broad land-use authority over soil erosion and sedimentation problems. However, since 1939, only one district (in Sioux County) has actually adopted regulations. The water management district, controlled by the county commissioners, is another important special district. This district has broad powers over both the water supply and sewers and sewage treatment. It also exercises authority over the drainage of wetlands and ponds.

Wyoming

Wyoming does have a state Land Use Planning Act (1975) which requires each local government, both city and county, to prepare and adopt a land-use plan. The plan must be prepared in conformance with a series of state guidelines, and then the plan must be submitted to the state for approval by the state land-use commission. Should a county or city fail to prepare such a plan, the state is empowered to do it. To insure consistency between local and county plans, the law also requires that the county plan include all local plans. Thus, the county plan is a composite of plans for the unincorporated areas as well as the incorporated areas.

Under extraterritoriality legislation, cities may review all subdivisions within one mile of the city limits. Cities are also permitted to exercise zoning authority for up to three miles from city limits, but at the moment there is much confusion surrounding the application of this provision. Thus, few cities have undertaken this responsibility.

The state does not have border to border coverage by regional councils. But a few regional councils do serve as the principal planning staff to counties and cities. In northeastern Wyoming, for example, a joint planning board was formed to provide planning services to a three county area. In three other counties, a single association was formed to provide planning services to a single county and all of the towns within the county. In southwestern Wyoming, one association covers two counties and eight towns and provides them with a full range of grant services. However, in this association, the council is shying away from planning activities.

Although there are a variety of special districts, the counties and towns control most services which are critical for planning. Conservation districts, however, do have wide ranging powers over soil and erosion control and may adopt land-use regulations. But to adopt such regulations, the district must have the approval of at least 75 percent of the land-holding voters and at least 75 percent of the land in the district must be reflected in that vote.

South Dakota

There are no state laws in South Dakota which mandate local planning activity. The state enabling legislation does allow cities and counties, but not townships, to prepare plans and adopt land-use regulations.

South Dakota, like North Dakota, does have extended coverage by regional councils. And like North Dakota, these regional councils provide a broad range of services to cities and counties. This includes grant and local technical planning assistance. Regional councils have assisted cities and counties in the preparation of plans and in the development and adoption of land-use regulations. This experience and expertise make the regional councils an extremely important source of advice and assistance.

The level of planning activity varies across the state. Only thirty-five of the sixty-seven counties have prepared a comprehensive plan. Only a few have adopted land-use regulations to implement their plans. As in other states, the planning commission has responsibility for developing plans and administering the zoning ordinance, while the final responsibility rests with city councils, city commissions, or county commissions.

Cities and counties house most of the important planning

functions. Although there are very few special districts, soil and water conservation districts have been given some authority in monitoring and enforcing soil erosion and sedimentation control. The exact function of the soil and water conservation districts in this area has yet to be established. To date it appears that the soil and water conservation districts will perform a technical function in evaluating complaints and monitoring performance in soil erosion and sedimentation controls.

One interesting feature of land-use law in South Dakota is a provision which allows citizens to participate in decisions made by counties on new plats. If the city has an approved street plan, that is a street plan adopted by the city, the city may make comments and recommendations on new plats which fall within a three-mile radius of the city boundaries.

An Extraterritorial Jurisdiction Law also provides for the establishment of joint subdivision regulations and zoning of this three-mile area. With such a joint effort, the city must prepare a plan for the three-mile area before adopting the regulations. When the regulations are adopted, the city and the county can make joint decisions on new plats. In practice, however, the joint planning and regulatory provisions have not been widely applied, and when they have been applied, they have not worked well. Thus, in a complex area like this, rural planners are cautioned to proceed very slowly if at all.

Montana

Although Montana has no law which mandates the preparation of local plans or land-use regulations, the state does mandate the review of subdivisions by cities and counties. The law, the Subdivision and Platting Act, sets forth basic review criteria which must be followed, but local officials have the final decision-making authority.

There are very few regional councils in Montana. What little planning activity takes place is conducted at the county and city level. For example, approximately 20 percent of Montana's counties have adopted plans. Far less than 20 percent have adopted zoning ordinances.

The enabling legislation for zoning is extremely complex. There are three zoning enabling laws. The City-County Planning Enabling Act provides for six different types of planning boards: (1) a county planning board; (2) a city planning board; (3) a city/county planning board; (4) a county planning board with city representation; (5) a joint planning board; and, (6) a combined planning board.

Each of these boards has different powers and different responsibilities. A combined planning board would have planning and administrative authority over a county and cit(y)ies within the county. However, a city/county planning board would have authority only over an area extending from 4.5 miles to 12 miles from the city. A county planning board may have representatives from the county. A joint planning board would be involved in plan preparation, but would not have any administrative authority. As the enabling legislation in Montana is extremely complex, local planners are advised to seek the expert assistance of state planners in setting up any local planning boards.

One interesting feature of the zoning enabling legislation is the law which provides for zoning by petition. The so-called 40 acre law allows landowners in an area 40 acres or larger to petition the county commissioners for a special zoning district. If 60 percent of the landowners make this request, the county commissioners, the county surveyor, and the county assessor sit as a planning commission for the area. This commission then prepares a plan for the district which may be followed by a zoning ordinance. Once completed, the county commissioners retain final regulatory authority over the district.

There are 108 different types of special districts. Of these, three are particularly important to local planners. The first, conservation districts, which blanket the state, have wide ranging authority over land use. These districts are empowered to prepare comprehensive plans for soil and water conservation, flood protection, and the development and disposal of water. The districts may adopt land use regulations to implement these plans if the regulations are approved by a majority of land-holding voters in the district. To date, very few conservation districts have adopted land-use regulations.

In addition to the conservation districts, there are special improvement districts for cities, and rural improvement districts for counties. Both of these improvement districts may be established to serve a variety of public purposes, including parks and recreation, streets, drainage, lighting, libraries, etc. In addition, the counties may also establish water and sewer districts and the same function may be served in cities by the metropolitan sewer districts.

Chapter II
Policies and Plans

Assuming that he or she has weathered the first few months of the new job, the rural planner will want to begin to work with the community to prepare a formal plan. Although planning for a rural county or municipality may be accomplished on an *ad hoc* basis—dealing with problems as they come up—in time this will be expensive and duplicative. The community may wish to try another route. Most likely a plan prepared for a rural area will serve best if it falls somewhere between a detailed blueprint in the form of a comprehensive or master plan, and total laissez-faire. There are degrees of comprehensiveness which are permissible and workable in preparing a plan. The planner starting to help his community work out an overall development guide will aim for flexibility, but will try to make certain that the community commits itself explicitly to those policies it wishes to follow. Some communities want a traditional master plan, with every functional system carefully considered; others would be more satisfied with a "policy plan"—a relatively short statement of community goals and objectives against which all future development proposals can be measured. What is important is that the planner avoid the attempt to foist an extensive textbook plan upon a community that does not want it. Alternative approaches will work as well.

This chapter will discuss some of the general procedures which the planner can follow in helping a community to articulate policies and decide on the kind of a plan it wants.

The Planning Process

To begin the process of preparing a formal plan, the questions which must be answered are, "Where are we now?" and "Where would we like to be in the future?" The answer to the first question is clearly easier to achieve.

Where Are We Now: Collecting Data on Existing Conditions

The process of collecting information on conditions that currently exist can take place at the same period as discussions setting future goals are taking place. Several categories of information will be needed before a community can make educated decisions about how it wants to proceed. Important items of information that will be needed are a description of the existing natural resource base (see below), existing land uses, and the economic trends which affect the region and the local community. Information about existing resources and land uses can be gathered by local citizens in many cases. Whoever gathers the information should certainly check and augment it by consulting local people. No one knows better than the residents exactly what land is being used for what purposes, and where areas of special interest are located. Assistance will have to be sought in addition from a number of regional, state and federal agencies who regularly gather such information. Regional social and economic trends, including population projections, can be learned from local regional agencies, from state planning offices or university extension services. (See pages 167–170 for a description of methods of population projection.) Local banks, business and newspaper people and elected officers are also excellent sources of information. Statutory law affecting planning and development must be clarified too. The requirements of state and in some cases federal law are important limitations and guides to future planning which are sometimes overlooked.

The presentation of background information is not to be considered an academic exercise. The meaning of this information must be made clear by the planner or elected official who presents it. There are important reasons why this information is collected and analyzed. The most obvious reason for having it on hand is that such information gives the citizens a clear picture of where they stand; the current situation of a community is not always as evident as it might appear. Local people often are not aware of changes which have occurred in their community and cling to beliefs about how it used to be. They are often moved to institute change only when confronted with facts about how it is now. But an equally important reason for gathering data is that the existing situation represents the limitations within which the community must work. The limitations presented by the natural resource base are of particular importance in rural planning, and natural resources are a unique value in rural communities. If the limitations posed by slope, water and soil, for example, are well understood, the community can spare itself problems and expense in the future. The need to recognize statutory limitations is also important; the community cannot undertake actions which may be challenged in court. The planner can serve a very important function if he or she is able to indicate clearly the implications for the future which the existing situation of the community presents.

Citizen Participation

"Where would we like to be in the future?" must be decided by the people of the area themselves. How does the planner start to involve citizens in the planning process? Public meetings, newspaper articles, radio and television programs, face-to-face interviews, short and simple mail questionnaires have all been used effectively in rural areas. In addition, the town or county's chief executive usually will appoint a special advisory committee, or he or she may use the members of the town council, to meet at regular times to consider the direction which the community wishes to go. Establishing a number of committees to represent particular interests or particular geographic areas is a good way to involve a large number of people working together in small groups. People often enjoy serving on such committees, and if the selection represents various interest groups, a valuable forum for interchange of opinion is provided. The planner can assist the mayor or the county commissioner by making certain that relevant information is not overlooked in discussion meetings, but the planner must be careful not to play a leading role; he is to act as a resource person.

Some rural areas report that a regular newspaper column reporting on planning issues prepared by the planning commission can give considerable help in establishing contact with citizens. The pros and cons of local issues can be presented, and the processes of planning and possibilities of various implementing tools can be explained in short weekly columns. Public reaction to these columns should be solicited.

It is important that maximum publicity be given to the initial phase of the planning effort. Times and places of meetings should be posted and announced on local radio and in newspapers. The names and phone numbers of the local planning commissioners or the planner should be available and direct contact should be encouraged. Those responsible for the planning effort must be visible and their work understandable. Those people who cannot attend public meetings should be encouraged to make their opinions known. There may be people who do not wish to express their views publicly; every effort must be made to give them a means of offering their opinions.

It would be naive to assume that a simple list of goals and means of achieving them will magically emerge. The planner must recognize that at best what is finally agreed upon as the most pressing problems or most desirable goals may only represent a compromise. It is for this reason that goals, plans, and implementation tools must be continually examined and reevaluated, and the notion of planning as a "continuous process" begins to make sense. Various techniques have been developed for ranking alternative goals which can be pursued by interested planners (Van Es, 1976; and Stuart, 1978.) Although the initial phase of the planning process takes time, some end point for this phase must be set at the beginning of the undertaking in order to encourage concentrated effort.

The planner finally must be able to act as a facilitator, to organize the results of this policy-making process, and prepare a list of the goals and policies which are of most interest to most of the members of the community.

The Policy Plan

In some communities the plan itself is no more than an elaboration of the policies selected in the first phase of the planning process. General principles rather than specific proposals are the heart of the policy plan, which is growing in popularity. The delineation of goals and objectives is considered a sufficient guide to future land-use decisions and no further elaborate land-use plans need be made.

The Office of Economic Planning and Development of the state of Wyoming identifies three steps in the usual policy planning approach: "(1) the identification of *opportunities or problems;* (2) the establishment of *policies* for resolving identified problems, or for taking advantage of the various opportunities that may exist; and (3) a discussion of various governmental *programs* that will implement the established policies." An example of the way in which a policy plan can be used to guide residential development from the State of Wyoming Planning Information Series, 1977, follows:

Opportunities and Problems
In Wyoming City there is a developer who plans to construct one hundred new housing units (opportunity) in a development known as Paradise Hills. However, the proposed subdivision is located one mile outside the city limits and it is not currently served by adequate water, sewer, and transportation facilities (problem). In addition, the proposed development is located on a hillside and a small manufacturing plant is situated within one-eighth of a mile of the proposed residential site (problem). The developer has petitioned the community for annexation and subdivision approval.

Policies
   1. Control land uses on the periphery of Wyoming City.
   2. Encourage new development to occur within the city limits or

immediately adjacent to Wyoming City.

3. Ensure that all developments are served by adequate water, sewer, and transportation facilities before final subdivision approval is granted.

4. Ensure that the developer pays a fair share of the cost for needed water and sewer lines and for the construction of roads when the development is located outside of the existing city limits.

5. Ensure that residential development will not occur in the immediate vicinity of industrial land-uses.

6. Take necessary measures that will prevent residential development from occurring on steep slopes where foundation and erosion problems are common.

Programs

1. Approve subdivision plans only when they are located within the general vicinity of existing water and sewer lines.

2. Offer property tax incentives for those developers who build within the city limits.

3. Enact an ordinance that specifies that development shall occur only on slopes of less than 12 percent.

In the hypothetical case of the developer petitioning for annexation and subdivision approval, the local planning commission should compare the developer's proposal to the policies and programs just described. Of first concern would be the location of the proposed subdivision one mile outside the existing city limits. If there were no contiguous development between this proposed site and the community, subdivision approval would violate the policy of encouraging new development to occur within the city limits or immediately adjacent to the community. In addition, the development does not have adequate water, sewer or transportation facilities, set forth for all development by another policy. In the latter problem, however, if the developer were willing to pay the major costs for water and sewer lines and for the construction of necessary roads, this requirement could be met.

Another problem is presented by the fact that the proposed subdivision is located within one-eighth mile of a small manufacturing plant. Allowing the residential subdivision to develop would violate the policy of not encouraging residential development within the immediate vicinity of industrial land-uses. An additional problem is the fact that the proposed development is located on a hillside. Depending upon the steepness of the slope, it may be undesirable to allow development to take place if the slope is greater than 12 percent.

Compared to the policies and programs described, the major problem with the proposed development is its distance from the community. This could be mitigated if the developer were willing to pay the costs of all water, sewer, and transportation facilities to serve the development. In addition, depending upon an evaluation of the degree and slope of the hillside in the proposed subdivision, the proposal should be denied if it appears that a hazard is present. (State of Wyoming, 1977, p. 71.)

Franklyn Beal in *Defining Development Objectives* indicates the particular advantages of a policy plan:

> ...if a plan designates a particular area in the Central Business District for multi-family housing, once the housing is built, or once it becomes obvious that the housing cannot be built (due to changing conditions or some other unforeseen circumstance), then the plan becomes outdated and useless as a guide for community decision-making. On the other hand, a clearly stated policy, like 'make the CBD a dominant feature of the region by enhancing it as the center for commercial, residential, and cultural activities,' remains in effect regardless of what happens to the housing proposal (Beal, 1968, p. 331).

Some issues which are likely to arise in preparing a policy plan in rural areas will concern:

1. *Boomtown growth*—particularly evident in communities experiencing a surge of development of energy resources. The community will have to face a demand for schools, housing, fire and police which the tax base may not be able to support for a number of years. If these problems are recognized in advance of development, the potential for degradation of environment and drain of fiscal resources may be mitigated. The community can benefit from the experiences of other areas which have negotiated with new industry for short term financial assistance or direct provision of services as a condition of their coming into the community (see references to *Negotiation* in bibliography). Such discussion can make clear that while large-scale new development may offer opportunities to the rural community it may also have serious costs.

2. *Decline*—the other side of the coin for many rural communities is the decline of agricultural employment and consequent loss of population. Economic development programs which concentrate on non-farm employment may be the primary goal in such communities. The pros and cons of development of recreational potential or second homes to attract tourism, or

the possibility of seeking out new institutions such as community colleges to locate in the area can be discussed as part of an overall policy planning program.

3. *Population changes*—as a result of declining agriculture and population loss, the population of some small towns may become increasingly elderly or low income. Special services may be required for these population groups. The possibility of regional cooperation between adjacent municipalities or counties and the pooling of financial resources and services may be sought as a matter of community policy. Chapters 7 and 8 discuss in greater detail approaches which have been taken to solving some of these problems.

4. *Preservation*—preservation of agricultural land, and/or of small town character is a goal of many rural communities. In some cases, this goal may be believed to be in conflict with the goal of attracting new development for economic development. Careful design of implementation tools, such as special zoning districts, performance controls, phased capital improvements programs, or special tax structures may make it possible for a community to accommodate both goals. Chapter 4 discusses some of these approaches.

The Comprehensive Plan

Although the policy plan has the advantage of flexibility, without careful follow-up it may become so general that it ends up as nothing more than an "apple pie and motherhood" statement. For this reason some communities still prefer the more traditional comprehensive plan.

The comprehensive plan can be found under a variety of names: the general plan, development plan or master plan. Whatever name the comprehensive plan goes under, it is characterized by a more thorough consideration of all major functional systems of the planning area than the policy plan and by its presentation of a "best" physical arrangement for future development. The elements of a comprehensive plan are discussed in most urban planning texts and are familiar to most planning students. Comprehensive plans usually contain the following elements:

1. Background: discusses the process by which the community arrived at the plan, and the methods of amending or updating the plan.
2. Goals, objectives and standards. The clear presentation of this section is as important to the comprehensive plan as to the policy plan. It justifies the implementation tools eventually selected. Such goal statements have been used in some cases as legal evidence that the community's zoning and subdivision ordinances are not arbitrary.
3. Existing conditions, including in some cases,
   a. Environmentally sensitive areas
   b. Areas or structures of unique historic interest
   c. Economic and social conditions, including population projections
4. A land-use element indicating future location and uses of land.
5. A housing element.
6. A transportation element.
7. A parks and recreation element.
8. A renewal or economic development element, including a CBD discussion where appropriate.
9. A financing element indicating the means for providing funds to undertake capital improvements.

Whether the community chooses to prepare a comprehensive or a policy plan may depend on time, money, and staff, as well as philosophical preference. The community which is undecided about what approach to take can find references to further sources in the Bibliography.

Whatever kind of plan is prepared, it should be subject to public hearings, and finally should be adopted by the local legislature. A plan does not usually have the force of an ordinance. Nevertheless, adoption gives any ordinances based on it further status.

Preparation of Implementation Techniques

Once the community's policies and plans have been decided upon, the planner and the planning commission can begin to design the implementation tools it wishes to use. The most common tools are land-use regulations, capital improvements programs, and special funding programs. Land use regulations can take a number of forms. Though zoning and subdivision ordinances and building codes are familiar procedures, other approaches may be taken: permitting procedures, public review processes and other flexible procedures are increasingly being used. The town may need to get some legal assistance if it is preparing new ordinances.

The community's capital improvements program (CIP) will also have a significant role to play in implementing the community plan. The capital improvements program is a schedule of major nonrecurring public expenditures for physical facilities, usually prepared for a 6-year period along with an estimate of costs and sources of revenues. The purpose of a CIP is to develop an orderly schedule of improvements needed by a community and to provide a means of evaluating the long-range needs of the community. Capital programming goes beyond just determining needs by providing a device for establishing priorities and offering a means of analyzing the city's ability to pay for major improvements. Not only can a CIP help to schedule and coordinate projects, it can help to clarify a desirable pattern of distributing funds. Capital improvements programming is increasingly used by cities and counties as an extension of city plans as well as a fiscal tool. Further information on the theory and methods of capital programming can be found through consulting the references suggested in the Bibliography.

The impact of capital improvements must be carefully considered. A decision to spend public funds to extend sewer and water lines, for example, or to develop or improve roads, almost inevitably will lead to increased development adjacent to these facilities. Therefore, the location of these key capital facilities should be carefully considered before programming to insure that development will occur where and when the community wants it. Too often haphazard provision of facilities encourages development in a pattern which is expensive for the community to service. Water lines which were intended to assist the farmer, for example, may result instead in break up of farms for subdivision.

Finally, new sources of funds may have to be sought to help implement the new planning program. The planner will have to be acquainted with the tax structure and the possibilities of local tax adjustment, the legality and acceptability of local development fees, as well as the intricacies of applying for outside grants.

Detailed discussion of some of the issues involved in implementation will be considered in the chapters which follow.

Chapter III
Using Natural Resources
as a Planning Guide

Rural areas are fortunate in still being able to make planning choices based on existing natural resources. Although it would appear self-evident that choices must be based on the land in rural areas, the method of land-use planning that starts with the natural resource base is sometimes overlooked by planners trained to deal with urban situations where the possibility of making such choices has long since disappeared. In recent years, increasing numbers of rural areas have recognized their special opportunities and have developed planning methods which take natural resources as their starting point.

Planning based on the natural resource base is motivated not only by the desire to conserve and protect desirable natural features (although this is of course an important point), but also by a belief that development of any kind— roads, residences and shopping centers—can best be located, with less present expense and fewer future problems, if based on an understanding of natural constraints. The natural environment can structure the optimum location of development and save the community problems in the future—problems with provision of water, for example, or with erosion, settling, and sedimentation. Once the natural characteristics of the land are mapped and classified, a clear physical structure which constrains or permits future growth often becomes apparent.

Preparing the inventory and classification of natural resources is an important part of rural environmental planning. Out of the variety of existing characteristics that can be looked at, the planner selects for analysis those which will have the most important effects on future development. It is clear that topography, soils and water are important. Topography dictates the location of roads and houses; clearing steep slopes for building is not only expensive but may create future problems affecting the stability of larger land areas. Soils have important characteristics which must be respected: permeability relates to the location of septic systems; bearing capacity affects the costs of new housing, and preserving agricultural potential may be necessary for the economic health of the community. Though it is hardly necessary to point out the value of a pure water supply, the relationships between the supply of water and other characteristics of the natural resource base are not always obvious. A natural resource inventory can help to point out important relationships between the various natural and man-made systems. Geology, vegetation, wildlife, and unique natural or man-made features all play different parts in maintaining the desired quality and unique identity of a given region.

This chapter provides a guide to some of the techniques involved in preparing the inventory of existing conditions, offers some aids to the planner or citizens making the inventories, and suggests some of the characteristics of existing resources which must be examined and interpreted.

Maps

A useful resource inventory is compiled by describing and mapping each set of natural features and existing land uses individually: topography, hydrology, soils, geology, vegetation, and wildlife are suggested as basic categories for maps. Other natural resource categories, however, may be selected. The primary sources of information will be existing maps, verified by field checking where possible, supplemented by reports, studies, and surveys.

It is important to keep in mind that along with maps and other printed documents, there is no substitute for firsthand information: local specialists such as hydrologists and geologists at nearby universities are frequently the most expert sources of information in a region. Not only will they be able to interpret configurations, statistics, and other data, but they will probably have recent information and field experience. Agencies working with maps should maintain close contact with those who compiled and published the maps. For example, any decisions based upon soil, geological, or topographic considerations should be made only after consultation with the regional offices of the Soil Conservation Service of the U.S. Department of Agriculture. Aside from their ability to interpret maps, they will have updates and amendments on hand.

Maps will be of little use unless they are able to be interpreted and evaluated easily. The identification of sub-areas for their intrinsic suitability for conservation or for future development might be the guiding principle in preparing a presentation. For each of the major data categories, factors related to *conservation* or to *development* should be selected and highlighted. For an initial planning effort a simple summary categorization of data will be helpful. For example, in presenting an interpretive map of slope conditions, "slopes greater than 25 percent—usually no development" may be represented by dark shading; "slopes from 15 to 25 percent—suited for development" and "slopes of 0 to 3 percent—acceptable for development if no ponding or erosion problems" should be shaded successively lighter. By such a presentation, major categories will be clear. What is important is to recognize that too much data may be as difficult to understand as too little. For purposes of clarity, or to highlight a variety of values, it may be useful to prepare more than one interpretive map for a given category. For example, a soils map may be prepared which highlights soils suitable for agriculture, and one which highlights soils suitable for construction.

Since each set of data (e.g., soils) should be recorded on its own map, it is essential to have a good base map, which acts as a reference point upon which subsequent maps are placed. Base maps should display all man-made features in the region: roads, political boundaries, and even individual structures, if the scale is small enough to permit it.

The base map should be of a convenient size for work in the field, and easily reproducible. It is important to keep it simple

and legible. Scale should relate to the capabilities of reproduc-
tion equipment readily available. If the map is to be repro-
duced in sections to be pasted together it should be divided in
such a way as to make matching easy. Sections should also be
divided in such a way as to be easily reproducible on available
equipment. If maps are to produce maximum benefits, they
should be readily available and relatively inexpensive.

It may be useful to have a base map prepared in two or even
three different scales or sizes in order to meet all eventual
demands. For all towns but those of very small size, it may be
desirable to have a base map with sheets at a scale of 1" =
200' or less for central areas which are densely settled. For
areas which are developed with a number of 50-foot lots, a
scale of 300 to 600 feet to an inch is about the minimum for
acceptable legibility. For a rural area which wishes to include a
central village with extended environs on its base map, ability
to measure within fractions of a mile is all that is needed. In
this case 1,000 feet or a half mile to the inch will be appropriate. The final choice will depend on the size of the community
and its particular needs. Combining maps of several scales for
the preliminary survey may be the most workable procedure.

The U.S. Geological Survey (USGS) maps at a scale of either
1:24,000 1" = 2,000 feet ($7\frac{1}{2}$ minute) or 1:62,500 (15-
minute) 1" = approximately 1 mile (the former being more
accurate than the latter) are convenient and useful references.
Land Use and Land Cover and Associated Maps are now being
compiled by the USGS for the entire country.

In 1974 the National Cartographic Information Center
(NCIC) was established by the USGS to provide information and
assist data users in obtaining both general and special cartographic information. They are an excellent source of help.

Topography and Slope

Land use is determined, to a great degree, by elevation and
slope. Historically, development progressed through lowlands,
into valleys, and around hills and mountains. Although this
general pattern still remains true, today there are far fewer

restrictions on developing steep slopes and other areas once considered inaccessible or undesirable. For this reason, the shape of the terrain must be known if land use is to be properly planned. As elevation increases, so do the costs of roads, utilities, and maintenance services, such as snow removal. As the degree of slope increases, so does the difficulty of building and supporting structures.

The development of hillsides must be approached with care because such development can affect the equilibrium of a region or district wider than anticipated. Care must be exercised when tampering with the harmony of slope, soil, vegetation, drainage patterns, and geological foundation.

Bad planning can disturb soil stability, causing erosion and a resulting loss of slope; careless removal of vegetation from hillsides deprives the grade of the cemental network of plant roots, alters established drainage pathways, or eliminates a natural wind screen. Such a loss of protection permits rapid erosion, which adds silt and other sediment particles to downstream waterways and sullies immediate water quality. Spring thaws or strong rains on unstable slopes can produce mass movements, such as landslides, slumps, and flaws, particularly in steeply sloping areas.

By the removal of vegetation, hillside development also increases runoff that would ordinarily be retained and transpired by trees and other vegetation. The detrimental effects of hillside disturbance are increased by the addition of impervious surfaces, such as paving and buildings, further reducing groundwater percolation, thus adding to the amount of runoff, destruction of water quality, and potential for flooding.

Furthermore, disturbance of hillsides can destroy a community's aesthetic resources. A range of hills frequently marks a community's boundary and provides an attractive scenic setting for homes and buildings. Degradation of hillsides as a result of erosion and loss of vegetation deprives a community of its attractive and distinct setting and decreases real estate values.

Through insufficient attention to the problems posed by erosion, runoff, and aesthetic damage, hillside development can have a far-reaching impact on a region's land, water, economic, and scenic resources. Yet with proper planning, hillsides can be developed in a manner compatible with hillside ecology.

Although there are many factors that determine where hillside development is appropriate, it is safe to say that low slopes (those with 1 to 10 percent grade) offer few major obstacles to development, although they are susceptible to erosion if careless removal of the groundcover occurs. Gentle slopes are capable of supporting low-density residential use, but more intense uses should be allowed only with caution.

Density should be lower on moderate slopes (10 to 25 percent grade) because severe erosion and land slippage may result when the groundcover is disturbed. Subsequent sedimentation is a serious possibility, fouling and clogging streams and disrupting the natural water courses. If the soils and drainage on moderate slopes are not conducive to construction, structural damage can result.

On extreme slopes (above 25 percent grade), development will almost certainly increase the amount and velocity of runoff, causing severe erosion. Since development is risky and very expensive, these areas might be set aside for recreation since they often are of great scenic beauty.

Slope in a region may be determined from a topography map, readily available from the National Topography Map Series of the USGS. Most states now have a complete coverage at 1:24,000 and 1:62,500. Relief is shown by 20-foot contour lines on 15-minute maps and 10 feet on $7\frac{1}{2}$ minute maps. If the use of contours is wanted for an overlay map, the USGS can furnish maps with only the brown overprint that indicates contour lines.

Other sources for topographic maps in some states are state geological surveys and state planning agencies. In addition, the U.S. Army Topographic Command has maps for some areas of the country. Soil survey maps usually provide some topographic information—mainly that relevant to erosion, location of ridge lines, and direction of drainage. If an area lacks current maps, the USGS will pay up to one-half the cost of topographic mapping carried out in cooperation with state or local governments.

It will be easy to use contour maps for public presentation if, instead of using an overlay of contour lines, the degrees of slopes are aggregated into three or more groups—low, moderate, extreme, etc.—and each assigned a different color. This will at once reduce the complexity of the map and, at the same time, highlight only those areas that have significant slope that will have an effect on planning development.

Hydrology

The principal reasons for controlling development on or near water are to protect watersheds, to preserve the quality and quantity of the water supply, and to prevent damaging floods. Urban areas require great quantities of water for industrial, business, and domestic use. In regions where agriculture is a major land use, water availability and quality are as important as soils. Since, in any case, surface waters are essential for regional aesthetic and economic benefits, they should be inventoried thoroughly.

The desired degree of control varies for the type of area where development would affect surface water. Permanent bodies of water—lakes, rivers, streams, estuaries, etc.—are valuable as a source of water supply, food, and recreation, for waste dispersion, transportation, and power generation. All lakes and ponds may become degraded, become marsh and then dry land. This natural evolution, called entropy, may be hastened by uncontrolled development since pollution and erosion resulting from urbanization can destroy the water's balanced nitrogen and oxygen cycles and its recreation potential.

Streams and creeks have a direct effect upon the quality and quantity of a region's water resources. Qualitatively, streams and creeks replenish groundwater, river flow, and reservoirs; they are a major natural source of water to the system and if they become polluted, then a region's entire water resource, both above and below ground will suffer. Quantitatively, streams and creeks may carry increased runoff or sediment from improper watershed development and increase or cut off regular water flow to groundwater formations. Similar quantitative effects can be seen, on a larger scale, in lakes and rivers.

Since streams and creeks contribute to a region's total water resource and general environmental well-being, the planning of development within a region must expand beyond the watercourses themselves and look to the whole concept of the watershed system—drainage, wetlands, lakes, reservoirs, and groundwater filtrations. Since streams and creeks are major networks that transport nutrients and sedimentation, as well as pathways functioning as routes for various birds and mammals, they are a matrix of the watershed, binding hillsides, woodlands, and wetlands into one inseparable, interdependent ecological community. Because streams and creeks are an intricate part of the hydrological and nutrient cycles, and because of their intricate relationship to so many environmental communities and processes, the health of the watercourses serves as an index to the health of the entire system.

Floodland is the land area adjacent to a body of water which is covered by excess water during periods of flooding. This water carrying capacity of floodlands is an essential function and is why floodlands are so valuable. Floodlands may be divided into zones based on the frequency of inundation, often categorized as channels, floodways, and floodplains. It is especially important to make these distinctions for land-use and development controls which are important since building on floodlands endangers human life and property. Furthermore, floodplains often provide valuable recreation land. Filling, damming, or leveling floodplains decreases storage capacity and increases flood velocity and the flood potential downstream. Agriculture is often an ideal use in floodplains as the soils are very fertile, there is usually substantial groundwater, and the effect on flat land is minimal.

Wetlands—tracts of low-lying lands that are saturated with moisture and usually overgrown with vegetation—act as sponges that absorb excess runoff and thus reduce flooding potential. They also provide important wildlife habitats and recreational areas and have educational and scientific value. Some wetlands have agricultural value; they often have scenic beauty. Wetlands are frequently found about estuaries—water passages where the tide meets a river current, especially an arm of the sea at the lower end of a river. As breeding grounds for a variety of organisms, estuaries are particularly intolerant of waste disposal, dredging, filling, and upstream pollution since these activities can destroy important animal and plant communities.

Subsurface waters in the form of aquifers—water-bearing layers of sand, gravel, or porous rock—are as important and delicate as surface waters. As a major source of water supply, their quality must be maintained and the removal of water from them must not exceed the rate of replenishment. Aquifers are replenished in recharge areas—areas of interchange between the aquifer and the earth's surface and the point where precipitation and surface water infiltrate the aquifer. Wise planning of development in recharge areas is particularly important because of the danger of polluting the water supply.

Aquifers act as reservoirs, filters, and a balance in the hydrological system of a community and region. They are natural reservoirs for groundwater used in drinking and irrigation and must be protected because the amount of groundwater entering the aquifers is used by many types of communities: some areas can draw upon surface water supplies, such as lakes and streams, for their drinking water and irrigation needs, but many communities, particularly rural ones, depend upon groundwater or wells drilled into aquifers for their water.

Percolation of precipitation through soil and overlying formations filters many impurities before they reach the aquifer; as groundwater moves through waterbearing formations of aquifers, it is filtered further. But this filtering property of aquifers is not absolute. Leaking septic tanks and sewage lines, unsealed landfill sites, and sewage and soil waste disposal sites can allow pollutants to pass directly into groundwater reserves where the water table is very near the surface, the soil mantle is very thin, or the aquifer is very permeable. In these cases, concern must be directed toward the quality of water entering the aquifer.

Similarly, pollution or depletion of surface water affects groundwater and can contaminate an entire system since aquifers are directly connected to lakes, streams, and wetlands through gradual seepage. Alternately, some of these lakes, streams, and wetlands replenish their water supply from the aquifer when conditions are dry. Therefore, pollution factors must be checked to maintain the aquifer-stream-lake-wetland reciprocal balance and attention must be focused on the quality and quantity of water exchanged between groundwater and surface reserves.

Because aquifers serve these three functions—they act as a reservoir, as a filter, and as part of the hydrological cycle—they are important regional resources and are particularly sensitive in terms of development. It is best to avoid development over deep aquifers.

Hydrology studies include subsurface water as well as surface water. The Water Information Group of the USGS has information in the form of maps, atlases, and reports that cover various characteristics of the hydrological cycle. They have a free publication for each state, "Water Resources Investigation," which includes a list of a selected number of reports prepared for each state. Depending on detail, the scale of the maps varies from 1:24,000 to 1:250,000. For surface water only, a local planning agency may request a copy of the blue overprint from the standard USGS topographic map. These hydrological maps and reports contain much information about the quality and quantity of ground and surface waters. For a given area, hydrological information includes analyses of the elevation levels of major floods, depth to mineralized groundwater, saline water, chemical qualities of surface water, and temperature of surface water. Aquifers, floodplains, and wetlands should be highlighted on the hydrology map.

Soils

Soil composition directly affects building and highway construction, septic systems, water availability, and agriculture. Since everything that touches the soil is affected by it, it is essential that accurate soil data are used in land-use planning. A soil suitability study should be used to assess (1) the engineering property of soils in order to determine the appropriate pattern of residential, commercial, industrial, agricultural, and recreational use; (2) the suitability of soils for sewage dispersion, drainage systems, and water storage; (3) the soil and plant relationship so that prime agricultural areas can be identified; and (4) the location of important mineral deposits.

Soils with a high moisture content, whether due to a high water table or poor drainage, are suitable only for floating or other specially built structures if supplied with public water and sewerage. Wet soils, important because they store water, can be easily contaminated if septic tanks are allowed. In development, draining and filling should be permitted selectively if they do not interfere with the water supply.

Dense soils inhibit and are often impervious to the free downward flow of water; such soils usually have a high proportion of clay in them. Impermeability may cause tanks to overflow and contaminate the water supply, and like wet soils, dense soils are unsuitable for development without public water and sewer systems.

Poor load-bearing soils are usually easy to compact because of their moisture content or because excessive internal spaces are present. (Filled land or industrial or municipal waste piles often have these characteristics.) Such soils are unable to support structures such as buildings and paved roads, and are thus generally unsuitable for intensive development. Recreation and agriculture, as well as certain types of light or flexible structures, are adaptable to poor load-bearing soils, but heavy structures require anchoring to bedrock.

If a local planner is unable to interpret soil types into appropriate use categories (e.g., soils good for residential development, soils for agriculture), the local Soil Conservation Service (SCS) office can prepare such interpretive maps and reports. For this reason, it is a good idea to work closely with the local office.

A soil survey is based upon aerial photography and the maps are usually printed at a scale of $3'' = 5,000$ ($3:60,000$) or $1'' = 1$ mile. They are accompanied by a discussion of the functional classification of the soils in the area based upon a nationwide classification system, including a description of each kind of soil and general information about the agriculture and climate of the area. Most surveys supply information such as the most important soils for potential agricultural uses, what types of wildlife are likely to be associated with certain types of soils, nonagricultural plant material and its relationship with soil types, likely flood and drainage areas, and soil properties affecting engineering uses. This basic information provides a suitable foundation for planning decisions.

Geology

Geology involves not only bedrock and other mineral foundations covered by a layer of soil, but also areas and planes of exposed rock. Geology has a fundamental bearing upon surface and subsurface drainage patterns and a site's ability to support structures.

In some areas, the underground formations are incapable of supporting heavy loads and development can cause subsidence, landsliding or other earth movement. These weak areas are usually associated with certain geologic characteristics, a type of bedrock or the manner in which layers of rock and soil are arranged, for example. Areas such as these may be capable of supporting only low-intensity development and may require special construction methods to assure slope stability.

Many problems arise because investigations often neglect to identify the nature and location of subsurface mineral deposits. Wherever mineral extraction is feasible, the detrimental effects of such extraction must be minimized and provisions must be made for site re-use after the extractive operations are concluded. With proper planning, mineral extraction can be accomplished without negative effects on the environment, but this is possible only if planners know beforehand where the deposits are located so that land use before and after the operation can be controlled. If mineral deposits are found after development has taken place, extraction operations must be precluded.

One of the problems encountered when collecting geological data is that too often they are outdated and have varying degrees of accuracy in many areas of the country. Furthermore, interpretation requires experts. Geological maps of

1:24,000 to 1:63,363 are available for only about 25 percent of the U.S. and smaller scale maps (1:250,000) are available for less than one-third of the states and approximately 40 percent of the country. Maps showing geological structure and mineral resources in a region are available from the USGS.

Vegetation and Wildlife (Biotic Resources)

Too often, if vegetation and wildlife are considered at all in land-use planning, it is only in terms of parks and other open spaces for recreation. Little thought is given to the ecologically delicate relationship among plants, animals, and man. Since uncontrolled development and the subsequent loss of groundcover can often have serious consequences, it is important that planners should have at least a working acquaintance with ecology and should gather as much information as possible about areas in their region sensitive to development.

Development should be watched especially in woodlands since they play an important role in the protection of watersheds. Aside from the aesthetic pleasures that trees, shrubs, and other vegetation provide, they also prevent erosion by binding the soil together with their roots. In addition, as water percolates downward, plantlife aids in its cleansing.

Unique vegetation habitats should be preserved for scientific and educational reasons. Virgin stands of forest, unbroken prairie, and other features support complex animal communities that are intrinsically important. The tolerance of these areas to intensive nearby development varies but must be taken into consideration in any event.

The green overprints of the USGS topographical maps may be used to determine dense woodland cover, but for a more detailed and accurate inventory, local sources have to be used. Wildlife and botany experts at nearby schools are often valuable aids for identifying unique habitat areas and routes of migratory animals that are worthy of protection. State fish and game departments may also have to be consulted. In short, gathering data on vegetation and wildlife is a piecemeal process. Site-specific information on biotic resources simply does not exist for most regions.

Conclusion

Increasing numbers of rural communities find that planning based on natural resources results not only in a more pleasing environment but saves them money. Using the natural resource inventory in conjunction with the traditional inventory of existing land uses provides a firm basis for sensible locational decisions.

Chapter IV
Zoning and Development
Permit Systems

Zoning grew up in the city, and settled down in the suburbs. When people build houses on the edge of Missoula or Cheyenne, they like zoning. They don't have to worry about fast-food restaurants being built next door or a mobile home being parked on the lot across the street. It is like insurance. They pay by giving up their chance to sell their land for a gas station, but in return they are guaranteed a neighborhood of houses like their own.

There is no love affair with zoning in small towns and rural areas; it will need some introductions or match-making.

When a planner suggests a zoning ordinance, he is likely to have an irate citizen respond by pounding his fists and saying: "You can't tell me what to do with my land. Next, you'll want me to have a *permit* to plow my fields." For these people, zoning is a political ideology. It is seen as an infringement on personal liberties. For them, if some fool wants to build a house that will slide down the hill, that's his business.

Every place has a vocal minority that holds this opinion. The difficulty for the planner in sparsely populated areas is that there is often no one on the other side. Most people will be indifferent to zoning, and everyone will probably have misconceptions about it. The planner cannot expect any basic acceptance or support for land controls. For most, zoning does not solve perceived problems; unless the town or rural area is experiencing development pressures, land-use is probably not a major problem. In small towns, the amount of development is small, and most people will develop their land in the same way as their neighbors have. In rural areas, distance is a buffer. Conflicts are few and generally can be handled on an *ad hoc* basis. Zoning an entire town or county seems somewhat like swatting flies with a sledgehammer.

Dislike of zoning does not mean that people are not interested in controls. Let a hippy commune appear with funny looking domes and untidy children waving at the cars on the county road, and someone will be in the office saying: "They can't do that. That's not the way we do things here." The same dislike may be expressed towards junk cars around a house or mobile home. Under these conditions, the planner must be careful of the way he uses zoning. Zoning brings some rules to the game, and the courts can decide if the community is playing fair, but it may sometimes be selectively enforced and it can become vindictive in certain cases.

Strategies for the Planner

Handyman and Technician

Most planners serving small towns and rural areas do not see themselves as power brokers; instead, they play the role of handyman or technician. These are not bad roles, particularly for the beginning planner or for the person who is pioneering planning in an area which has had no planning. In this role, the planner uses land-use controls for doing some minor repairs without doing a total overhaul. For example, the planners from a regional agency in South Dakota were called into a small town because the citizens were concerned about the prospects of apartment buildings. Once the planners started working with the town, they discovered that the town did not object to apartment buildings per se; instead, the people were concerned about the streets becoming clogged with cars and about the apartments attracting single people living together— communes. The regional agency suggested an ordinance that required three off-street parking spaces for every family unit and that said that no family unit could have more than four unrelated individuals. This took care of the problem without a comprehensive plan and a zoning ordinance.

From the planners' point of view, this was a good solution to the problem. The town simply did not need a comprehensive zoning ordinance which tied down all the expected uses. There is certainly no need to overregulate. If the worries are minor, as in this case, then it is possible to solve the problem with a simple ordinance that directly addresses the specific problem. Such ordinances are within traditional police powers of local governments to protect the health, safety, and welfare of their citizens. The important legal consideration to remember is that such ordinances must apply equally to all people in similar situations and to try to figure out the consequences. In this example, the ordinance applied to all housing in the community. It did, however, have one unintended problem: it ruled out convents, which was not the community's intent.

Using bits and pieces from traditional land-use controls to tackle specific problems is common practice. Many places have a floodplain ordinance or a wetland ordinance or a mobile home ordinance without having established formal zoning. These ordinances can be instrumental in convincing the local population that land-use controls have their place. It is not unusual for a small town or rural area to begin with a junk car ordinance, move on to a mobile home ordinance, and end up with a comprehensive plan and zoning ordinance.

Insurance Agent and Fortune Teller

Another strategy for the planner is to act as the community's insurance agent or fortune teller. In doing his plans, the planner is not just identifying current problems, but he is also looking ahead to see what may be around the next corner. This job of assessing the risks that a community or region may be taking by doggedly continuing its current policies is difficult. It is easier for people to complain about their current problems than to figure out what they want for the community five, ten, or twenty years from now, but this future orientation is important for land-use controls. The planner is hired to givef professional advice about the future: what the probabilities are of things going wrong, and what can be done now to reduce those probabilities.

The risks for a community may involve physical danger, such as houses being built in flood-prone areas or on unstable slopes, or the risks may be social. The land may be changing ownership. A check with the records can document if, when land changes hands, it is being bought by people outside the community: corporate farmers, second home buyers, or others. The risks are different if most of the land transfers are internal to the current population or if the land is being bought by outside people, who may not use the land in ways the community is used to. There may also be risks of quick, dramatic change; if there are natural resources, such as coal, that are available for exploitation, a quiet village may suddenly become a boom town.

If the risks of future change are substantial, it may be important for the planner to convince the governments and the people that zoning is necessary, even if repugnant. Remember, the basic reason for land controls is self-interest. This self-interest is described well in a pamphlet by the extension service of Michigan State University.

> Regardless of where you live or what your interests may be, you surely value your property. You would like your home, your farm, your place of business, your summer cottage—whatever you own—to be worth as much a few years from now as it is today.
>
> But, without zoning, many things can happen to your community. Everyone is more or less free to use his property in nearly any way he pleases. The use may be in harmony or in conflict with the interests of the community. It may seriously injure the value of your property. It may even destroy the enjoyment you have had in your property.
>
> As property changes hands in your neighborhood, do you know what the new owners will do? If heirs, will they continue the former use? Or will they sell to a stranger because they live elsewhere or do not care to continue the former use? Then how will the stranger use the property?
>
> Injuries to your property may be due to mere thoughtlessness on the part of neighboring property owners. They may come from I-don't-care newcomers. They may arise from someone's

desire to exploit a location or resource for a particular use at the expense of all other property owners.

You won't have a very definite answer until your town or county has enacted a zoning ordinance governing the future use of property. While zoning cannot change existing conditions, it can protect the future value of your property.

Zoning is not only in the individual's interest, it is in the community's interest, too:

A few years can bring many changes to a community.

Unless changes are guided, most communities tend to grow like Topsy. Some become quite a hodgepodge in the course of time, often with mixed-up land uses that cruelly hurt each other.

When this occurs, then property values begin slipping. But taxes tend to go up. Special assessments may even be levied to meet the cost of doctoring up the hit-and-miss developments. Thousands of dollars must often be spent to change the makeshift roads or streets into a more useful transportation *system*—to create a safe sewage disposal *system*—to provide an adequate fire-fighting or water *system*.

But hit-and-miss is not easily revamped or redesigned into an efficient system.

It is better to have had a plan to begin with. The expense is less both in taxes and in costs to the property owner. The results are better. (Michigan State, p. 3-4.)

There are lots of horror stories that illustrate what can happen if a government does not take care to protect itself from future changes. But there is a success story that tells it better. Northampton County, Virginia is an isolated rural community on the Delmarva Peninsula. Brown and Root, an international construction company, bought acres of land for a huge industrial complex without the knowledge of the county government. The vice-president of Brown and Root and the governor of Virginia jointly announced the news to the county: they were going to have a platform fabrication plant for off-shore oil rigs; 1,500 new workers would soon be arriving. For a county with only 3,650 families, this meant boom troubles. Fortunately for the county, they had a zoning ordinance already in place that zoned most of the county "agriculture-conservation." Brown and Root needed to have their land rezoned to industrial in order to build their plant. During the process of arranging that rezoning, the county designed provisions that protected their groundwater from being polluted,

provided a job training program so that the county's unemployed would have a chance at the new jobs, and developed a
staging plan so that the county would not go through a sudden
boom and bust as a result of an influx of new workers. It all
came from the good luck of having passed a zoning ordinance.
It was nothing complex; it just stated that they expected the
agricultural lands to be used for agriculture.

Innovator and Sly Fox

Finally, there are two other roles which experienced planning
directors from the Old West Region recommend—be crafty or
be creative. The first role is Machiavellian. This role is summarized in the advice: "Do whatever you want, just don't call it
zoning." The planners giving this advice have come to the conclusion that it is politically impossible to get traditional zoning
accepted in their communities; yet, they see lots of problems
that need the regulation inherent in zoning. Their solution to
the problem is to work through informal negotiations with each
individual who is planning to build something new. They feel
that it is critical for the planner to develop the power of persuasion and political powers. These abilities, of course, only come
from experience and time in the community.

Central to this role, obviously, is knowledge of what is going
to be built before it is built. One secret to successful negotiation
is to get to the individual before he or she has invested so much
money that no change in plans is possible. Once the material
has been ordered or ground broken, there is probably little the
planner can do. To obtain this foreknowledge, the planners rely
on the permit systems that are already accepted by the people
in the community. For example, one suggestion is to keep in
close touch with the public utilities. Everyone accepts the fact
that electricity or water or sewer must be assured. By keeping
track of these applications, it is possible for the planner to know
something about people's plans. Another suggestion is to use
platting—the device for officially recording ownership changes
or *lot* subdivisions. In South Dakota, state law says that the
county commissioners must approve plats; so, it is possible to

ask for detailed information when a person applies for plat approval. As one director said, "Just to fill out the form, the guy has to give you all the information you need." Building codes are often used in the same manner.

An example of how this tactic works was given by a planning director in South Dakota. One of the criteria that the county commissioners use in approving plats is whether the new development is on existing roads. "We say, for public health and safety, we don't want school buses riding on inadequate roads—only on county oil. Now this is a land-use control technique, but it is stated in terms of helping out the county school system."

The second role planners can play is that of the innovator. Planning directors for several governments in the Old West Region have been developing land control systems that they feel are more compatible with the rural small town setting. Most of these systems fall under the rubric "development permit systems." The prime difference from traditional zoning is the lack of districts which divide the land into residential, commercial and industrial uses. Instead, the development permit system sets up standards by which each development is reviewed, and acceptance or denial of the development is based on whether the proposed project meets these criteria. In practice, the systems operate like a hybrid of subdivision and zoning. The standards generally include consideration of the availability of public service (water, sewer, etc.) such as subdivision ordinances require, and they generally include consideration of compatibility with surrounding uses, much like zoning. These systems are discussed in detail later in this chapter.

The practical realities that these innovators are confronting are both technical and political. On the technical side, it is difficult to predetermine the best places for future land use. In a largely undeveloped area, there are so many options for locating commercial, industrial or residential use that it becomes impossible to pin down those locations with any certainty. There is no strong justification for a use being located in a particular spot until the point at which developments start infringing on each other. As a result, governments that have passed zoning ordinances find themselves constantly rezoning.

What happens in practice is that land is zoned after the fact. As opposed to urban areas, in rural areas one does not zone undeveloped land. An application for a subdivision comes in, and then the zoning is given to go along with it. There are no billboards saying, "This land zoned commercial."

The political side of the problem also relates to the number of locational options available for any particular land use. One planning director explained it this way: "Someone may want to put in a gas station, and you sit there with the zoning board and they say, 'Yes, we have to zone an area for gas stations.' And they say, 'If we zone that for gas stations, then he's going to make the money and I don't get a chance. What if the guy comes to me and asks me to sell my land?' You set performance standards and require a permit. This puts it back on the free market, and then, everyone is happy." The performance standards to which he refers are the accumulated development policies passed by the government. They are both detailed specifications, such as the typical regulations controlling the use of septic systems, and much more general policies, such as a statement about protecting residential neighborhoods from uses which create glare, noise, or odor. These performance standards are discussed in more detail later in this chapter.

The same planning director found that his commissioners were more willing to put stringent requirements on development through a permit system than with traditional zoning. He also found that these requirements were more acceptable to the developers. He said, "When they build that motel, they'll comply with everything, just as long as you don't tell them to put it on the other side of the highway."

The Basics of Zoning

Whether the planner chooses to use traditional zoning or not, it is good to understand the basic principles involved, since all the other systems of regulations are variations from this original model. Also, zoning is beginning to lose some of its stigma in some rural areas. In Iowa and Colorado, for example, rural and small town zoning is becoming a general practice.

It is impossible within the scope of this book to give a complete treatise on zoning. Just the compilation of all the special zoning districts used in rural and small town areas would fill a book of this size. The fact of the matter is that most zoning ordinances are adaptations of ordinances written for other towns. There are two reasons for this. First, a zoning ordinance is an exercise in legal writing—references to appropriate state legislation, legal definitions, title and application, and provisions for appeals or variances. Much of this material is known as "boilerplate;" the specific wording will be the same for any community. Consequently, it is unnecessary and costly to start from scratch in writing these provisions. They can be taken from either the ordinances of other governments in the state or from model legislation provided by the state office of community affairs.

The second reason is political. Most communities—unless they have had a great deal of experience with zoning—feel more comfortable using a model that has been successful in a community similar to their own. By using ordinances from other towns, they can avoid some of the errors or pitfalls of a first ordinance. The other community's experience acts as a testing ground for specific definitions or particular provisions.

It is necessary for the planner to put together some files that will aid in writing ordinances. There is an abundance of printed material on these subjects, but it is especially good to start a file of ordinances from towns or counties similar to one's own. Currently, there are some general texts on zoning (these are listed in the Bibliography) which provide a good base. It will also be necessary to collect material on specific problems an ordinance might address: floodplain zoning, feedlot zoning, mobile park zoning—whatever the special provision might be for the town.

A zoning ordinance is generally made up of two parts: (1) a map showing the location and boundaries of each zoning district; and (2) an accompanying text which specifies the zoning requirements.

The basic aim of zoning is to segregate incompatible uses. As discussed earlier, this is both the strength and weakness of zoning. By designating specific areas for residential, commercial, or agricultural uses, zoning provides one of the easiest forms of regulations to administer. The landowner will know from the ordinance itself what he can or cannot do with his land. Likewise, it gives the best protection to the current land uses, and the person building a home at a particular site will know what the surrounding land can or cannot be used for. On the other hand, for communities with large amounts of undeveloped land, it may be impossible to draw these lines without closing off too many options.

There are means of getting around this problem. Most small towns, for example, use few districts. For those areas in which it makes sense to draw strict boundaries, it is done, and the rest of the land is left in a more general category. As the community grows and the land-use patterns become better established, the ordinance is amended to reflect these changes. But to begin with it is likely to have just three districts: residential, commercial-industrial, and agricultural.

The Philosophy Behind Use Districts

In standard zoning the entire jurisdiction is divided into districts based on present and desired uses. The districts are not necessarily equally restrictive, however, and if there are areas in which the community is satisfied to allow any type of activity, the zoning would allow it. Generally, however, the zoning districts reflect certain principles:

Compatibility of Uses

Since one of the basic purposes of zoning districts is to separate uses that conflict with each other in some specific way, those uses that are compatible may be grouped together. The idea of compatibility does not, however, mean that districts should be used for only one kind of land use. Single-family residences, duplexes, apartments and locally-oriented retail stores can all be compatible with each other if adequate amounts of land are required for each unit, off-street parking is required, and traffic controlled.

On the other hand, the development of a significant number of residences in agricultural and ranching areas, particularly if occupied by former town dwellers not familiar with farming operations, can result in significant complaints about the effects of agricultural operations. They may result in legal action to stop such normal agricultural practices as night plowing and harvesting, or the use of insecticides and pesticides. A strong wind can easily blow dust and chemicals into nearby residential areas. In one Nebraska case, for example, a developer proposed a mobile home subdivision on the perimeter of a pivot irrigated field. Herbicides and pesticides were both applied through the irrigation system which would have endangered the residents. Basic zoning prevents these problems.

Mobile homes present another example of a use which is sometimes felt to be incompatible with traditional single-family development in some communities. In others, it is permitted on standard lots in residential districts with the units placed on permanent foundations.

Communities vary greatly in their tolerance of the kinds of land uses that are acceptable. Uses which appear to be incompatible need to be examined according to the standards of each community. It is up to the framers of the ordinance to determine what the particular community views as a problem and wants to control.

Appropriateness of the Land

The issue of the appropriateness of the land for particular uses was discussed in the previous chapter. This is a conceptually simple, but sometimes technically complex issue; for example, the soils in a particular area may make certain areas inappropriate for residences using septic systems, and the land should be designated for some other use. If an area is some distance from a major highway, it may be inappropriate for industrial or commercial use. Similarly, floodplains should not be developed for residential or commercial use, but may be used for parking or yards when buildings or homes are on its boundaries. These issues should be fully considered in developing a scheme of zoning districts.

Locational Needs of Uses

The issue in determining locational needs is whether a particular use must be near some other use or public facility. Agricultural processing operations may benefit from being adjacent to agricultural lands. Certain kinds of commercial uses may need to be near residences. Implement dealers may find it desirable to be on the edge of town where they have more room to display equipment. Similarly, industrial operations require good transportation access and therefore should be located near major highways or rail lines.

In some cases, the locational *desires* of particular land users will not be the same as the public desires regarding where those uses should be. This can be particularly troublesome with commercial activities seeking highway strip locations that may create problems because of traffic patterns. There may also be a problem with second homes or other residential developments that seek scenic locations appropriate in terms of the character of the land, but which will result in expensive extensions of roads, school bus routes, or sewer and water systems.

Public Service Effects

The effects of the location of land uses upon public services and facilities should also be considered. Land use patterns have been demonstrated to have significant effects on public service costs. The location of medium density (three dwelling units per acre or more) residential and other development adjacent to small towns where water and sewer extensions can be economically provided is clearly preferable from a cost standpoint to its location some distance from those services.

More subtle impacts on public services also occur. Scattered residential development in rural areas may result in the dedication of new roads to the county and the increase of road maintenance and plowing costs. School bus routes may have to be extended to pick up children in new areas. Fire protection areas may have to be enlarged and, to maintain response times, equipment or stations added. In some areas, second homes, both scattered and in developments, have also resulted in police protection problems during the months they are unoccupied.

Residential Districts

Once it has been determined how the land will be divided, the text of the ordinance is written. For each district there is a statement of purpose, an itemization of future uses of land and property that will be permitted, and standards or conditions under which permitted uses may be carried on, such as minimum lot sizes to insure safety for sewage disposal. For purposes of illustration the following is the "R" Residential District for Clark County, South Dakota:

"R" Residential District Regulations

Section 501. The intent of the "R" Residential District is to provide a stable environment for residential development free from incompatible uses.

Section 502. Use Regulations. A building or premises shall be used only for the following purposes:

1. Agricultural and horticulture uses excluding farmsteads.
2. Single-family dwellings.
3. Two-family dwellings.
4. Multiple dwellings.
5. Public parks, playgrounds, and community buildings.
6. Public libraries.
7. Public schools, elementary and high, or private schools having a curriculum equivalent to a public elementary or public high school and having no rooms regularly used for housing or sleeping purposes.
8. Churches, but any church that is on a new site shall provide off-street parking space upon the lot or within two hundred (200) feet thereof, which space is adequate to accommodate one (1) car for every five (5) persons for which seating is provided in the main auditorium of the church exclusive of the seating capacity of Sunday school and other special rooms.
9. Golf courses, except miniature courses and driving tees.
10. Accessory buildings and accessory uses, customarily incident to the above uses (not involving the conduct of a business), including a private garage, home occupations, the use of a lot or portion thereof for a vegetable or flower garden, and the keeping of small animals and fowl, but not on a commercial basis or on a scale reasonably objectionable to adjacent property owners. Accessory uses shall also include public building bulletin boards and temporary signs not exceeding ten (10) square feet in area, pertaining

to the lease, hire or sale of a building or premises, and church bulletin boards not exceeding twenty (20) square feet in area.

An accessory building that is not a part of the main structure shall be located not less than sixty (60) feet from the front lot line.

Section 503. Parking Regulations. Whenever a structure is erected, converted or structurally altered for a dwelling, there shall be provided accessible parking space on the lot to accommodate one (1) automobile for each dwelling unit.

Section 504. Height Regulations. No building shall exceed two and one half (2½) stories nor shall it exceed thirty-five (35) feet in height except public, semi-public, or public service buildings, hospitals, institutions or schools, when permitted in a district, may be erected to a height not exceeding seventy-five (75) feet if the building is set back from each yard line at least one (1) foot for each two (2) feet of additional building height above the height limit otherwise provided in the district in which the building is located.

Section 505. Yard and Lot Area Regulations.

1. Front Yard:
   (a) There shall be a front yard having a depth of not less than thirty (30) feet except as provided in Article XIII hereof.
   (b) Where lots have a double frontage, the required front yard shall be provided on both streets.
   (c) Where a lot is located at the intersection of two (2) or more streets there shall be a front yard on each street side of a corner lot. No accessory building shall project beyond the front yard line on either street.

2. Side Yard:
   (a) Except as hereinafter provided in the following paragraph and in Article XIII, there shall be a side yard on each side of a building, having a width of not less than ten (10) feet.
   (b) Wherever a buildable lot at the time of the passage of this Resolution has a width less than required in this district, the side yard on each side of a building may be reduced to a width of not less than ten (10) percent of the width of the lot, but in no instance shall it be less than four (4) feet.

3. Rear Yard: Except as hereinafter provided in Article XIII, there shall be a rear yard having a depth of not less than thirty (30) feet or twenty (20) per cent of the depth of the

lot, whichever amount is smaller.

4. Water and Sewer Requirements: Minimum standards shall be those contained in Extension Bulletin No. 665 and shall be in effect until the South Dakota Department of Environmental Protection adopts minimum standards for disposal of waste and for waste disposal systems. Water supply well shall be located a minimum of one hundred (100) feet from any sub-surface absorption system.

Using the above example it is easy to see how each district's regulations fit together.

Statement of Purpose

One of the most frequently overlooked parts of the zoning ordinance is the statement of purpose for each zone. In the above example, the county has only one residential classification and it does not provide for any special exceptions to its basic uses. Therefore, the statement of purpose is simple and straightforward: "to provide a stable environment for residential development." If a community has several residential zones, it would be necessary to distinguish the purpose of each. For example, a community may have an older part of town it wishes to preserve in a single-family residential style. The area may be beginning to experience a slight decline with the introduction of nonconforming mixed land-uses. If the community is serious in its intent to retain the single-family flavor of this area, it should say so in the zoning ordinance in such a way that there is no question about what the community wants within the zone. This is helpful in two ways: (1) if the ordinance is challenged in court, the courts will generally examine whether the intent of the zone is reasonable and within the purposes of zoning, and whether the related specific provisions are consistent with the intent of the zone. In many cases, so long as the intent and provisions are reasonable, the courts will refuse to second-guess the legislative body that adopted the ordinance. (2) The statement of purpose or intent will give the zoning officer guidance in the daily administration of the ordinance.

Permitted Uses, Uses by Special Exception and Accessory Uses

After the statement of intent, the regulations will list the uses that are permitted within the district. (These are also known as "Uses by Right.") This section of the ordinance catalogues all the possible uses of the land; any use must be listed before it can be allowed in the district. The list in the above example is for the most part self-explanatory, but it is useful to explain some items in the list.

The first item states that the "R" zone can be used for agricultural and horticulture uses excluding farmsteads. When delineating the boundary of zone, it is logical to include adjacent undeveloped land to allow for expansion of the primary use of the district. However, since it cannot be predetermined when that land will be developed for residential purposes, some other use of the land must be provided so that the landowner does not lose the use of his property. In the Clark County example, the spare land in the district can be continued to be used for agricultural purposes.

Item eight permits churches into the residential zone, but places special conditions on that particular type of use. In this example, churches are required to provide off-street parking at a ratio of one parking space for every five seats in the main auditorium. When zoning districts get more complicated than this one, there is often an entire list of uses that can only be done under special conditions. These are called uses by special exception or conditional uses. They are often listed separately from the uses by right, and instead of simply being approved by the zoning officer, they must go through additional review by the board of adjustment to make certain they meet the additional requirements. However, if the additional requirements are as simple as parking requirements or locational requirements, then it is better to work these into the text of the regular use requirements.

Item 10, accessory buildings and accessory uses, is a particularly difficult section to write for small towns and rural areas. Accessory uses and structures are those secondary activities expected and accepted on a particular site, such as garages, animal shelters, storage sheds, etc. In urban areas, it is often a matter of simply limiting accessory uses to garages, but in small towns many more activities may go on around a particular residence. It is clear that there is no harm in allowing people to do baby-sitting in their homes or possibly running a beauty parlor in the basement; these uses do not create disturbances for the neighbors. But on the other hand, problems may arise when someone is working on two or three of his neighbors' cars in his backyard or wants to keep a flock of geese.

There is really no way to list or define all these uses or structures. Consequently, it is necessary, as in the example, to give general guidelines of what is acceptable. The phrase "but not on a commercial basis or on a scale reasonably objectionable to adjacent property owners" essentially leaves the final determination up to the zoning officer. Such a phrase gives the government the power to arbitrate disputes when someone registers a complaint about a neighbor.

Dimensional Requirements and Other Standards

Finally, the text of the ordinance will also lay out all the conditions that must be met by the uses of that district. These standards include the height of buildings in feet and/or stories, the minimum size of front, side and rear yards, minimum lot width, minimum lot size, and requirements for water and sewer.

Origcnally, the intent of these requirements was only to ensure adequate light, air and protection from fire hazards. As zoning has developed, their use has expanded to include such purposes as preserving interesting street faces, preventing buildings from blocking sight lines at intersections, and keeping potentially noxious uses at significant distances from adjoining property.

Figure 1. illustrates the major dimensional requirements that can be treated in a residential district in a small town.

Yards

Front yards are measured from right-of-way lines or, where the entire steet is not in public ownership or where there are problems with actual street locations diverging from recorded rights-of-way, they may be measured from the center-line of the traveled or paved roadway. Side and rear yards are measured from lot lines.

Figure 1.

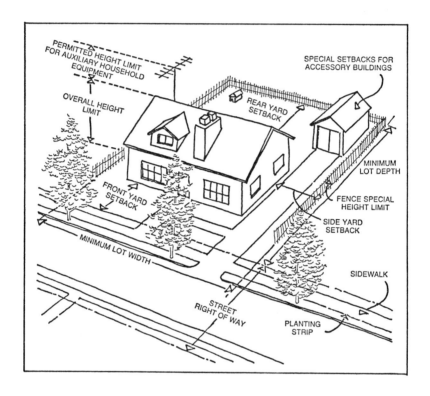

In the Clark County example, these yard requirements change for the uses that are permitted to go above the 35 feet of residential structures. They must add one foot of yard space onto each yard for every two feet of additional building height. The primary purpose of such a provision is to make sure that neighboring residences are not shaded by the larger structures. In addition, these institutions and churches will also have more people using them, and the additional yard space will provide space so they will not be spilling over onto neighboring lawns.

Minimum Lot Width and Depth

Depth is often not used, but rather is the natural result of the area of the lot divided by the required width. Width is measured either at a public street or given as average width with a smaller minimum at the street to accommodate odd shaped lots. Width is generally more important in residential districts since it assures access of fire fight equipment.

Height

Either the height in feet or number of stories may be specified. Appurtenances, such as antennas, are often exempt from building height regulations.

Special Setbacks for Accessory Buildings

Sometimes garages and other accessory buildings are permitted in required rear and side yards, although many ordinances exclude accessory buildings from any required yard.

Lot Size and Density

The minimum lot size is specified in dimensional requirements. In areas without public sewer systems, it may be set as whatever is required to obtain approval of a septic tank. In areas with sewers, it can be used to set the overall eventual pattern and density of development with significant effects on public facility and service costs. In agricultural areas, it can be used to discourage development.

In metropolitan areas, large lot sizes have been used to prevent development of low- and moderate-cost housing.

While this abuse is not widely reported in nonmetropolitan areas, it is a possible abuse in and around growing small towns. Larger lots are simply more expensive, and particularly if not large enough for use in areas of soils suitable for development with on-site sewer and water systems, significantly more expensive to develop with public services. This drives up the cost of housing.

Commercial and Industrial Zoning

Along with a residential zone, most small towns will have a commercial or an industrial zone. These zones follow the same pattern as the residential zones. The following "C-I" District is from Ward, South Dakota:

"C-I" Commercial Industrial District

Intent: The intent of the "C-I" Commercial Industrial District is to provide for business establishments serving the needs of trade area residents, especially retail and service businesses. Permitted uses are intended to create a business district, free from conflicting land-uses.

Permitted Uses: The following uses and structures shall be permitted in the "C-I" Commercial Industrial District:
1. Retail and wholesale sales;
2. Finance, insurance and real estate services;
3. Business services including any warehousing and storage services;
4. Churches, welfare and charitable services;
5. Eating and drinking places;
6. Communication and utility uses;
7. Automobile filling stations and parking;
8. Agriculture and horticulture;
9. Public buildings and grounds.

Minimum Yard Requirements: Permitted uses shall have a minimum front yard of ten (10) feet, minimum side yards of ten (10) feet, and a minimum rear yard of twenty (20) feet.

Special Exceptions: The following uses may be permitted as special exceptions in the "C-I" Commercial Industrial District by the Board of Adjustment, subject to such requirements as the Board deems necessary to protect and promote the health, safety and general welfare:
1. Junk yards, provided that the area is enclosed or screened from public view as required by the Board of Adjustment;

2. Other industrial or commercial uses determined by the Board of Adjustment to be consistent with the intent of this district.

This particular zone was chosen to illustrate two points, one about yard requirements and the other about special exceptions.

The provision of side yard and rear yard requirements in a commercial district is fairly unusual, but presumably this was done to follow conventional practice within the town, which does not have a typical main street environment. A much more common yard and area requirement for commercial establishments would be like that in the Clark County ordinance:

Section 604. Yard and Area Regulations.

1. Side Yard: Where a lot is used for any of the commercial or industrial purposes permitted in this district a side yard is not required except on the side of a lot abutting on an "R" Residential District, in which case there shall be a side yard of not less than nine (9) feet.

2. Rear Yard: In all other cases a rear yard is not required except where a lot abuts on an "R" Residential District, in which case there shall be a rear yard of not less than twenty (20) feet in depth.

3. Intensity of Use. When a buildable lot is improved with a single-family dwelling, two-family dwelling, or a multiple dwelling, or when living facilities are erected above other uses the intensity of use regulations are the same as those required in the "R" Residential District.

This illustrates how specific provisions are customized to promote the particular type of development a community wants.

The second point that should be noted is the use of the special exception procedures for industrial development. Since the town has no current industrial uses, it has allowed prospective industrial developers to use the special exception procedure, rather than requesting a zoning change. Normally, uses by special exceptions must be listed in the same manner as the uses by right. If the board of adjustment turned down an industrial use, the town might be challenged in court for the vagueness of this provision. Also, the provision is an unnecessary and probably illegal delegation of the legislative body's authority. It should be the responsibility of the legislative body to determine what is or is not appropriate to a particular district. The elected representatives should have the final power to say yea or nay on these types of questions.

The Third Zone—Agriculture, Conservation, and Rural Use Districts

It may be relatively easy to distinguish residential zones and commercial zones in small towns, but it is likely that the town's boundaries also include undeveloped land. As discussed earlier, at the time of zoning it may be impossible to know what this land will eventually be used for. No particular land-use pattern has been established. And it is with this land that controversy will probably arise.

There are two approaches to this undeveloped land: one restrictive and one unrestrictive. It is an explicit policy decision to be made by the community.

Restrictive Approach

Small towns, like suburban communities, are sometimes plagued with sprawl. Knox County, Illinois, for example, had the problem of a roadhouse opening up outside of town. A farmer on the zoning board described the problem: "It sits out there with no police protection. I don't know how many times it has been broken into and robbed. Or how many drunken brawls they've had. It's a wonder there haven't been more accidents as people who've been drinking pull out into traffic. A tavern is a hazard anywhere, but especially in the country." This example is probably the most dramatic, but other uses may also create problems: unsightly junk car yards that just keep growing with the years, or Tastee Freezes that create traffic problems along a normally high-speed highway, or private dump grounds that become a nuisance to their neighbors.

Sometimes these problems may be as much the reason for zoning as the protection of the residential and commercial areas within town. In this situation the town generally zones the land for a specific use, such as agriculture, as is the situation in Ward, South Dakota. All the land that is not zoned residential or commercial-industrial is zoned agricultural:

"A" Agricultural District

Intent: The intent of the "A" Agricultural District is to protect agricultural land and uses from incompatible land-uses and to limit residential, commercial and industrial uses to those areas where they are best suited by reason of their requirements for public services and sound development.

Permitted Uses: The following uses and structures shall be permitted in the "A" Agricultural District:
1. Any form of agricultural activity, but excluding feed lots and sales or auction yards or barns which require approval from the Board of Adjustment;
2. Single-family dwellings;
3. Public parks and recreation areas.

Permitted Accessory Uses: The following accessory uses and structures shall be permitted in the "A" Agricultural District:
1. Accessory uses and structures customarily incidental to permitted uses and structures when established within the space limits of this district;
2. Home occupations;
3. Roadside stands for sales of agricultural products grown or produced on the premises.

Special Exceptions: The following uses may be permitted as special exceptions in the "A" Agricultural District by the Board of Adjustment subject to such requirements as the Board deems necessary to protect adjacent property, prevent objectionable or offensive conditions and promote the health, safety and general welfare:
1. Airports;
2. Cemeteries;
3. Commercial or private recreation areas or developments such as golf courses, campgrounds, drive-in theatres, riding stables, race tracks, swimming pools, etc.;
4. Extraction of sand, gravel, minerals and petroleum or natural gas;
5. Public buildings or facilities erected or established and operated by any governmental agency;
6. Radio and television towers and transmitters;
7. Utility substations.

This zoning is clearly designed to keep these nuisance uses out of the open countryside.

In addition, as the statement of intent suggests, this restrictive approach to the surrounding land is also designed to encourage more compact development that can be easily serviced by sewer, water, police, and fire, thus representing a cost saving to the community. This purpose is more clearly stated in the "C" Conservation District for Fairfield Heights, Illinois, a district that is used for the same permitted uses as the agricultural district in Ward:

Section 203.0. "C" Conservation District

The "C" Conservation District encompasses areas within which natural topography creates practical difficulty for compact urban development. Site location for buildings may be difficult on small tracts, adequate and safe traffic circulation systems are problematic, engineering of utility systems and storm water drainage entail special circumstances and difficulties, and erosion can become a significant consideration. This can result in disproportionate or burdensome expenditures of public funds for the provision of necessary supporting roads and public facilities. It is the intent and purpose of this district to provide for appropriate densities to preserve and enhance the natural conditions of such areas and to reduce the disproportionate cost of public facilities, by providing for appropriate uses and density patterns.

One problem should be mentioned with these restrictive open land districts. Unless the zoning is done at a county level or in conjunction with county zoning, they can create "leap-frog development." The businesses that normally would spring up along the highway leading out of town will now be on the same highway but just outside the town limits. What was out in the country will be further out in the country.

Unrestricted Approach

The other situation a planner may find is a community that is concerned about protecting its residential areas or commercial areas from disruptive uses, but is essentially unconcerned about how the undeveloped land is used. In this situation, the third zone may be called "rural use district" and consist of a long catalogue of uses that are currently taking place in that area.

One extreme model of this approach is called "residential restricted zoning." It is popular in Iowa, and the state of Iowa has made special provisions in its enabling legislation to allow such zoning. With this type of zoning, there are only two districts: a restricted residential zone, and an unrestricted zone. The residential zone provisions look the same as those discussed earlier, but the rest of the land is classified as "unrestricted." This second zone is essentially not zoned; the land can be used for any purposes which the landowner wishes—including residential. The people in these towns are only concerned about protecting current residential areas.

County Zoning

When rural counties are situated next to growing urban or metropolitan areas, the zoning ordinances become as intricate and ornate as urban zoning. In these cases, the zoning is attempting to counterbalance strong, natural market pressures for converting open space into urban development. In recent years, there has been considerable experimentation with regulations that are designed to preserve prime agricultural land from being used for housing, to protect particularly scenic areas from overdevelopment, or to protect the government from servicing development that is scattered over huge spaces. In these cases, the county ordinances may include many districts and provisions not generally seen in small town zoning ordinance. Such provisions might include:

— Urban service districts that prevent residential and commercial development from occurring outside of the area served by the city's water and sewer systems;
— Agricultural preserves that prevent the subdivision of farms into small lots;
— Rural center zones that protect small crossroad settlements; or
— Density transfers or purchase of development/zoning rights that allow a farmer to capture some of the development potential of his land without taking it out of production.

However, where these urban development pressures do not occur, county zoning does not look much different from small town zoning. It is likely to have one or two more districts, but that is all. In some regions, for example, these additional regulations are likely to be concerned with resource exploitation—coal or oil, or recreational developments.

Dunn County, North Dakota's ordinance, a particularly fine example of brevity and clarity, illustrates how these additional concerns can be incorporated.

The natural resource exploitation is incorporated into the agricultural district regulations in the following manner: oil and gas exploration and oil and gas production are both permitted uses in the agricultural district. However, these activities must file additional information with the local government to assure that the operation is being conducted in a reasonable manner. These requirements read as follows:

(1)) Oil and gas exploration

The provisions of this section shall not apply to any digging, drilling or excavation for agricultural purposes, the operation of coal mines, oil and gas drilling and production and digging, drilling or excavation by Dunn County and its incorporated cities. The operators must furnish the following to the Code Administrator:

(1) Evidence of compliance with Section 38-08.1-04, N.D.C.C., "Filing of notice of intention to engage in drilling.";

(2) Plan drawn to scale showing the location of lines to be explored;

(3) Schedule of commencement and completion of operations;

(4) Upon completion of operations, a final plan drawn to scale, showing the actual survey location of all seismic exploration lines, and if applicable, the location of all shot holes;

(5) Evidence that the surface owner has been notified in writing of the operator's activities;

(6) Notification that all wire flags and/or other objects related to the exploration activities have been removed;

(7) Evidence that permission for the use of water has been obtained from surface owner before exploration activity begins;

(8) Evidence that the operator has posted a bond as required by Chapter 38-08, North Dakota Century Code, and the Rules and Regulations of the North Dakota Industrial Commission.

(m) Oil and gas drilling and production

The operator shall submit the following data and documents to the Code Administrator prior to any drilling operation:

(1) The legal description of the tract of land on which the well is located;

(2) The location of the proposed well;

(3) The name of the owner of the mineral estate lying in and under the proposed well site;

(4) The location of all buildings within one-fourth (¼) mile of the proposed well site;

(5) The name and address of the drilling contractor;

(6) Approximate date of commencement of operations; and

(7) A copy of the drilling permit issued pursuant to state or federal regulations.

Coal exploration and coal mining, as well as other subsurface mineral exploration, are listed as conditional uses. This gives Dunn County more power to review both the development stage of coal production and the plans for reclamation of the site:

(f) Coal exploration

The provisions of this section shall not apply to any digging, drilling, or excavation for agricultural purposes, the operation of coal mines and the digging, drilling or excavation by Dunn County and its incorporated cities. The applicant for a coal exploration permit shall meet the following requirements:

(1) A copy of the approved North Dakota State Industrial Commission Permit Application Form for Coal Exploration.

(2) A copy of the completed North Dakota State Industrial Commission Coal Exploration Compliance Bond Form.

(3) Upon completion, the operator shall file with the Register of Deeds, the actual location of the testing.

(4) The duration of permit for coal exploration shall not exceed 90 days.

(g) Coal mining

These provisions shall not apply to excavation of coal for private non-commercial uses. The applicant shall meet the following requirements:

(1) Copies of all non-confidential information that was submitted to the Public Service Commission concerning site operations, locations, and ownership patterns.

(2) A copy of all information submitted to the North Dakota Public Service Commission concerning site reclamation.

(3) Evidence of approval by the Public Service Commission for operation of the mine or excavation, if required by state law.

(4) Conformance to all State and Federal laws relating to the preservation, removal or relocation of historical or archaeological artifacts, and to reclamation of strip-mined lands.

(5) To post performance bond for reclamation of the site, with the County Auditor, if not already posted with the state.

The provisions for other subsurface mineral mining follow basically the same format as the coal provisions. The agricultural district concludes with a section on the excavation and mining of sand, gravel, and similar materials. For these activities, the county requires a reclamation agreement in writing, and prevents any excavation or process within 300 feet of an adjacent property line or within 500 feet of an existing residence.

By incorporating these provisions into the agricultural district, rather than making a separate mining or mineral recovery district, the county government has made a clear policy statement concerning possible conflicts between agriculture and these other industries. The county, first and foremost, defines itself as an agricultural county; these other activities must be carried on so as to minimize the disruption to agriculture.

With these regulations, it is clear that the process of administration is more important than the specific content of the regulations. The regulations simply set up assurances that the county government will be knowledgeable about the oil and coal companies' activities, and that the county will have a chance to review the company plans before operations actually take place. What is actually done with this review power depends upon the government's skills in negotiation: how clearly they know their bottom line for these activities and how sophisticated they are in reviewing the technical documents submitted by the coal and oil companies.

The other major concern of western counties will be recreational development. Here again, Dunn County's ordinance represents a particularly clear example. This county has set up a special recreational district, and the primary concerns are the regulation of tourist and trailer camps and the regulation of second homes or recreational homes within the district.

The regulations read as follows:

3.4 R-Recreational District

Permitted Uses:

(a) Agriculture

(b) Public parks and outdoor recreational facilities including golf courses

(c) Churches, schools and related facilities

(d) Hunting, fishing and trapping

(e) Raising of game animals, waterfowl and fish

(f) Harvesting of any natural crops

(g) Ski slides and resorts

(h) Communication and power transmission lines and other public utility lines

(i) Accessory buildings or structures to any permitted uses

2. Conditionally Permitted Uses:

(a) Recreational parks, tourist and trailer camps
   The applicant shall meet the following requirements to obtain a permit:

   (1) The minimum area or campground shall be 5 acres and maximum number of recreational trailers shall be 15 units per gross acre.

   (2) A site plan showing the boundary of property, topographic information with contour intervals of no more than 5 feet; arrangement of streets, drives and access roads; location of service buildings; location and dimension of camp sites; location of sanitary facilities; location of water supply.

   (3) Proof of compliance with the requirements of North Dakota State Health Department and North Dakota State Laboratories Department.

   (4) Approval of the County Commission for ingress and egress to the property.

(b) Single family dwelling units, cabins and summer residences on a minimum of 40 acres of land.

Other Aspects of the Ordinance

While the specific provisions of each district are the most important parts of any ordinance, two other parts of the zoning ordinance are worth mentioning. They are the zoning map and the provision on non-conforming uses.

Figure 2. City Map of Ward, Moody County, South Dakota

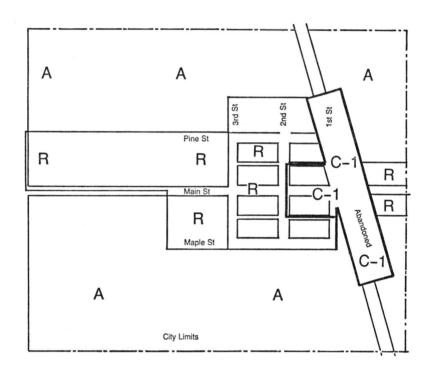

Ward Zoning

   A   Agriculture
   R   Residential
   C-I   Commercial-Industrial

Source: Town of Ward Zoning Ordinance

Zoning district boundaries should be clearly shown on the map and for the sake of clarity and ease of interpretation should follow discernible borders. Streets and roads, railroad rights-of-way, and property lines are usually distinct and are often followed. Where districts or special provisions are applied to special land features such as floodplains, slopes or wetlands, the boundaries of those features need to be delineated and clearly mapped. These will not usually follow property lines and will require more interpretation through either field examination or careful examination of maps.

The map can be as simple as that for Ward, South Dakota, which is printed on the first pages of their ordinance.

In theory, a zoning ordinance applies to both existing and new development and is therefore retroactive. Most zoning ordinances, however, have a special clause which permits the continuance of existing uses that are nonconforming. The most common provisions simply provide that existing nonconforming uses may be continued after adoption of the ordinance, may be maintained, but may *not* be enlarged, rebuilt after substantial destruction by fire or other catastrophe, nor resumed if discontinued for a period of time (commonly one year). Generally, very few nonconforming uses are eliminated by these provisions. Zoning is, in fact, protective and preventative, but not remedial.

Some communities have tried to go further and eliminate nonconforming uses. Some have had the benefit of specific state enabling legislation providing for amortization of nonconforming uses, while others have not. When this is done, nonconforming uses are classified into several types, generally as follows:

1. Nonconforming use of open land—junk yard or used car lot.
2. Nonconforming signs, advertisements, and similar light structures.
3. Nonconforming use of a conforming building—a small shop in a house in a residential district.
4. Nonconforming use of a building specifically designed for that purpose—a factory in a residential district.
5. Buildings conforming as to use but not in conformance with dimensional or other requirements of a physical character. (Delafons, p. 228.)

Each type of nonconformity is then made subject to different requirements, depending on the seriousness of the problem and the amount of investment involved. A conforming use in a nonconforming building, type 5, would generally be left alone. Low investment uses such as signs would be required to be eliminated within, say, three to five years. Others would be phased out over a period that reflected the economic life of the facility. This is essentially conceptually similar to depreciation or amortization for income tax purposes. If an industrialist is depreciating his factory over twenty years, it can be argued that at the end of that period he has recouped his entire investment and can be required to end or remove the use.

This approach has both practical and political limitations and is not used very often. Industries are constantly investing and re-investing in both plant and equipment in order to remain competitive. They would, in fact, be confronted with difficult choices much earlier than the end of the amortization period. In addition, most people will tend to view this kind of provision as a form of public condemnation of private property, even if the period is reasonable and corresponds to depreciation used for income tax purposes.

PAS Report No. 280, *The Effect of Nonconforming Land-Use Amortization,* published in 1972, found that amortization provisions were most commonly used for billboards, that most communities had not adopted such provisions, and that many of those that had did not enforce them consistently. The major reasons given for nonenforcement and lack of adoption were that nonconforming uses were not priority problems, that judicial invalidation was feared, and that homogeneity was not preferred over the existing pattern.

Often, severely conflicting uses can be dealt with in other, more specific ways. If the problem is traffic, traffic control measures may be instituted, often with the help of the owner of the nonconforming use. If appearance is the problem, landscaping may be carried out cooperatively in many cases. If it is a problem of air or water pollution or another clear health hazard, state and federal laws or general nuisance laws may be used to stop the practice.

Administration of Zoning

Once an ordinance has been written and adopted, then it must be publicized and enforced. In urban areas the administration of zoning is a big job. It is not unusual to find planning commissions spending 80 percent of their bi-weekly meetings on requests for zoning changes or other zoning matters. Except for boom towns, this generally will not be the case for rural areas. The volume of development will be small, and, if the ordinance is well written, the amount of necessary administrative time will be small.

Making sure everyone knows about the zoning ordinance may be a bigger job than reviewing applications. Once a building is under construction or built, it is not likely that the community is going to force the individual to take it back down or stop construction. Therefore, it is critical that the planner make sure that people do not ignore the zoning ordinance. As one step in this process, Kings County, Wyoming had the state penitentiary make signs reading: "Kings County is zoned; Building permission required." These signs were placed along the county roads. Since everyone eventually has to drive by one of these signs, ignorance of the fact that there is a zoning law becomes doubtful.

In terms of zoning administration, the experienced planning directors believe that it is particularly important to remember that the final authority for the administration of land-use controls rests with either the lay boards—the planning commission or the board of adjustment—or with the elected officials. They feel it is important to keep the roles clear. As one planning director put it: "The planner sits out in the audience, and the planning commission gets the questions. Never let the Board push you out there in front. Someone on the planning commission should explain the ordinance, and if he gets stuck, then he can ask the planner for an interpretation. Always remain in the role of technical advisor. Otherwise, you're some character who is forcing an ordinance on them."

Development and Adoption of Zoning Ordinances

Zoning ordinances are usually drafted by the planning board in consultation with the jurisdiction's attorney. It is common to find planning directors complaining about the conservatism of municipal attorneys, particularly when drafting zoning ordinances. This conservatism comes from their role of protecting the local government from possible law suits. If a community wants its attorney's stamp of approval on a zoning ordinance, it is essentially asking him to put his professional reputation on the line. Consequently, he is likely to be conservative. As one municipal attorney in Connecticut explains it: "If the planning board writes the ordinance, I can generally defend their ordinance. But if they want me to write it, that's another matter. I have to be careful and make sure there are no controversial sections. It is my reputation which is at stake." In any case, it is typical for the planning department and the planning board to take the lead in the actual drafting of the ordinance. The municipal attorney is likely to review and comment on drafts.

Local governments often develop zoning ordinances in the absence of a formal comprehensive land-use plan or a land-use policy plan. However, a zoning ordinance is strengthened substantially in the eyes of the courts when such documents exist and there are clear links between the plans and the zoning ordinance.

Public hearings are required by most state laws in the process of developing and adopting a zoning ordinance. In some states a planning board hearing and a governing body hearing are both required. Citizens generally participate with far more vigor in zoning hearings than during development of a comprehensive plan. The reality of regulation sparks real concern with the land use proposed for a person's own land as well as his neighbors. It is advisable to provide for preliminary public discussion meetings as well as formal public hearings.

It is likely that during the adoption process a number of changes will be made by the governing body as to boundaries or specific district provisions. This is inevitable and desirable. Adopting an ordinance is a political act subject ultimately to the indirect approval of the electorate at the polls; it is natural that political judgments will be added by the governing body as a complement to the more technical judgments made by and included in the recommendations of the planners and planning board.

Routine Administration

The zoning ordinance will designate an official who will be responsible for basic administration of the zoning ordinance, including granting approval to uses by right that meet all requirements, determining when special reviews are required, and managing the procedural aspects of special exceptions and variances. In order to provide a basic administrative mechanism, either separate zoning permits are required or, in jurisdictions with a building code, a combined zoning and building permit is often used with a space to indicate that zoning approval has been given.

In rural areas it is often difficult to find someone who is readily available and capable of handling these responsibilities. The county or village clerk is often designated, but may not be the most appropriate person. In most counties there is a sanitarian responsible for administering the sanitary code and in some, a building inspector responsible for the building code. Often, the most expeditious arrangement is to designate one of these to administer the zoning ordinance, sanitary code, subdivision ordinance and building code. In some areas, small towns will find it acceptable to have their codes administered by county personnel.

In other cases, a regional planning agency may provide code administration services, sometimes with delegated state authority to handle state permits and reviews as well. A single person may serve several communities by a circuit rider approach, similar to traveling preachers and judges.

In general, it is better to have full-time administrative services by qualified staff with offices located in a different locality than to have part-time local service. If an applicant has to wait for the one day a week that a part-time official is available in order to apply for a permit, temptations to ignore the ordinance may well win out. Part-time services may also result in delays of decisions on special exceptions or other review procedures, an additional temptation to evasion.

Fees may be established as part of the ordinance to cover part of the costs of administration. There is generally a fee schedule with larger fees for larger or more complex developments such as new industry. In urban areas, these fees can become substantial, but the advice from rural planning directors is to keep them low. Don't expect to recapture your administrative costs by charging fees; instead, use only nominal fees to make sure that the applicant is serious about the application.

Amendments

Amendments to the map or text require the approval of the governing body originally adopting the ordinance. In the case of amendments to the map, special notice must be given to adjacent or nearby property owners affected by the proposed amendment. In the case of text amendments, general notice is sufficient. Public hearings are desirable and often required. Some states and localities also provide that in the case of map amendments, the objection of a specified percentage of affected or nearby property owners (such as 20 percent within 500 or 1,000 feet) results in the requirement of a two-thirds or three-fourths majority by the legislative body to pass the amendment.

Variances

Variances are a relief valve given where the literal enforcement of the ordinance would result in unnecessary hardship to a particular property owner. They are decided by the board of adjustment on a case-by-case basis after notice and public hearing; special notice to nearby property owners is good practice. Variances are granted as to height, bulk, placement of buildings, yards and other requirements, when the variance is in harmony with the intent of the ordinance, will not be injurious to the neighborhood, and is not conferring any benefit on the particular property owner not already enjoyed by other residents of the district. Special conditions should exist that do not affect other land or buildings in the district, and that were not created by the property owner. *Use* variances almost never meet the requirements for variances, and should not be granted.

If, for example, an ordinance requires erection of all future dwellings on lots having widths no less than 75 feet, and a land owner finds himself with only a 70-foot lot wedged in between other land owners, the board of appeals may vary the 75-foot requirement and permit construction of the dwelling on the 70-foot lot. But the lot must still be *used* only for a dwelling.

A board of appeals does not have power under the guise of a variance either to disregard or amend the ordinance under which it functions. The board cannot change its fundamental terms nor rezone land for other uses, as is sometimes believed. Only the elected officials may amend or change any part of their ordinance.

Development Permit System

As discussed earlier, the heart of zoning is specifying which uses go on which lands. A zoning ordinance traditionally consists of "use" lists and maps which specify, for instance, that single-family residences, schools, and churches are compatible and can be located in one zoning district, but mobile homes are not and must be put in another section of the community. This kind of ordinance requires the drafters to list many types of present and (if possible) future uses, and then decide which are compatible and which are not. Needless to say the task is difficult and frequently results in arbitrary decisions—particularly in sparsely populated areas with considerable open land.

In the 1950s, APA developed a concept of industrial performance standards for zoning ordinances. The performance criteria were in terms of such measurable outputs as air pollution, noise, vibration, and glare. Thus, a processing plant that because of advanced technology performed in a clean, quiet manner would be permitted near residential uses where previously it would have been required to be in another section of town. Since then, this idea has been used for regulating residential and commercial uses as well.

The history of zoning and land regulations has demonstrated a slow but steady movement toward replacing specification codes with performance codes. Such techniques as planned unit development, floating zones, special use permits, and industrial performance zoning have all been attempts to regulate a particular use or activity on the basis of its performance. These techniques have added flexibility or discretion to traditional zoning by establishing a list of criteria by which development proposals will be reviewed on a case-by-case basis, rather than predetermining what will or will not be allowed.

Such flexible land controls appeal to rural and small towns, and a number of communities have developed this style of regulation. The local government does not grant permission for development in advance of receiving a proposal and analyzing its impacts on the community. In all areas where growth could conceivably occur—farm or vacant land and blighted areas slated for redevelopment—the existing zoning is replaced by a permit system. There are no uses by right in such areas, except the existing uses, and few, if any, prohibited uses. Every development or redevelopment activity is required to obtain a permit.

One of the simplest of these permit systems is that developed by Farmington, Maine. Farmington's land-use ordinance prohibits "adverse effects" from land-use change. It states: "Land use changes that will have an adverse effect on the character of their surrounding areas are prohibited. No land-use changes shall be permitted without Planning Board approval pursuant to this article."

Land use change is defined as altering the use of a property from one category of use to another, and the "surrounding area" is defined as all property within 500 feet of the proposed development. For example, if an individual owns a piece of property and the majority of the surrounding property is used for single-family residences, then the landowner has two options. First, he can conform to the majority use and build a single family residence, in which case he will not need a permit. However, if he wants to build a multi-unit residence, a commercial structure, or a recreation facility, then he will have to have a permit from the town.

In Farmington's system adverse effects are determined by a vote of the affected property owners and the board of selectmen. Each property owner within the 500-foot limit, the property owner requesting the permit, and the selectmen are each given one vote. If a person says that the development would have an adverse effect, he must give his reason. The vote does not have the force of law; it is simply advisory to the planning board. The board can turn down a development even if the majority of surrounding property owners approve. However, one can assume that it would be difficult politically for the planning board to go against the majority wishes of the landowners.

Although this system is appealing because it is so simple and so democratic, it can run into trouble because of its total lack of criteria by which adverse effects are to be measured. Some rural planning directors are leery of such a radical system because it is so open to pressure politics. As one director stated: "Some good old boy will do some arm twisting and get a majority of people to sign his petition; then, if it is a bad development, you are in real trouble."

The Development Permit System created for Breckenridge, Colorado is at the opposite end of the spectrum in terms of its complexity. Breckenridge is a small old-time mining town in the Colorado mountains which has received intense development pressure associated with skiing and other recreational resources. It uses a point system similar to those developed as a growth control mechanism for rapidly growing suburban communities such as Petaluma, California, Ramapo, New York, and Boulder, Colorado.

Kirk Wickersham, the consultant who developed the system for Breckenridge, explains it this way:

> Implementation of a Permit System requires an integrated set of social, economic, public service, environmental, and design policies for a community. It is neither legally nor politically sufficient simply to abolish zoning and wait for proposals to come

in, approving those that strike the fancy of politicians, and rejecting the others. Government must indicate, in advance and to all alike, the types of impacts it seeks from new development and the impacts that will not be tolerated.

Where the Permit System replaces zoning as a basic regulatory mechanism, the policies are adopted directly into law, and issuance or denial of the development permit is based upon them. Policies can be either absolute or relative:

- Absolute policies either require some feature (such as compliance with health regulations when using wells and septic systems) or prohibit something (like building in an avalanche chute). Failure to implement a relevant absolute policy defeats the proposal.

- Relative policies encourage or discourage features by allocating positive or negative points to the proposal based on its performance. Relative policies can be "weighted"—that is, an important policy can be assigned a value of "five" while an unimportant policy is only assigned "one" or "two." The development's score on each policy consists of its performance points multiplied by the importance value of the policy.

To be approved a development must achieve a total net score—for all relative policies of zero or better; density bonuses are awarded for higher scores.

The location and sequence of new growth can be guided through a policy that requires new development to be served by a complete range of public facilities. Extension of the public facilities into new growth areas can be programmed by local government to conform to policies relating to urban form and public fiscal balance. (Wickersham, Jr., p. 6-7.)

As yet, there is little experience with such weighted point systems in rural areas. The suburban communities using similar systems have found some difficulty administering them. The various values given each development criterion are harder to develop than the traditional use list; some of the communities, such as Ramapo, have found that their formulas have become outdated as economic and development conditions change. As a consequence, the point systems have the same arbitrary character that sometimes plagues traditional zoning.

There is, however, a third model of the development permit system which fits somewhere between the totally open system of Farmington and the complex weighting system of Breckenridge. Byron and Ten Sleep in Wyoming's Big Horn Basin are examples of this style of permit systems. The development codes of these communities essentially combine the type of standards found in subdivision codes and zoning codes into one comprehensive list of development criteria—what these ordinances call "performance standards."

The commercial development section from the Ten Sleep ordinance gives a clear picture of how these ordinances are written and how they operate:

Chapter VII. Performance Standards

Section 1. *Commercial Development.* In order to check unnecessary sprawl and encroachment on agricultural land as well as prevent an undue strain on available resources and the tax payers' dollar all commercial development shall conform to the following standards:

a. No commercial development will be allowed without a thorough analysis of the effects of that development on the Town's water supply and distribution system, sewage collection and treatment, fire protection and streets. To accomplish this the following information should be provided by the applicant:

1. An estimate of the amount of water required by the development on a daily basis.
2. An estimate of the amount and type of sewage effluent to be generated daily.
3. An estimate of the amount and type of solid waste to be generated daily.
4. A letter from the Fire Chief stating that the present fire protection service can adequately protect the proposed development.
5. An estimate of the number of employees including an estimate of the number who will reside in Ten Sleep.

b. All commercial development shall be located on Main Street or in an orderly manner to the East of Ten Sleep. A waiver will be granted only if sufficient evidence can be shown to the Council that no adequate site is available in the above named area. An application may be rejected on the basis of lack of an adequate site.

c. All commercial developments located outside the urban limit line shall be provided with an individual water supply, water distribution, and sewage disposal system separate from the Town's facilities. Approval of the water and sewage systems by the Department of Environmental Quality must be presented.

d. The applicant shall bear the full cost of any extension, expansion, or upgrading of Town facilities, including streets, necessitated to accommodate the development.

e. All commercial developments inside the urban limit line must be connected to town water and sewer.

f. The Council may require pre-treatment of a commercial development's effluent before entering the Town's sewage system.

g. Any commercial development not located on Main Street must provide off-street parking adequate for employees and customers.

h. Safe access to public streets must be provided at all commercial developments.

i. No commercial developments shall be allowed inside the Town Limits which houses or sells livestock.

j. All structures or extensions of structures shall be at least 10 feet from all streets and 3 feet from all property lines or alleyways. A distance of 15 feet from property lines is requested if the adjacent lot is solely residential.

k. Any street extension not indicated in the Master Plan from a commercial development to an existing public street shall be considered a private road and shall be maintained by the applicant.

As the above provision illustrates many of the requirements that one would find in a commercial district in a standard zoning ordinance are also found in the development code. Both the Ten Sleep and Byron codes go as far as outlining suggested locations for such uses. In this case the codes say: "All commercial development shall be located on Main Street or in an orderly manner to the East of Ten Sleep." In one sense the town has two commercial districts; however, there is more flexibility than in the standard commercial districts since the town is willing to consider other locations.

The other provisions typical of zoning are the requirements concerning off-street parking, safe access to public streets, standard set-backs, and a buffer distance from residential uses.

What is present in Ten Sleep's ordinance that is not found in the usual zoning ordinance are the provisions which are similar to those of a subdivision code. These provisions include the information about the estimated daily water needs, the amount and type of sewage effluent, and the generation of solid wastes. In addition, the requirements for the applicant to contribute to any public costs arising from the development, such as upgrading streets or extending water facilities, are sometimes found in subdivision codes but not in zoning ordinances.

The particular provisions that development should "bear the full cost" are not necessary for a development permit system. They simply happen to be the policies of these particular towns. Generally communities wish to encourage the expansion of commercial facilities, and the public is willing to support basic public services without special exactions on each new development.

From the point of view of administration, the development codes are clearly more difficult to administer than traditional zoning. Under traditional zoning most development will only require verification that it is indeed in the right zone. The only development that requires much administrative time is that which needs a change in zoning or some variance from the zoning regulations. In these cases it would be necessary to go through planning commission or board of adjustment hearings.

This is not the case with development codes. Every development requires a formal analysis of the effects it will have on the community, and the application must go through formal review procedures in front of the town council. The review procedures for Ten Sleep include provisions for a site inspection by the town council, public hearings on the proposed activity, review and comment on the application from appropriate agencies, and an evaluation of the application in terms of its conformity to the master plan for Ten Sleep. After the hearings, reviews, and evaluations, the town council can approve the application, or approve it with special conditions, or reject it (accompanied by written reasons).

For Ten Sleep and Byron, the increase in administration has not been a burden. It is unlikely that either town has more than ten applications a year; consequently, there is no real problem following the more complex procedures. The staff who developed these ordinances feel that the ordinances may not be appropriate for boom town situations, where everything "is going crazy," but they do feel that the ordinances work well for the towns for which they were designed.

Conclusions

As a planning tool and a guide to land use, rural zoning is in its fourth decade. Although it has had grudging acceptance at best in some states, it is gaining in respect. In addition, the last few years have seen significant experimentation to adapt land controls so they better meet the needs of rural areas. It is likely that the planning departments in rural areas will be making a significant contribution to the way we care for the land.

In conclusion, however, it is good to remember that zoning is not the only technique to promote sound development. To be effective it must be used along with subdivision regulations, building codes, public investment policies, and property tax policies. None of these activities by local governments can stand alone, and this wider use of planning and land-use controls will depend heavily on local leadership. People will have to take the time to become informed of the alternative approaches to managing their community's resources. It is the people who serve on governing, planning, and zoning boards who are the real key to effective land-use controls.

Chapter V
Rural And Small Town
Subdivision Regulations

Section I—Basic Considerations

- X sold off lots along the road over a period of five years, completely surrounding his farm with new houses. Along one road, he left no interior access points, effectively "land-locking" his farm.
- Y subdivided a 40-acre parcel off of his farm and sold the lots. But the roads are not paved and they are impassible for two months a year. Now the residents want the town to rebuild and pave the road.
- Q came out from the city and started subdividing a 20-parcel "estate" subdivision, only to find no one interested in buying at the moment. He started building roads, sold off a few of the most scenic (and interior) parcels, but never finished the roads and other improvements. Now the owners of the interior parcels want someone to finish the roads and provide winter road service.
- Z took a hillside with a view and divided it. But his parcel was narrow and to get access, he built a steep road that is difficult to negotiate in snow and tends to wash out down the hill. Winter road service is impossible and some of the lots will require expensive and special construction to be built on.
- M built a "rustic" community for summer residents with "scenic" 12-foot roads. Fire vehicles cannot get through and pass other vehicles safely, and some residents are now living there year-round.
- P sold off 20-acre parcels to people and did not have to inform anyone. Now the volunteer fire department is no

longer sure where people are living or not living and where
the access roads to these homesteads are.

These are examples of some of the problems which good
subdivision ordinances might have prevented.

This chapter is about subdivision regulation and how subdivision regulation can be used to prevent similar problems in
rural areas and small towns. It is designed to complement
model ordinances prepared by APA, a number of states, and
regional planning agencies. (See Bibliography.)

In rural areas, subdivision regulations are easily as important
as zoning, and often more important. Zoning determines the
uses to which parcels can be put, as well as the size of parcels
and hence density. In many cases in rural areas, however,
there is little public concern as to whether particular parcels
are used for recreation, housing or commerce. Instead the
concern is that, whatever the use, there be adequate roads and
fire access, utilities and sanitary conditions. The community is
concerned that any lots sold should be able to be built on and
that steep slopes and floodplains be protected from development because of hazards that may result. Subdivision regulations address these concerns.

The historical development of subdivision regulation reflects several purposes. Initially subdivision regulation was
used "to provide a more efficient method of selling land,
permitting a seller to record a plat of his land by dividing it
into blocks and lots, sequentially numbered and laid out."
(Freilich and Levi, 1975, p. 2.) This tended to reduce costs of
maintaining land records and prevent conflicting deeds. It
provided for great improvement in the system of keeping land
records and minimal protection to the buyer.

After 1928, subdivision regulations were also used to require that certain internal physical improvements be made in
the subdivision under the general authority of the police
power. Concern focused on the basics: streets and utilities
and layouts. Following World War II, the use of subdivision
regulation broadened to include provision of open space and
school sites and to require that these and streets be dedicated to the municipality. Most subdivision regulation still
remains in this phase and extends to requiring developers to

provide all improvements internal to the subdivision at their expense as well as their share of bordering streets, to insure that the subdivision is basically linked to the rest of the community.

In the 70's, in some localities there has been increasing concern with the relationship between the subdivision and the rest of the community. Attempts have been made to link approval to the availability of adequate facilities off site as well as to consistency with overall plans for capital improvements and community growth.

Today subdivision regulations commonly accomplish several of these purposes. Subdivision regulations:

• Assure the accuracy of land records.
• Require that any lots created are laid out reasonably in relation to topography and conform to zoning, sanitation and other regulations if appropriate.
• Restrict development in areas where hazards will result.
• Require that streets, public utilities, and other facilities be adequate as to design and construction and that those facilities necessary for a particular subdivision are included within it.
• Require the subdivision or owner to pay his fair share of costs of the subdivision.
• Assure that the subdivision relates to the overall plan for the community, and particularly that planned major streets, parks and other public facilities are either provided by the subdivider or reserved for public purchase.

Subdivision review also provides an opportunity to negotiate with the subdivider over the specific design and improvements. Even though it is desirable that local standards and policies be clear, subdivision review is a design process and there is room for difference of opinion on whether a particular design meets the regulations. Hence there is room for negotiation.

When a rural community or small town develops subdivision regulations, it faces a number of issues that should be resolved to local satisfaction. Sometimes state law will be controlling. In other cases, model regulations will contain provisions that are not fully appropriate or which a community can exceed. If, after consideration, the community adopts the provisions of a model regulation, it must understand what it has adopted and be able to defend the regulations against criticism.

Are All Divisions of Land "Subdivisions?"

In principal, any division of land into two or more separate parcels, no matter how large, might be considered a subdivision. In practice, not all divisions are subject to subdivision regulations. Those divisions that do not significantly affect the overall plan of the area, or do not require public improvements or require the creation of new roads, are often exempt from regulation. Small subdividers and local farmers often object to the effort and cost involved in meeting the requirements for some divisions. As a result, divisions such as the creation of one or two 2-acre lots per year or sale of large, off-road parcels are often exempt. Over a period of years, exempt divisions can result in an overloaded rural road network, land-locked interior parcels, and fragmented farmland. On the other hand, in most rural areas creation of 20-acre or larger parcels is likely to create relatively few road or other public service problems, although it could still fragment ownership of productive farm and forest land.

These problems are addressed by carefully drafting the definition of a subdivision. States define a subdivision in state statutes, but often permit localities to develop a "stricter" definition if they wish.

The chosen definition of a subdivision should be based on analysis of what kinds of divisions will create public problems, for example, in providing fire protection, school bus service, road maintenance, sewer and water or other sanitation. Some subdivisions may create a hazard due to mistreatment of the natural environment such as floodplains, slopes, wetlands, or water recharge areas. Others will affect land ownership patterns in such a way that future use of the land, according to reasonable community plans, is threatened by developments such as solid strips along roads, or by developments that are so scattered that the viability of agriculture is destroyed. Divisions of land that are not likely to create such problems are made exempt from subdivision regulation through the wording of the definition and a listing of exemptions. Several sample definitions are shown below.

Definition (Freilich and Levi, Model Subdivision Regulations, p. 144)

Subdivision. Any land, vacant or improved, which is divided or proposed to be divided into two (2) or more lots, parcels, sites, units, plots or interests for the purpose of offer, sale, lease, or development, either on the installment plan or upon any and all other plans, terms, and conditions, including resubdivision. Subdivision includes the division or development of residential and nonresidential zoned land, whether by deed, metes and bounds description, devise, intestacy, lease, map, plat, or other recorded instrument. [2.1]

This is the most restrictive, all inclusive definition possible.

Minor Subdivision. Any subdivision containing not more than three (3) lots fronting on an existing street, not involving any new street or road, or the extension of municipal facilities, or the creation of any public improvements, and not adversely affecting the remainder of the parcel or adjoining property, and not in conflict with any provision or portion of the Master Plan, Official Map, Zoning Ordinance, or these regulations. [2.2(3)]

Major Subdivision. All subdivisions not classified as minor subdivisions, including but not limited to subdivisions of four (4) or more lots, or any size subdivision requiring any new street or extension of the local governmental facilities, or the creation of any public improvements. [2.2(3)]

Definition (Wyoming Department of Economic Planning and Development, Model Subdivision Regulations, June 1976)

Subdivision. For municipalities: the division of a tract or parcel of land into three or more parts for immediate or future sale or building development.

For counties: a division of a lot, tract, parcel or other unit of land into three (3) or more lots, plots, units, sites or other subdivisions of land for the immediate or future purpose of sale, building development or redevelopment, for residential, recreational, industrial, commercial or public uses. The word "subdivide" or any derivative thereof shall have reference to the term subdivision, including mobile home courts, the creation of which constitutes a subdivision of land.

Three lots, no matter how large. No comment is made about the time period over which the divisions occur. This is a

*common "loophole." It permits sequential divisions without
review that may, over time, amount to a fairly substantial
subdivision.*

**Definition (Montana Department of Community Affairs. "Montana
Model Subdivision Regulation." June 1975. pp. 7-8.)**

Subdivision: A division of land so divided, which creates one or
more parcels containing less than twenty (20) acres, exclusive of
public roadways, in order that the title to or possession of the
parcels may be sold, rented, leased, or otherwise conveyed, and
shall include any resubdivision; and shall further include any condominium or *area, regardless of its size, which provides or will
provide multiple space for recreational camping vehicles,* or
mobile homes. A subdivision shall comprise only those parcels
less than twenty (20) acres which have been segregated from the
original tract, and the plat thereof shall show all such parcels
whether contiguous or not. Provided, however, condominiums
constructed on land divided in compliance with the Montana
Subdivision and Platting Act are exempt from the provisions of
the Act.

*20 acres should cover almost any division likely to cause
public service problems.*

a.   Rural Subdivision: A subdivision within which development
     is not more than one dwelling unit per acre exclusive of
     public roadways, and which is located one mile or more
     from a third class city, two miles or more from a second
     class city, or three miles or more from a first class city.

b.   Urban-Suburban Subdivision: A subdivision within which the
     density of development is greater than one dwelling unit
     per acre exclusive of public roadways, or which is located
     within one mile of a town or third class city, two miles of a
     second class city, or three miles of a first class city.

There are five key elements in these definitions:

• *The size of lot considered a subdivision.* If a size is set, some
  developers will divide lots just bigger. In Wisconsin's enabling
  law, for example (not shown), 1.5 acres is the dividing line
  although localities can set larger (stricter) limits. As a result
  there are many divisions of land into lots of 1.6 acres, thereby
  evading the definition of a subdivision. Others use larger sizes,
  for example, the 20 acres in Montana. One argument in setting a
  size is that farmers trying to transfer a building site to a child
  should not have to go through the rigors of subdivision review.

• *The number of lots at one time over some period of years.*
  Some definitions exclude a single lot no matter how small if it is
  an isolated division. If there will be an average of more than one

lot per year, it is considered a subdivision. This ends up being enforced only when an owner attempts to sell, for example, the fifth lot in the fourth year. At best, it only slows down the unreviewed divisions, since all the subdivider has to do is wait.

- *Whether the lots are already served by a public street or not.* If streets or municipal utilities are involved, even one new parcel could count as a subdivision regardless of size. If no new streets or utilities are involved a less restrictive definition would apply.

- *Whether the definition covers only lots developed for sale or also those for lease, mobile home sites and condominiums.* Some state's law may constrain local choice by restricting the definition to sale. This is not uniform, however, and the options should be explored. If a community is also carrying out a zoning ordinance and has site plan review procedures for larger developments including apartments and commercial enterprises, they may be covered there. If leased developments and condominiums are not adequately reviewed under zoning, a definition similar to the sample from Freilich and Levi's *Model Subdivision Regulations* will cover. That definition appears to cover all possible situations other than a current owner building on a currently recorded panel. It also creates enough ambiguity about what might be *excluded* that a planning board determination would be required in some cases.

- *Allowance of specified exemptions.* Maine exempts gifts to blood, marriage or adopted relatives, sales to abutting landowners, and lots kept for one's own use for five years. Montana exempts intra-family transfers as long as the lot is recorded and the deed transferred simultaneously. Only one transfer is allowed. The most important exemptions are usually those relating to transfers within a family and these appear to be increasingly common in agricultural, ranching and other rural areas.

As a practical matter, definitions that reflect these distinctions would require four types of subdivisions.

- *Exempt Divisions of Land.* A division or series of divisions creating an average of less than one lot per year (five lots in five years), creating very large lots and not requiring public sewer or water extensions or a new public street can be exempt from the standards and requirements. The farmer or rancher selling off an occasional parcel to provide cash will not, therefore, be subject to full regulations.
  To keep the planning board (and the volunteer fire department) up to date, however, exempt divisions should be required to be filed as a survey and reviewed by the planning board for accuracy before the division is recorded.

- *Small Subdivisions (5 to 25 or 50 parcels).* Small scale subdivisions are likely to be the projects of local residents with the technical aid of the local land surveyor. The challenge in regulating these divisions is to deal with the limited resources and (in some cases) experience of local residents while protecting the public interests that led to regulation in the first place. The standards and improvement requirements should be the same as for larger subdivisions, including guarantees that improvements will be built. It is sometimes possible, however, to develop a simpler, two-step review process for smaller divisions. Review proceeds directly from a sketch plat to a final plat. Public meetings, on-site inspection, reviews and negotiation can be focused on the sketch plat; the final plat is then developed and reflects the agreed-upon design, thus saving the cost of preparing the extra set of drawings and documents. It should be emphasized, however, that all standards should be followed.

- *Subdivisions of Over 50 Parcels.* Large subdivisions in rural areas and small towns are often projects of developers from outside the community. They will generally be better financed than local subdividers. They may be both subdividing and building houses for sale. The procedures and requirements for large divisions may be somewhat different than for smaller ones. If any significant public investments or expenses are requested, such as a sewer extension, there should be provisions requiring that the developer prepare a market study that satisfactorily demonstrates that the market will absorb the project. Otherwise, public expenditures are risky. Environmental impact statements can be required, probably even if not required for smaller divisions since the prospective impact can be presumed to be larger. The fee schedule may provide that any costs of hiring consultants to review a large development may be assessed against the subdivider. The fullest review process, involving sketch plat, preliminary and final plat reviews should be used. Large divisions will often be developed in stages and require provisions for approval of both the whole and subsequent parts. There will also have to be guarantees that improvements will be built (see section on administration, following).

- *Intra-Family Transfers.* Some states and localities make distinctions between intra-family transfers and other transfers where the particular type of division would otherwise be subject to review. Montana in its Model Subdivision Regulations, June 1975, provides that the transfer of ownership and the recording of the division must occur simultaneously to prevent abuse. Only one such transfer is permitted. Administratively, these would be treated as any other exempt division of land and would be submitted to the planning board for informational purposes.

What Can be Required by Regulations?

The heart of subdivision regulation is its requirements for improvements, dedication of land to the public, reservation of sites for public facilities, standards for improvements, design requirements, and determination of who pays for what. These provisions assure that necessary public facilities are provided in a subdivision, that the quality of the improvements is adequate, that the public is protected against hazards resulting from the misuse of the natural environment, and that the layout is safe and serviceable.

A community can choose what it will require. Whatever the local government expects in terms of public facilities, open space, land for street and roads, reservations for school sites or fire stations, etc. should be provided at the time of subdivision. To do so later—or on verbal assurances of a subdivider—is not likely to work.

Dedication, Easements, Reservations, and Maintenance

The subdivision regulations will provide for dedication of public rights-of-way; recording of easements for utilities, drainage or other purposes; reservation of school and other public facility sites (to be purchased later); may require dedication of public open space; and may be used to assure private maintenance of private streets or other common facilities. In a few states, localities may be permitted to accept ownership of streets without becoming responsible for all services and maintenance. Freilich and Levi's *Model Subdivision Regulations* contain a full range of these provisions.

In developing these requirements, several issues need to be considered:

- *Streets.* Street rights-of-way are generally required to be dedicated, including the land required for planned major streets included in the subdivision. For example, if a major two-lane arterial is planned through the area being subdivided, the subdivider is usually required to dedicate the land but only improve the road to, say, collector standards. In some ordinances, this has been left rather ambiguous. If it is ambiguous, it provides room for negotiation which may or may not be to the community's advantage.

- *Homeowner Associations.* If streets, sewers, water systems or other facilities are not dedicated to the public or are not accepted for maintenance as well as ownership, there must be provision for maintenance. This is usually in the form of a homeowners' association and the regulations may specify that any such association must be approved by the local government as part of the subdivision review process. In many cases, homeowners' associations have not fulfilled all of their responsibilities and local governments have taken full maintenance and service responsibilities, regardless of the original agreement. As a result, many communities now require dedication of all common facilities in subdivisions and that they meet local standards. This applies to "seasonal" second home developments as well.

- *Open Space Dedication.* Many communities require open space dedication as discussed later. Courts have upheld the rights of communities to require open space so long as it is necessary to serve the people in that subdivision and not the community at large. Communities may also reserve additional space or collect fees-in-lieu-of dedication to use to purchase open space.

Reservation Requirements. Reservation requirements protect sites for such planned community facilities as schools, wells, and community-wide parks. They require that those sites be formally shown on a comprehensive plan and/or official map, and that the community be prepared to buy them. Without reservation requirements, the community may not be able to prevent a subdivider from including the site in his plat.

- *Easements.* All required easements should be required to be shown on plats. Utility easements, containing electric, phone and other utilities, are frequently now provided along rear lot lines. Drainage easements are also often required as are access easements. Suitable legal documentation attached to deeds will be required. The register of deeds procedures should be coordinated with those of the subdivision regulations.

What Improvements Should be Required?

What improvements to require of the subdivider and standards for improvements are central issues in subdivision regulation. This discussion will divide improvements into "basic" and "optional" ones. The ones shown as basic seem to be the minimum that a community should require—streets, sanitation, water, storm drainage, utilities, survey monuments, reservations. Others, including parks, sidewalks, etc., may be necessary or desired in some communities but not others. For example, sidewalks and street lights may be necessary for safety in a subdivision in a village or another higher density subdivision, but not in a low density one. The idea of "optional" may be incorporated in the ordinance as "at the option" of the planning board. The treatment of various improvements as options at the discretion of the planning board also provides more opportunity for negotiation with subdividers.

Who Pays for Improvements?

Typically, improvements within the subdivision are the sole responsibility of the subdivider. This does not necessarily mean the subdivider pays, however. For example, electric and gas utilities file rules on extensions with state utility-regulating agencies that include a free extension limit for each new customer. Sewer and water utilities, public or private, often have similar rules.

Subdivision regulations will cross-reference or restate these other requirements. Generally, the developer or subdivider should take the risk in developing the subdivision; the community should not carry costs related to facilities used solely by people within the subdivision. Requiring the developer to take the risk involved in paying for improvements also helps insure that the developer will check the market.

The costs of improvements will be built into the lot or house prices and included in mortgages. They are paid off over a long term and result in a reasonably fair deal for developer, new residents and existing residents.

Some communities allow special assessment districts to be established for new subdivisions. The local government installs the required improvements at its cost and places a special assessment against the property. Commonly, the buyer pays the assessment. Some communities also finance the assessments through special assessment funds and allow buyers to pay the assessment over a period of years.

If the subdivision is slow to sell out, the local government is left holding the assessments. Basically, use of special assessments helps small subdividers with limited access to capital, but puts the risk on the local government. If a community wishes to assist subdividers/developers in this way, it should first make sure that there is a strong market for the project by requiring that a market analysis be prepared by the subdivider.

Some improvements will also serve more than the subdivision. Collector or interceptor sewers and water mains are the two common examples. Generally, collector sewers and the like are fully provided by the developer/subdivider. The rationale is that all other subdivisions will have similar amounts of collector sewers and hence this segment is for the use of the residents of this subdivision.

Interceptor sewers and main water lines may, however, serve much larger populations and provide excess capacity for future growth. These costs are not usually charged directly to a developer, although a pro rata share of the cost is borne by each developer. There are two basic alternatives that are equitable. One is for government to pick up the cost and charge each developer a pro rata share as a tap fee or other charge. The second is to require the first developer to pay the costs and recover them from subsequent developers who use the facility. The second approach is preferable as it places risk and cost burden on the developer. In the case of proposed leapfrog subdivisions, the first cost may be sufficient to discourage the subdivision and result in development of other land closer to services.

In many cases, the specific details of handling the costs will be subject to negotiation within general policies that place the costs attributable to the subdivision on the subdivision.

Improvement guarantees should be also required as discussed in Section IV—Administration.

What Are Appropriate Improvement and Design Requirements?

Development of improvement requirements and standards involves both matters of policy and technical questions. Whether to require paved streets, for example, is partly a matter of policy concerning whether paved streets are preferable for dust control, aesthetic or equipment-access reasons. It may also be a technical matter related to whether fire equipment can cope with unpaved streets, whether adequate drainage and road stability require paving. Once it is decided whether to require paving or not, engineers must assist in determining what kinds of base and surface are necessary in a particular locality. The principles of examining both policy and technical questions apply to all improvements and related standards.

Traditionally, standards for subdivision improvements have been specification standards: "Streets constructed of 8" of crushed rock surfaced with 4" of bituminous concrete," for example. Growing awareness of alternative techniques for solving the same problem has led to use of performance criteria and "certified professional design" in some cases. This is particularly the case with storm water management where storm sewers are often not necessary if the design of the subdivision itself includes open or vegetated areas or ponds to hold run-off. The regulations might, for example, provide that storm run-off not exceed the run-off prior to development, that the plan be certified by a licensed engineer, and that it will be subject to review by the Soil Conservation Service and the local consulting or municipal engineer prior to approval by the local government. In the discussion of specific improvements, this question will be raised where appropriate and sources of technical assistance noted.

The technical nature of improvement standards requires that the planner or planning board draw on the expertise of others in developing requirements and reviewing proposed subdivisions. Engineers, land surveyors, landscape architects and soils scientists are all involved. In larger cities and some counties, the services of engineers are usually available in the engineering department or public works department. Since this is not the case in rural areas, consulting engineering services may be necessary. The Soil Conservation Service of USDA, which has offices in virtually every county in the United States, is also an extremely important source of advice and assistance with regard to soil suitabilities and treatments for roads and septic tanks, storm water control practices, and other questions.

Section II—Improvements

This section is organized in three parts: basic improvements, optional improvements and improvements for special types of subdivision. Both general requirements and development of standards are discussed. Standards and examples shown should be considered illustrative.

Basic Improvements

Basic improvements are those that should be required of virtually all subdivisions in all communities. The standards of the improvements should be varied, however, depending on the size and the character of the community. The question of whether particular improvements are to be reserved, provided in easements, or dedicated is dealt with in the following discussion of each.

Streets

Streets improved to adequate width and standards for the function and loads expected should be required and the expense borne by the developer. Streets should generally be dedicated to the locality. In the case of multi-family or PUD subdivisions where the owner or a homeowners' association takes permanent responsibility for maintenance, streets may be improved to municipal standards but not dedicated if provisions for maintenance satisfactory to the community are made. Where a street shown on the master street plan, such as a major arterial, is of a function and size greater than that which may reasonably be attributed to the subdivision, the subdivider may be required to dedicate the entire right-of-way, but is often only required to improve it to collector standards. This is a negotiable issue, of course, with additional costs carried by the local government.

Width of street, right-of-way, and paving and curbing requirements in various situations should all be specified in the regulations. (Sidewalks are discussed as optional improvements. See page 126.) Some communities have developed separate design manuals, containing detailed specification standards and design requirements, which have the advantage of segregating material of greatest concern to the engineers, site planners or surveyors actually designing the subdivision.

General Requirement, (Frederick County, Maryland)

Section 38A-55. Street and Sidewalk Construction.

A. Street Construction

The subdivider shall provide for the complete construction of street improvements, including drainage facilities (except driveway entrance drainage pipes), as provided in section 38A-72 of this ordinance and in accordance with the specifications of the Frederick County Design Manual.

> *"Open Section" is without curbs and gutters. "Closed" section is with curbs and gutters.*

Open Section Construction, as specified in the Design Manual, may be utilized when the median lot size is ten thousand (10,000) square feet or greater. Closed Section Construction, as specified in the Design Manual, shall be utilized where two-family and multi-family developments are proposed and where the median lot size for single-family dwellings is less than ten thousand (10,000) square feet. Closed Section Construction may also be required by the Planning Commission where it would be desirable to continue Closed Section Construction that is existing or proposed in adjoining developments.

Standards. Standards as to width, right-of-way, curbing and construction and paving types should be established by the locality. These standards, however, need to be related to local conditions and should not necessarily be simply adopted from elsewhere, such as model subdivision regulation or state highway standards. An excellent discussion of the question, with good consideration of both public and builder concerns with cost and maintenance, can be found in *Residential Streets: Objectives, Principles and Design Considerations,* Urban Land Institute (ULI), American Society of Civil Engineers (ASCE) and National Association of Home Builders (NAHB), 1974, available from ULI, 1200 18th Street, N.W., Washington, D.C. 20036.

Width. Residential streets, as opposed to streets serving primarily through traffic, are usually lightly loaded. Their width relates to their function, parking policy, snow storage needs, convenience and access for emergency vehicles, and only secondarily to traffic volumes. Their right-of-way needs relate to presence or absence of sidewalks and placement of utilities. If utilities are not in the right-of-way and the pedestrian system is internal or there is none, extra right-of-way may not be needed. The exception would be streets expected to become through, major streets as other areas develop. ULI/ NAHB/ASCE present a hierarchy of streets ranging from "place" to "arterial" in the manual, *Residential Streets,* which differentiates residential streets from state, county or town highways. (See Figure 1.)

Residential Streets argues that unimpeded two-way flow is not required on streets below "subcollector"—here drivers are cautious and not particularly inconvenienced by occasional waiting. Narrower streets below the subcollector level also encourage greater caution.

Width is also influenced by parking: if it is provided for residents and visitors within lots, it may be preferable to eliminate street parking, or provide it only on one side. In snowy climates, width must also be provided for snow storage.

Consideration of these factors produces somewhat different results from those of the common recommendations, such as are found in Freilich. Overall development density receives only peripheral consideration—a factor that contributes to vehicle volume—in preference to function and number of units served by a particular street. In rural and small town situations, where the range of development densities is limited, the functional approach is worthy of the most consideration so long as the major streets or county highway plan considered overall volume and capacity questions.

It is recommended that the standards derived from ULI *et al* and shown in Figure 1. be considered, compared with standards in state or other local sources and with local experience. These apply to streets and roads *within subdivisions only.* For the major street system, including state, county and town roads that now function or will function as arterials, state standards should be used.

Figure 1. Street Width

Conditions	Paved Width
Collector or Sub-Collector 2 moving lanes parking both sides	36 feet
Loop Sub-Collectors generally not connected to an arterial, parking 2 sides, alternating flow acceptable	26 feet
Lanes and Places including cul-de-sacs to 300', parking 1 side, with snow likely	20 feet
Special Situations with maxi- mum speeds of 10–15mph serve topo, cul-de-sacs of 3 du's, loops up to 10 du's	16 to 18 feet

Source: ULI, *et al., Residential Streets,* pp. 22-23.

If parking is not desired or required, widths can be reduced by eight feet per parking lane. It is doubtful that streets should be reduced much below twenty feet even without parking. Under alternating flow, it is assumed that there is some place into which an approaching vehicle can pull over.

Rights-of-way are commonly 20 to 30 feet wider than paved widths where utilities and sidewalks are required. Planning sources use 30 additional feet almost uniformly, regardless of utility or sidewalk needs. The building industry prefers twenty feet only if sidewalks and utilities are involved, and less if utilities are in rear property line easements. Their argument is, of course, partly land consumption, but also that unnecessary public maintenance requirements result.

As indicated earlier, streets that will be arterial highways in the future should be improved to highway standards rather than residential street standards. These commonly involve shoulders, 50 mph or greater design standards, and right-of-way adequate to provide for these factors.

Construction, Curbing and Paving. Construction, curbing and paving requirements also relate to local factors. The base of the road, where gravel must be brought in, etc., relate to the underlying soil conditions. Some soils can be made into suitable road base by addition of chemicals and the expense of removal and replacement avoided. The Soil Conservation Service of USDA (SCS) has developed engineering soil maps. Technical assistance on this question is available from SCS offices.

The method of storm drainage selected will affect whether curbing is needed or desirable. Storm sewers commonly require curbing to divert water to inlets, while on-site retention methods generally do not require curbing. Curbing requirements may therefore be made contingent on the storm drainage system.

Climate and resulting frost or other problems are important variables as well, affecting the kind of base, surface and drainage needed for durability. It may be desirable to omit curbing and install gravel rather than hard surfaced roads. Shoulder, curb or edge treatment may also be specified to allow natural vegetation to grow back up to the road edge rather than a gravel or other edge.

Again, given the number of possible concerns in construction and paving, local standards should be developed in conjunction with the SCS, local engineers, road and highway departments, and possibly developers.

The requirements in the regulation may include the usual construction and paving for various situations, but should provide for variation with the approval of a local engineer or road department. In any case all improvement plans for roads should be certified by a licensed engineer.

Sewer and Water

It is required that provision be made for sewer and water services generally acceptable to health authorities. Subdivision regulations will prohibit subdivisions, usually by reference to state or county sanitary requirements, in areas where adequate sewerage disposal cannot be obtained. Often, however, these requirements are designed primarily for individual, scattered sites and should be modified for subdivisions to provide for soil testing on each lot or at a number of test sites spaced across the proposed subdivision.

In many cases, it will be clear whether a public system is a reasonable requirement or whether on-site private facilities must be used. Where public systems exist, or will exist within 1,000 feet at the time the subdivision is built, requiring public systems is usually economically justifiable. The permissible increase in density will more than compensate for the cost of the system and an extension to reach the subdivision. Where the subdivision is in an area where no public system will reach within ten or twenty years, and the proposal is for large lots or parcels capable of supporting wells and septic tanks, that approach will be preferable. Unfortunately, a large proportion of proposals will fall between these two extremes.

Commonly, a proposal will be made for a subdivision in an area that is likely to be served in five to ten years. Some ordinances, such as Freilich and Levi's model, would require a capped sewer system, and allow septic tanks and wells to be used in the interim. In the meantime, the cost of providing a capped system on lots large enough to insure adequate functioning of septic tanks is generally prohibitive. The requirement may have the effect, desired in most cases, of dissuading the subdivider. An alternative is to require lot sizes and layouts that permit resubdivision at a later time.

A second alternative is the designation of service areas for water and sewer systems. The service areas could be developed as part of required water quality planning and management activities or independently, based on long-term population expectations and cost-effectiveness analysis of system alternatives. The service area would need to be amended frequently—every two or three years—to conform to growth rates and the specific costs involved in extending service to a particular area. An area proposed for subdivision but not in the service area would either be developed with septic tanks with provisions for resubdivision, or denied as premature. (The cost-effectiveness questions are complex and are treated in greater detail elsewhere. For example, a subdivision in an area expected to be served within five years might be more economically developed with a capped system and interim septic tanks than to install sewers later. Cost analyses can consider such questions, and policies can be developed for sub-parts of a service area, that is, those to be served in two years, five years, or ten years.)

Subdividers in fringe and outlying areas wishing to develop higher density subdivisions may propose package or community sewer and water systems. There are management problems, both present and future, with such systems and they may not meet state and federal requirements. They should not necessarily be banned, however, but their use should generally not be encouraged in areas where municipal systems are likely in the foreseeable future.

Water systems should generally provide full fire flow capacity. There may be some situations, however, where the groundwater is of poor quality and a small pipe community water system is proposed in a subdivision of one-acre or larger lots instead of wells. This presents the community with a dilemma regarding fire protection since fire flow capacity is not provided. Some people are willing to pay the costs of small pipe water systems in one-acre or larger lot subdivisions where the risk of fire spread may not be too severe. Whether these types of facilities will be considered acceptable should be a matter of policy, determined in advance of requested approvals, after consultation with fire officials and health officials. Which types of systems may be found acceptable under varying conditions should be specified in improvement requirements.

Both sewer and water systems are often handled by reference to applicable county and state health requirements;

those requirements are generally controlling unless the subdivision standards are "higher."

Where on-site systems will be used for water or sewer it is important to require that each lot be required to be tested for a source of water and adequate drainage for waste disposal. This is basically a consumer protection requirement to protect unsuspecting buyers, but also protects the locality in the long run from failing wells and septic tanks requiring extension of municipal systems.

General Requirement (Dane County, Wisconsin)

8.63 Sewage Disposal System

(1) In Type I Subdivision, provision for private sewage disposal systems shall be specified as by Chapter H65 of the Wisconsin Administrative Code and the County Sanitary Ordinance.

> *Types I and II were defined in the definition of a subdivision.*

(2) In Type II Subdivision where public sanitary sewers are available at the time of platting, the subdivision shall be provided with sanitary sewers to each lot within the subdivision.

(3) In Type II Subdivision, where public sanitary sewers are not available at the time of platting, provision for private sewage disposal systems shall be as specified by Chapter H65 of the Wisconsin Administrative Code and the County Sanitary Ordinance. In addition, the subdivision shall be provided with sanitary sewers to each lot within the subdivision.

> *Other ordinances use distance as a criterion of availability. 500 feet is common, but too short in most cases. Assuming smaller lots with sewer and water facilities, a subdivider can pay for a sewer or water extension and still have a marketable subdivision in terms of price. 500 feet may be too long for a 5-lot division, while one-half mile may be "affordable" for a 150-lot division.*

(4) For purposes of this Ordinance determination of whether sewer facilities will not be available to the subdivision within a period of two (2) years shall be made by the Agency after review of sewer facilities, plans, and pro-

grams affecting the area in which the subdivision is located.

General Requirement (Butler County, Pennsylvania)
5.08 Water Supply Hydrants

1. Where public water is available adjacent to or within five hundred (500) feet of the subdivision or land development, the developer shall connect to the public water system, and a letter of intent from the water utility shall be filed with the Planning Commission stating:

    a. That the development can be served with an adequate water supply;
    b. That sufficient static and flow pressures for fire protection are available at peak demand; and
    c. That the proposed plans for the water supply system have been designed to meet the requirements of the water utility.

2. Where the subdivision or land development occurs in an area that has been designated by the municipality or by the authority or by the company serving it as an area to be connected within a period of two (2) years, the Planning Commission may require the developer to construct the necessary water mains and provide an interim water supply.

3. Where public water is not available, the developer shall provide individual water supply systems on each lot, or a supply system serving the entire plan or clusters of lots or buildings, acceptable to the Pennsylvania Department of Environmental Resources.

4. All water supply systems shall meet the requirements of the Pennsylvania Department of Environmental Resources as to quality, quantity and pressure.

5. Water distribution lines shall be not less than six (6) inches in diameter.

    This is the minimum size for fire protection.

6. Fire hydrants shall be provided, spaced not farther apart than five hundred (500) feet, where connection has been or will be made to a public water system.

Standards. Some regulations provide detailed standards and engineering criteria with regard to load and demand estimates, pipe sizes, slope of pipe, etc. These do not appear justified at this time. There are a number of innovations under development in systems for small communities, including pressure systems, vacuum sewers, management systems for individual and group septic tanks, and the like. While this development complicates matters and creates a greater need for prior planning in the area, it also means that subdivision regulations should cross-reference approval of other authorities rather than incorporate the separate requirements.

It is suggested that a provision be developed requiring approval of health authorities and the local consulting engineer, and that standards in the subdivision regulation be limited to designation of which types, locations and densities of subdivisions will be required to have public or community systems rather than individual facilities.

Storm Drainage and Grading

Current practice is moving away from storm sewer systems to more general requirements that some system of drainage through grading, natural storage, etc., be provided to manage the expected runoff and protect adjacent lots in the subdivision and land not part of the subdivision. This is considered to be cheaper and environmentally more sound: natural water flow is disrupted less with fewer effects on groundwater recharge, resulting in less pollution from runoff. The requirement should reflect this flexibility of methods, as should the related design standards.

General Requirement (Montana Model Subdivision Regulations, June 1975)

8. Grading and Drainage

a. The subdivider shall provide a complete grading and drainage plan with accurate dimensions, courses and elevations, showing the proposed grades of streets and drainage improvements.

> *The way these provisions are written establishes desirable flexibility.*

b. The subdivider shall provide suitable drainage facilities for any surface run-off affecting the subdivision; these facilities shall be located in street rights-of-way or in perpetual easements of appropriate widths and are subject to approval by the governing body.

c. Each culvert or other drainage facility shall be large enough to accommodate potential run-off from upstream drainage areas.

d. Drainage systems shall not discharge into any sanitary sewer facility.

e. The grading and drainage system shall be designed and certified by a registered engineer.

f. The grading and drainage system for a minor subdivision may be designed and certified by a registered engineer or, with the approval of the governing body, may be designed in consultation with the Soil Conservation Service or other authorities.

g. All drainage systems shall meet the minimum standards of the Montana Department of Health and Environmental Sciences, as required by Sections 69-5001 through 69-5005, R.C.M. 1947, and all regulations adopted pursuant thereto.

Standards

The sample shown cross-references state requirements, and the wording of the sample establishes flexibility with regard to how they are met. There is a growing body of information on how to handle storm water by other than building storm sewers, partly as a result of the U.S. Environmental Protection Agency's Water Quality Planning and Management program (Section 208). That agency and the Soil Conservation Service are a readily available local source of information. In addition, *Residential Storm Water Management* by the Urban Land Institute, American Society of Civil Engineers and National Association of Home Builders, 1975, available from ULI, treats the basic considerations involved.

The objectives of storm water management are to prevent flooding of lots and within the subdivision, to avoid water load in downhill or downstream areas by keeping both storm water on site and runoff to what they were before development, and to prevent water pollution resulting from runoff from the subdivision.

The options for dealing with storm water include a storm sewer system as well as on-site measures. The on-site measures which relate to the basic design of the subdivisions, are much preferred since the water does not have to be treated. They include retention ponds that can also be used for recreation—these can sometimes be created by using roads as dams, and by minimizing paved areas, drainage ways and easements that may lead water to open areas. These measures must be carefully designed and reviewed in terms of long-term maintenance requirements such as potential siltation or algae growth in retention ponds.

All drainage and related grading plans should be certified by an engineer, subject to review by the local engineer and Soil Conservation Service.

Utilities

(Gas, Electricity, Telephone, and Cable TV). The installation of gas, electrical and telephone utilities is required by subdivision regulation. In areas where cable tv is in use it should be required as well. The subdivider makes arrangements for installation with the private utility providing the service, and will make financial arrangements with the utility according to the rules and rates on file with the state regulatory agency. Many localities include the utility companies among the reviewers to insure conformance. Private utilities should be included in financial guarantees of improvement costs and inspections to insure that all improvements are installed.

It is increasingly prevalent to require electric lines, telephone cables and cable tv to be installed underground. There are both aesthetic and maintenance advantages, as well as reduction in service interruptions due to storms. This requirement will generally not apply below a certain density for cost reasons, but the cost questions need to be explored locally with the utility company to determine a cut off point. For technical reasons, power lines above a certain level of voltage may not be able to be buried.

As natural gas service is becoming increasingly difficult to obtain in some parts of the country, it may become an optional requirement in the future, with provisions requiring an attempt to obtain it, and if obtained, its installation at the time of construction.

General Requirement (Frederick County, Maryland)
Section 38A-51 Gas, Electric and Telephone Utilities
Extensions of electric distribution lines necessary to furnish permanent electric and telephone service to any residential, commercial or industrial subdivision, shall be made underground in accordance with Public Service Commission Rules and existing tariffs. Electric transmission and distribution lines of 138 kv or greater shall be exempt from the underground requirement.

Cable tv should be added if in use in the area.

Standards. Utility company standards will apply to the more technical aspects. Local decisions relate to whether to place electric and telephone lines underground as discussed above and where the lines shall be placed. In recent years, above-ground utilities have increasingly been placed in an easement along rear lot lines rather than along streets. There are often both aesthetic and cost advantages to such a placement, although access for maintenance can be a problem. Underground utilities are often required to be placed in such an easement, rather than under streets. In case service is needed, the street does not have to be torn up, although the residents may plant shrubbery, place storage buildings or build fences in the easements. The advantage of street placement of underground utilities is that a separate trench does not have to be dug and the utilities can be installed at the same time as the street is torn up for installation of sewer and water systems. The building industry favors an in-street location. (See NAHB, *Land Development Manual,* 1974, Chapter 14, p. 236). Freilich and Levi provide language for underground installation in rear lot line easements.

Survey Monuments
Monuments are required so that the platted lots and streets can be rechecked at some future time should disputes or questions arise. The standards and requirements are suprisingly uniform, despite the fact that monuments are supposed to be frost-proof and the frost line varies. Most requirements

set them only 24 inches–30 inches deep even in areas of
42-inch and 48-inch frost penetration. The monument requirements are covered by improvement guarantees and permanent monuments *within* the subdivision are often placed
after major construction is completed to avoid their being
disturbed by construction equipment.

General Requirement (Butler County, Pennsylvania)
5.03 Monuments and Markers
1. Monuments shall be set permanently:
   a. At the intersection of all lines forming angles in the
      boundary of the subdivision or land development; and
   b. At the intersection of all street lines.
2. Markers shall be set permanently at all lot corners.
3. Monuments shall be made of pre-cast concrete with a
   minimum diameter of six (6) inches and a minimum
   length of thirty (30) inches, and shall be set flush with
   the finished grade. A brass pin shall be set in the top of
   each monument and scored or marked to indicate the
   exact point of crossing of the intersecting lines.
4. Markers shall consist of magnetic metal pipes or bars at
   least twenty-four (24) inches long and not less than
   three-quarters ($\frac{3}{4}$) inch in diameter, and shall be set flush
   with the finished grade. They shall be scored to indicate
   the exact point of crossing of intersecting lines.
5. Any monuments or markers that are removed shall be
   replaced by a registered engineer or surveyor at the
   expense of the person removing them.

Standards. Included above.

School Sites and Other Public Facilities
Reservation of sites for schools, parks in excess of dedication requirements, and fire stations and the like are usually
shown on the community master plan. When they are included in the land being subdivided they are "reserved" for
public use, but must be purchased. These facilities are not
subject to dedication requirements or fees since they generally are not attributable only to a single subdivision and it
would be rare that a single development would provide adequate demand to justify dedication of the whole site. This

contrasts with park and open space requirements, where even one acre may be a useful park to the small number of people in a subdivision generating only that much need for recreation space as determined by local standards.

Freilich and Levi's *Model Subdivision Regulations* include ordinance language for provision of land for other public uses— sites to be reserved as part of an overall planning effort and shown on official documents, such as the comprehensive plan or an official map.

Optional Improvements

Open Space Dedication or Fees in Lieu

In subdivisions above a minimal density such as 1 dwelling unit (du) per 2- to 5-acres, there is little argument that the residents generate a need and demand for public or semi-public parks and open space. Reasonable requirements may be related to lot size and fees required if no suitable land exists on the site. It is generally recommended that a fixed, per lot fee be used and placed in a neighborhood park fund. Such a fee, however, would need to be periodically updated to remain current with rising land values. An alternative is a fee based on *developed* market value of the land in the subdivision. This type of fee is based on the assumption that the land later bought to serve the neighborhood's needs will be bought from another subdivider in the process of developing at the price he would obtain from the market. Until that time, the money should be retained in a neighborhood park fund and invested. The problem of assuring that the investments yield as great a return as the inflation of land costs rests with the community.

Some communities are also reported to be exacting a fee to use to develop the park. This has emerged in areas where the developers want the park developed right away as a marketing point in their subdivision and offer to defray the costs. (Lamont, 1978). It is unlikely that such a mechanism would be popular in areas where most developers would not do it voluntarily, although it appears a legally reasonable extension of the dedication requirements.

See Freilich and Levi, *Model Subdivision Regulations* for ordinance language for parks, playgrounds, and recreation areas.

Small towns and low density areas may find it more advantageous to provide larger community parks which are not treated by dedication requirements, but can be reserved and purchased. Low density areas, in particular, may provide ample space for residents with community-wide parks of much greater benefit. On the other hand, in small towns that are growing substantially it *is* important to provide space within newly developing areas, since as time goes by and more development occurs, the "rural" fringe will be further away.

Sidewalks

Sidewalks and pedestrian ways are well established in subdivision regulations. Sidewalk requirements are generally related to the function and traffic expectations of the street system, and may not be required at all in low density subdivisions, or may be required on one side only.

The traditional sidewalk requirement relates to the density of the area, the function of the roads involved, and the continuation of existing sidewalks in lower density areas. Areas of 10,000 square-foot lots or smaller would commonly require sidewalks.

Standards

Sidewalks are usually four feet wide and paved. Concrete paving is not necessary in most cases, although a proper base is needed to avoid heaving in frost-prone areas. Local engineers should have knowledge of local soil and climatic conditions, and can assist in developing paving base and minimum slope (to prevent icing) requirements.

Street Signs and Names

Requirements that the subdivider provide street signs and street names relieves the community of the cost of the signs and the basic task of inventing street names. The community, however, must still double check for duplication.

Street Lighting

Street lighting is not likely to be needed in small town and rural subdivisions, but may be reasonably required, if desired. Roadway lighting standards, including standards for local streets and roads, are available: "Roadway Lighting" Publication RP-8, Illuminating Engineering Society, 345 East 47th Street, New York, New York 10017, $1.50 to members of IES, $2.25 to nonmembers. These are the American National Standards Institute Approved Standards, July 11, 1972. In considering these or other street lighting standards, energy consumption must be considered as a long term cost factor.

Numbered Fire Markers

If numbered house markers are required at the driveway entrance to facilitate locating driveways in emergencies, they may be required as a subdivision improvement.

Trees and Landscaping

Many urban jurisdictions require street trees and seeding or sod. Most rural areas will be satisfied with requiring final grading and soil stabilization for environmental protection, and leave more cosmetic landscaping to the residents. In small towns where street trees are in place in already-developed areas, the requirement of street trees is certainly reasonable and relieves the jurisdiction of a cost they would otherwise incur.

Mobile Homes and Other Special Subdivisions

The requirements for design and improvements discussed so far apply to all divisions of land that meet the definition of a subdivision. This generally includes planned developments, mobile home developments, and commercial or industrial subdivisions. To the extent that any standards or requirements need to be different for special types of subdivisions, they must be spelled out in the regulation or in separate regulations.

Mobile homes are most often treated differently, with special lot size and development requirements. Planned Unit Developments and Industrial and Commercial Subdivisions are subject usually to essentially the same standards as any other subdivision. In PUDs the key issue is to provide adequate flexibility to allow a good design and to coordinate zoning and subdivision approvals. Most model ordinances provide such language. In industrial and commercial subdivisions standards for streets and utilities may be different in order to handle heavier loads. Depending on state law, condominiums may be covered by the subdivision regulations.

Mobile home developments, however, remain the most common and often the most troublesome special type of subdivision. In rural areas and small towns, they may be proposed at a density that is otherwise unheard of in the community. Hence, the normal standards for utilities, streets and design may be inapplicable or at best less than fully appropriate.

The first question that a community must answer is whether it is willing to permit developments of such density. If the standard lot size of conventional construction is 10,000 to 12,000 square feet in a small town, what is the justification for 4,000 square-foot lots in a mobile home subdivision? Similarly, if in open country areas standard construction is permitted only on one-acre lots, why should mobile home developments be treated any differently? There is, after all, no great difference in sewerage, water and fire protection needs between the traditional subdivision and a mobile home one. While these are questions traditionally addressed in zoning, there are many communities that may not need or want zoning but do regulate the density of mobile homes as part of a subdivision regulation or through a separate mobile home ordinance. Thus, wherever the attempt is made to regulate mobile home subdivisions, these questions should be addressed.

In fact, mobile home subdivisions may be the only ones proposed for higher density development in rural areas. This is largely the result of the workings of the housing market. The mobile homes represent a lower cost living option with more desirable conditions than apartments in many cases. Hence, those who can afford larger houses or standard construction may also be able to afford standard lots or acreage, while those considering mobile homes cannot. As a result, the regulations on mobile homes may need to consider issues not faced elsewhere.

For a detailed guidance on regulation of mobile home subdivisions, see *Environmental Health Guide for Mobile Home Communities,* U.S. Public Health Service, Center for Disease Control, Atlanta, Georgia, 1975, and Planning Advisory Service Report 271, "Regulation of Modular Housing, with Special Emphasis on Mobile Homes." Since these reports were published, construction standards have been set nationally (1975). In other respects, however, they are still relevant. General site planning principles still apply as well.

The following ordinance excerpts illustrate some of the differences between regulation of a standard subdivision and a mobile home subdivision. It is recommended that for the most part standards not be lower than they would be in any other subdivision of similar density.

Mobile Home Park Developments (Frederick County, Maryland)
(3)(e) Street construction and design standards

i. Ownership. All streets shall be privately owned and maintained by the owner.
   In other single-family development, dedication is required.

ii. Pavements. All streets shall be paved to County pavement standards.

iii. Grades. Grades of all streets shall be sufficient to insure adequate surface drainage, but shall be not more than eight (8) percent. Short runs, with a maximum grade of ten (10) percent, may be permitted, provided traffic safety is assured by appropriate paving, adequate leveling areas and avoidance of small radii curves.
   Steeper grades than usually permitted in subdivision.

iv. Curb and gutter. All streets shall be provided with a concrete or asphalt curb and gutter.
   Usual for this density.

v. Intersections. Streets shall intersect at approximately right angles. A distance of at least one hundred (100) feet shall be maintained between center lines of offset intersecting streets. Intersections of more than two (2) streets at one point shall be avoided.
   Usual.

(4) Walks

a) General requirements. All developments shall be provided with safe, convenient, paved pedestrian walks of a

three (3) foot minimum width. Sudden changes in alignment and gradient shall be avoided. Location of walks
are subject to Planning Commission approval.

4 feet wide usual.

b) Individual walks. All mobile home stands shall be connected to common walks, to paved driveways or parking
spaces connecting to a paved street. Such individual
walks shall have a minimum width of two (2) feet.

Usually silent on on-lot walkways.

(5) Mobile home stands. The area of the mobile home stand
shall be improved to provide adequate support for the
placement and tie-down of the mobile home, thereby
securing the superstructure against uplift, sliding, rota-
tion and overturning.

a) The mobile home stand shall be constructed so as not to
heave, shift, or settle unevenly under the weight of the
mobile home due to frost action, inadequate drainage,
vibration or other forces acting on the structure.

These are critical lot improvements to assure safety.

b) The mobile home stand shall be provided with anchors
and tie-downs, such as cast-in-place concrete "dead
men," eyelets imbedded in concrete foundations or run-
ways, screw augers, arrowhead anchors or other devices
securing the stability of the mobile home.

c) Anchors and tie-downs shall be placed at least at each
corner of the mobile home stand, and each shall be able
to sustain a minimum tensile strength of twenty-eight
hundred (2,800) pounds.

Water, sewer, underground utility, parking, and street lighting requirements would all be those appropriate to the density
of the development and expected loads. They would not be
different than a single-family development of the same density
class, i.e., less than 10,000 square feet per lot.

Section III—Design Requirements

Design requirements in subdivision regulations address several major issues and problems associated with new development in rural areas and small towns. Design requirements address development in areas of potential natural hazards, protection of the character of the land, traffic and pedestrian safety, convenience to residents and other users of new development as affected by layout, and some aesthetic aspects of development.

Design requirements cannot be fully specified since the character of land varies from place to place. The requirements together with the three-stage subdivision review process discussed later provide an opportunity to develop safe, workable and environmentally sensitive subdivisions.

In designing subdivisions there are a number of general considerations important to both the subdivider and the planners reviewing subdivisions. These are discussed generally in "Caring for the Land" by Bruce Hendler, APA, 1977, and more specific guidance can be found in a text on site planning.

Both *Site Planning* by Kevin Lynch, MIT Press, 1971, and *A Guide to Site and Environmental Planning,* by Harvey M. Rubenstein, John Wiley and Sons, 1969, are good texts on site planning.

The major design considerations include:

- Relate streets and buildings to the topography in order to reduce steep street grades, disruption of natural drainage ways, concentration of run-off in street channels, and improved aesthetics.
- Minimize cutting and filling and removal of natural vegetation in order to reduce disruption of natural drainage and minimize aesthetic changes.
- Produce lots that are appropriately shaped and sized for building purposes.
- Provide blocks or clusters of lots that minimize the overall length of streets and public facilities.
- Provide street patterns and intersections that minimize traffic problems.
- Provide pedestrian ways that are separated from vehicular traffic and that go to the places pedestrians want to go.

- Provide recreation space of appropriate kinds for both children and adults.

Design regulations, along with informed and careful review, make it possible to achieve these design objectives through subdivision regulation. The remainder of this section covers those design regulations.

The design of a subdivision is required to conform to applicable zoning codes and the characteristics of the site. In the absence of zoning, minimum lot sizes for sewered and unsewered developments can be specified in subdivision regulations in the section on lots.

A general statement regarding the uniqueness of the site is often included, which is primarily a statement of policy, but is also a statement that the concept of the general welfare under the police power includes preserving natural features. Courts have ruled that the general welfare is an inclusive, broad concept and extends to essentially aesthetic and value preference matters as well as more precisely definable impacts of land development on people's health. Frederick County, Maryland handles these two points clearly and in few words:

Land Requirements (Frederick County, Maryland)

1) The land-use pattern of the Comprehensive Development Plan and the District Regulations of the Zoning Regulations shall form the basic theme of the design pattern of the proposed subdivision.

2) The subdivision design shall take advantage of the uniqueness of the site reflected by the topography, soils, the wooded areas, water bodies and the relationship to adjoining subdivisions and land-uses, both proposed and existing.

Development of Environmentally Sensitive and Hazardous Areas

Development in floodplains, along fault lines, on steep slopes and in landslide areas may be prohibited in subdivision regulations or special requirements may be applied to assure that hazards are avoided.

The specific hazards will vary from place to place. Most common is prohibition in floodplain areas, in part due to national concern with flooding and flood insurance programs. Other hazards are also important, however, and in developing regulations natural resource specialists at the nearest university or in the extension service should be consulted to be certain that the key hazards have been considered. A key reference for planning and regulation in such areas is *Performance Controls for Sensitive Lands* by Charles Thurow, et al, APA, PAS Report 307/308, 1975.

Preservation of Natural Features

The requirements of the sections on uniqueness of the land and development in hazard areas notwithstanding, it is desirable and common to prohibit changing the character of the land through bulldozing, cutting of trees, and removal of natural vegetation, prior to approval of the plat. It is required that the major natural features and trees be retained, thus preventing changes in the character of the landscape. From the developer's perspective, the retention of the natural features and trees where they are at all significant usually improves the sale value of the lots in the subdivision. Construction costs, however, may be higher when trees and other features are retained and must be worked around. As a result, many developers in the past, and a few today, clear sites before developing the plan or commencing work.

Some communities have had administrative problems with this kind of requirement. Some developers will strip the land before they initiate the subdivision review process. This may be dealt with first through attempts to educate developers and by establishing a reputation of being helpful (within limits) to subdividers. The cost vs. increase in value question is helpful here for persuasion purposes. It can next be dealt with by confronting possible offenders where stripping is occurring and future subdivision is expected; as a last resort, fines and court injunctions may be used if it can be proven that the stripper is intending to subdivide. (A general ordinance requiring a permit for such activities regardless of subdivision plans would make it easier to enforce this through the courts. In many communities, however, that would constitute an unacceptable intrusion into practices on the land and exceed the locally acceptable limits of regulation. Such a regulation is legally permissible, however.)

The provision on this question shown in Freilich and Levi's *Model Subdivision Regulations* is clear on the question of preservation of natural features.

Preservation of Natural Features and Amenities (Freilich and Levi)

(1) *General*. Existing features which would add value to residential development or to the local government as a whole, such as trees, as herein defined, watercourses and falls, beaches, historic sports, and similar irreplaceable assets, shall be preserved in the design of the subdivision. No trees shall be removed from any subdivision nor any change of grade of the land effected until approval of the preliminary plat has been preserved, and all trees where required shall be welled and protected against change of grade. The sketch plat shall show the number and location of existing trees, as required by these regulations and shall further indicate all those marked for retention, and the location of all proposed shade trees required along the street side of each lot as required by these regulations.

Erosion and Sedimentation

In addition to the storm drainage and grading provisions to reduce runoff discussed above in the Improvement Requirements section, it may be desirable to require measures during construction, and later to assure that erosion and resulting sedimentation of streams is controlled.

Erosion and sedimentation problems are not limited to areas of steep slope. They can occur in gently sloping agricultural areas, particularly where contour plowing and other protective measures are not being followed. When such areas are developed, the ground is susceptible to erosion once its vegetative cover is stripped. Measures for dealing with the problem focus on preserving vegetative cover during construction and quickly restoring it afterwards, as well as on structural and design measures. Addressing these issues can be required in the grading plans. *Performance Controls for Sensitive Lands* contains a full discussion of these issues.

Solar Orientation

As an energy conservation measure, there is increasing concern with orienting housing to take maximum advantage of sunlight for heat in northern climates. This is important whether full scale solar collection systems are to be used, there is to be passive "collection" through windows with storage in a masonry wall, or only incidental heat is to be picked up through the windows. Orienting streets from east to west rather than north to south will tend to produce lots amenable to orienting houses to take best advantage of sunlight and protecting their access to it in the future. This occurs because the southern exposure is protected by either a yard or a street. If streets are oriented north-south, adjacent buildings can block solar access unless complex regulations on placement of buildings on lots are used.

Streets and Intersections

Design requirements for streets are among the best developed of subdivision design provisions, reflecting both their importance for safety reasons and the fact that they were among the first issues covered by subdivision regulations. Overall layout, grades, alignments, use of cul-de-sacs and intersections are usually covered along with the width and paving requirements discussed above under improvement standards. Streets, through their relationship to topography, relate to environmental design questions and their orientation to solar access. Street plans and designs will be developed in interaction with the other aspects of the design of the subdivision as the site plan is developed. The requirements that must be met are subject to clear delineation, although there will be a number of ways to meet those requirements in each design situation. This is an area where careful examination by reviewers and negotiation with the subdivider can result in improvements in meeting the spirit as well as the letter of regulations. Many rural jurisdictions do not find it necessary to include all provisions discussed here.

Relationship to Topography

Relating street patterns to the existing topography helps reduce costs for cutting and filling to meet grade requirements and contributes substantially to the environmental sensitivity of the overall design.

Figure 2, taken from Michigan's "Model Guide for an Ordinance Regulating Subdivision of Land" provides a clear example of what this means.

Grades and Alignments

The maximum grade of streets is controlled to insure that roadways can be negotiated in all weather conditions, the minimum grade is regulated to assure drainage, and in cold climates, reduce or prevent icing. The horizontal alignment of curves (sharpness of curve) is controlled to assure safe curves at expected driving speeds and the vertical curve (the curve over the crest of a hill) is regulated to assure that there is adequate visibility over the crest to see a small object in time to stop. Minimum straightaways or tangent distances on reverse curves are also required.

There is greater variation than might be expected in these requirements. Grades relate in part to climate. Horizontal alignments and tangents relate to design speed and assumptions about how maneuverable vehicles are. Vertical alignments relate to design speed and assumed stopping distances. The variation in regulations from different parts of the country appears to be the result of different assumptions by the highway departments of various states. In order to assure conformance with those requirements and with unique climate and topological conditions, it is recommended that the state highway department be consulted and Freilich and Levi and the ULI publication, *Residential Streets,* cited earlier be used for reference and further background.

Overall Street Patterns

Subdivision regulations include a listing of several principles on the layout of streets, the use of cul-de-sacs, treatment of frontage on arterials, and other questions. Ordinance excerpts shown below illustrate the regulations, with sketches shown to further clarify the intent of the regulations in some cases.

Figure 2. Streets and Topography

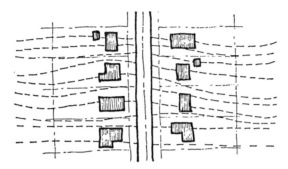

*Poor- Street running perpendicular to
slope creates excessive grades ...*

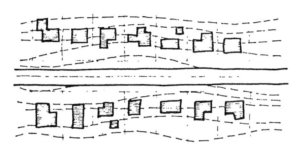

*Poor-Lots on one side higher than others.
Retaining walls may be needed...*

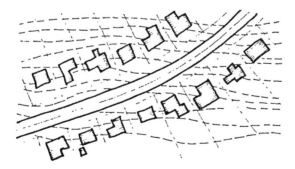

*Good - Avoids excessive grades
and costly retaining walls...*

Source: Michigan, *A Model Guide for an Ordinance Regulating Subdivision of Land*, 1968.

Discourage Through Traffic (Boulder, Colorado)

Local access roads shall be laid out so that their use by major through traffic will be discouraged.

Frontage on a Public Street, but not a collector or arterial (Boulder, Colorado)

Each lot shall be provided with the minimum frontage on an approved public or access road as specified in the Boulder County Zoning Resolution. Lots are generally not permitted to front on or obtain direct access from a collector, arterial or other high type road. The feasibility of a suitable driveway from the access road to a usable building area on each site must be demonstrated for each lot.

Prohibition of access from a collector or arterial is commonly met by providing reverse frontage lots, and where the roadway is an arterial or freeway, buffering may also be required. Regulation of distance between access points is an alternative and is discussed below.

Intervals Between Streets and Driveways (Butler County, Pennsylvania)

In general, local and minor streets, and collector streets shall not adjoin into the same side of a major or arterial street at intervals of less than eight hundred (800) feet.

> *This distance should be set in light of local topography and weather conditions affecting distances. Add driveways if state law permits.*

This requirement helps reserve the capacity of the road and provides adequate stopping distances. The sketches below show this applied to use of a series of cul-de-sacs and common driveways. If reverse frontage is required along roads classified major arterial or higher, this might be applied to major collectors and minor arterials. The use of common driveways is highly recommended to reduce access points on the highway. (See figure 3.)

Use of Cul-de-sacs (Scotts Bluff, Nebraska)

Local streets shall be so planned as to discourage through traffic. Cul-de-sacs are permitted where topography or other conditions justify their use. Cul-de-sacs shall normally not be longer than six hundred (600) feet and shall terminate with a turnaround having a diameter of not less than one hundred (100) feet.

Figure 3. Minimizing Highway Access

With cul-de-sacs

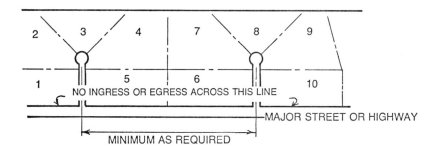

With common driveways

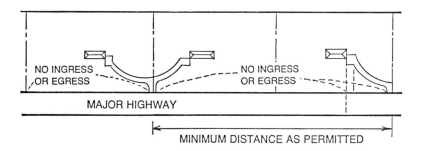

Source: *Frederick County Subdivision Regulations*, 1975.

> *Both the length and the size of turnaround are subject to local determination. Some also set a maximum number of houses served. The key concern is emergency vehicle access.*

Figure 4. illustrates the requirements for cul-de-sacs.

Figure 4. Cul-de-Sacs

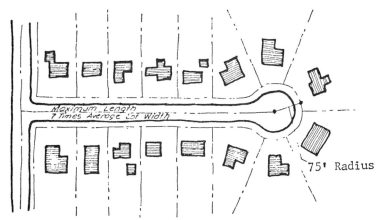

Source: Michigan, *A Model Guide for an Ordinance Regulating Subdivision of Land,* 1968.

Reserve Strips (Codington County, South Dakota)

There shall be no reserve strips in a subdivision except where their control is definitely vested in the county or township under conditions approved by the County Board as authorized by these regulations.

> *Reserve strips and plugs prevent adjoining lands from using streets provided as part of a subdivision. From the public standpoint, they help prevent divisions that would otherwise be subject to regulation from escaping by use of an existing street that is part of an adjoining subdivision. If not placed in public control, however, they can leave what are known as "spite" strips.*

Intersections.

The design of intersections is regulated for reasons of safety. The angle (as close to 90° as possible), the number of streets that may intersect, off-sets of intersections on opposite sides of streets, and required sight triangles are all included.

Intersections (Missoula County, Montana)

1) Intersections. The following items apply to intersections:
   a) No more than two (2) streets shall intersect at one (1) point.
   b) Streets shall intersect at right angles, except when topography dictates, and in no case shall the angle of intersection be less than sixty (60) degrees.
   c) Two (2) streets meeting a third street from opposite sides shall meet at the same point, or their centerlines shall be off-set at least one hundred twenty-five (125) feet.
   d) Intersection design shall provide acceptable visibility for traffic safety.
   e) Intersections of local streets with major arterials or highways shall be kept to a minimum.

Grade of Intersections (Freilich and Levi)

Intersections shall be designed with a flat grade whenever practical. In hilly rolling areas, at the approach to an intersection, a leveling area shall be provided having not been greater than a two per cent (2%) rate at a distance of sixty (60) feet, measured from the nearest right-of-way line of the intersecting street.

Intersections on Curves (Frederick County, Maryland)

Few ordinances prohibit intersections on curves, but Frederick County, Maryland suggests that where necessary they be on the outside curve to preserve sight distance.

Visibility at Intersections (Butler County, Pennsylvania)

Clear Site Triangle

At the intersection of two or more streets, the driver of a vehicle shall have an unobstructed view, to both his right and left, of at least one hundred fifty (150) feet on arterial streets and seventy-five (75) feet on collector and local roads, as measured along the center lines of the intersecting streets.

> *The distances might be reviewed with local or state highway engineers. Distance relates to speed of roadway being entered. State standards may differ.*

CLEAR SIGHT TRIANGLE

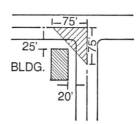

Figure 5. Intersections on Curves

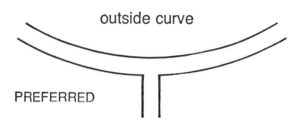

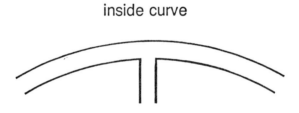

Intersections on curves where unavoidable should be on the outside rather than on the inside of the curve to allow for maximum sight distance.

Source: *Frederick County Subdivision Regulations*, 1975.

Lots, Blocks and Clusters

The subdivision regulations sometimes include additional minimal standards on blocks, lots and provision of pedestrian access. Length of blocks, numbers of lots per block, shapes and proportions of lots and related matters are covered.

Clusters of houses, for example, using systems of cul-de-sacs or other designs are not usually explicitly covered since the provisions for cluster developments suspend the normal design requirements to the extent that they are applicable. The requirements are basically drawn for subdivisions using curvilinear or grid street systems. Reviewers must exercise care in applying the requirements to assure good design that meets the spirit of regulations, not just the letter, and takes advantage of opportunities for variations of patterns to protect special natural features or other opportunities for improved design.

Lot Size and Shape (Frederick County, Maryland)

(1) The size, width, depth, shape, orientation and yards of lots shall not be less than specified in the Zoning Regulations for the district within which the lots are located and shall be appropriate for the type of development, the use contemplated and future utilities.

If no zoning, lot sizes may be specified.

(2) The relation of the depth of any single family lot to its width at the building restriction line should not be greater than three (3) to one (1), and only one (1) principal building shall be permitted on any such lot. Flag, or pipe-stem, or panhandle lots are permitted, except, however, not more than two (2) such lots may have adjoining driveway entrances to a public right-of-way.

This is intended to enhance usability of lots. Varies from place to place. Some places prohibit panhandle lots as an abuse intended to contribute useless land to meet minimum lot area requirements.

Figures 6 & 7 illustrates these provisions.

A general rule of thumb is for the lot depth not to exceed the lot width by 2 to 1 to 3 to 1. However, Lot "f" is much beyond this and is rather wasteful.

Lot "d" restricts house location a great deal, limiting future additions or accessory structures while "b" would require a stringing out of accessory structures with both front and rear yards severely limited in use.

Lots "a" and "c" offer the most utility and are most easily and economically served by utilities.

Lot "e" is acceptable; however, house siting is most probably best oriented in the direction of the arrow. Extension of utilities to this lot may be more expensive than conventional lots.

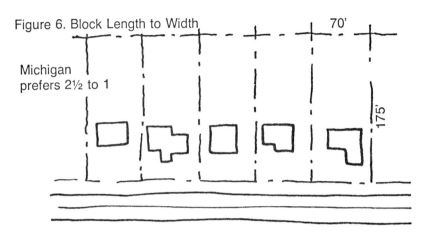

Figure 6. Block Length to Width

Michigan prefers 2½ to 1

70'

175'

APPROXIMATELY 2½ TIMES THE WIDTH

Source: Michigan, *Model Guide for an Ordinance Regulating Subdivision of Land*, 1968.

Figure 7. Lot Shapes

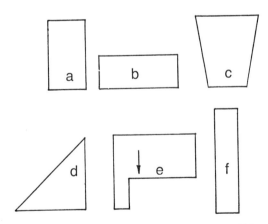

Source: *Frederick County Subdivision Regulations*, 1975

Section IV—Administration

The model subdivision regulations provided by the various states and those by Freilich and Levi contain generally excellent administrative provisions. They are applicable in rural areas and small towns, as well as to cities. This section does not duplicate the detailed provisions for administration but focuses on important issues in the administration of regulations and the review of proposed subdivisions.

General

Subdivision review is administered by the planning agency, with approval generally granted by the planning board. In some states this power rests exclusively with the governing body, while in others the governing body may not want to delegate it to an appointed body.

The review process includes obtaining necessary state and other local agency reviews and, in an increasing number of states, performing an environmental assessment of the subdivision. Hearings are often held on subdivision applications and are generally good practice. Time limits are often required by state law and are good practice even where not required. To a developer with money tied up in land, time delays in obtaining approval can be costly, help push up the cost of housing in the subdivision, and may affect his attitude regarding negotiating features of the subdivision plan. Local knowledge of the requirements of the state or other bodies, and the careful integration of those requirements with the local review timetable can help speed the process. This may also help foster cooperation from the developer and improve the possibilities of negotiating improvements in the overall design.

Negotiation

As indicated earlier, there is room for negotiation in subdivision regulation and review. It is an opportunity for the community to assure that the design and improvements are what it wants, and fit the character of the community.

The flexibility for negotiation comes from several places in subdivision regulation including:

- Making certain improvements optional at the discretion of the planning board;
- Exaction requirements which may vary from subdivision to subdivision;
- The normal range of opinion or reasonable disagreement over any design matters;
- The ability to waive or relax requirements such as street width or construction;
- The ability to delay approval of the project due to debate over whether the subdivision meets the spirit and letter of the regulations.

Typically, negotiation focuses on park and playground provisions, layout and design that may reduce the number of lots but be more attractive or environmentally sound, and who pays for various expensive items not clearly prescribed by policy or ordinance. The constraints that operate are both legal and natural. On one hand, there are limits to the power of the community to require concessions of a developer. On the other hand, speedy approval saves a developer money. There is, of course, a point at which a developer would rather sue than concede.

As in any negotiation, it is desirable that the planner be well aware of what the community wants and the minimum it will accept.

Environmental Impact and "Public Interest" Reviews

Subdivision review is a key opportunity to evaluate the overall impact and desirability of a subdivision on the community. Many communities now require environmental impact reviews which may include a broad range of environmental, social and economic factors. Montana communities are required to find in writing that the plat is in the public interest after considering the environmental review, need for the subdivision, public opinion, effects on agriculture, effects on local services, taxation, natural environment, wildlife, and public health and safety generally. Many communities now routinely require a fiscal impact statement or cost-revenue study before approval will be given.

The Montana mandate to deny plats not in the public interest is unique. Since it is established in state law, communities are less likely to be challenged for denying a proposed plat on the basis of public interest. The principle that subdivisions can and should be reviewed for impacts on the community, the environment, and the public purse, however, is reasonable and increasingly common as part of the review of subdivisions. The extent to which the findings of these reviews can be used to deny a particular subdivision will depend on state law and the extent to which specific standards or general public interest requirements are embodied in the regulation. In general, for example, it is unlikely that denial of a subdivision solely because it would have a negative financial impact on the community would stand up in court. Those findings, however, could be used with the developer to negotiate a design, mix of housing, or cost-sharing arrangements more favorable to the community.

Where environmental, public interest, fiscal or other reviews are required, the subdivider should be required to provide all the information necessary to evaluate the impacts. In addition, if professional planning, engineering, or other consultants are necessary to review the adequacy of the information submitted, their fees may generally be included in processing fees charged the developer.

Fees

Fees are customarily charged to cover the costs of reviewing subdivision applications, including the cost of reviews by outside professionals. In addition, there are usually fees charged for inspections to determine compliance during the construction stage. Recent research on fees (PAS Report 325, 1977) shows total fees ranging from $3.00 per subdivision to $300 plus an add-on per lot for both preliminary and final reviews.

Inspection fees are commonly set as a percentage of the estimated costs of improvements. Overall fees should not exceed reasonable costs of review or they may be judged a tax on development, which is usually not permissible as part of the regulatory process. Consultant costs can be either embedded in the fee structure or charged directly.

Not all communities charge all their costs; some view the processing of development applications as a public service, while others see fees as a way of discouraging development.

What is to be Submitted?

The exact form of documents, required contents, number of copies and other requirements for each plat are specified in subdivision regulations. There are slight variations from state to state with state model regulations or state law specifying the detailed requirements. Different requirements will apply to sketch, preliminary and final plats. See sample checklists at the end of this chapter.

It is important to be certain that all necessary documents are submitted at the final plat, including: properly executed easement and dedication documents, proof of ownership and signatures of all parties with equity interests, title opinion, title insurance on dedications to the locality if necessary, dedications in the proper form, etc.

Variances, Amendments, Appeals and Re-Subdivision

Special requirements and procedures are often provided for these procedures. Among the problems that may need to be considered are whether public hearings are required for variances or for re-subdivision. Some communities treat a re-subdivision the same way as a subdivision, while others may abbreviate the process. It has been pointed out, however, that the first re-subdivision of a 49-lot subdivision makes it a 50-lot subdivision. Different procedures may apply to the larger divisions and hence re-subdivision could, conceivably, be used to avoid the requirements.

Improvement Guarantees

Experience with incomplete unimproved subdivisions has led to requirements of guarantees that improvements shown and required will be built. The legal basis is discussed fully in Freilich and Levi, pp. 57-76. There are several options, discussed at some length in PAS Report 298, *Subdivision Improvement Guarantees*, January 1974.

First, the subdivider may simply install all improvements before final plat approval and before being permitted to sell or transfer any parcels. Since this requires significant front end investment, few subdividers choose this approach.

Performance bonds are an alternative. The subdivider purchases such a bond from a bonding company in an amount adequate to pay the cost of the required improvements. Often 125-150 percent of estimated cost is required to protect the locality. In many areas of the country, however, such bonds are not readily available and as a result other techniques have emerged.

Escrow accounts involve the developer depositing cash in the bank in such a manner that the community can obtain it if improvements are not completed. Property, including stocks or land, can also be put in escrow for the same purpose.

A letter of credit may also be used, with a bank, in effect, guaranteeing the improvements.

In using any of these options, the community still places all the risk on the subdivider and can require that the escrow property, bond, letter of credit, or whatever be developed in a way that is acceptable to the community (and its attorney).

There are two other methods. A special assessment or special service district may be created. The district or local government then makes the arrangements to finance and install improvements and costs are placed on each lot as a special assessment. This relieves the developer of the problem of obtaining financing and assures that improvements will, in fact, be installed. It shifts to the locality the risk that the subdivision is not needed and will not sell, however. In addition, the pay-back period for special assessments under state law may not be as long as the pay-back period for a mortgage, increasing the monthly cost to the homeowner or lot owner.

The final option is to provide a permissive waiver of guarantees for subdivision sections of under 25 lots or 50 percent of the subdivision. The presumption is that the refusal to approve subsequent sections of the subdivision will provide sufficient incentive to assure completion of improvements. If there is a strong market for the subdivision, it might, but if the developer misjudged the market, the local government may be left with a partly completed subdivision.

It should also be required that all improvements to be accepted by dedication be received free of any liens and encumbrances.

Review Procedures

The actual procedures for subdivision regulation usually provide for a three-step review. Some states set maximum time limits on review. Time delays are costly to developers who are buying and holding land waiting approvals. Local residents subdividing part of their holdings are somewhat less financially affected by delays, but are still affected. It is not unheard-of for communities to delay approvals as a way of discouraging development. If development is either wanted or inevitable, it is preferable to keep time delays to a minimum while providing careful review for conformance with both specific standards and environmental, public interest and fiscal questions.

The same review procedures can be applied to planned unit developments and mobile home subdivisions, even if they are regulated by separate or additional ordinances. For local simplicity, it is important to devise one review procedure for any development that the planning board or governing body is going to review. It prevents confusion due to different time limits or procedures and prevents mistakes such as a missed review deadline that can, in some states, constitute approval. (See figure 8.)

Figure 8. Subdivision Review Procedure

Sketch Plat

Informal Review
Staff or Planning Board

Minimize time. If staff review, should not be more than one week turnaround. Planning Board should review at next regular meeting and allow developer to be present.

Preliminary Plat
Submitted

Referred for Review
(as needed or required)
- Soil Conservation Service
- Consulting or City Engineer
- Highway Department
- Health Department/Sanitation
- Planning Boards
- Etc.
- Public Notice/Hearing

Set reasonable time even if state law does not require it. 60 days with mutual continuance for additional 60 days is reasonable. More time might not be. If hearing is to be held, set for approximately 30 days. Sometimes there are "trigger mechanisms" used to allow public to call a hearing.

Approve, Deny or Conditionally
Approve

Specify reasons in writing to be safe. Conditions should be formally marked on the face of the plat. Resubmissions of denied plats may get an accelerated view, but at least that should be an option of the planning board.

Final Plat Submission
and Approval

Final check point on improvements installation (or guarantee), deeds and other property documents for dedications, easements, etc.

Pre-Application or Sketch Plat

Many ordinances require and almost all recommend a pre-application review of the proposed subdivision to discuss the concept with the subdivider. This conversation is not binding on any party. It occurs at a regular meeting of the planning board or is delegated to a staff planner. The purpose is to

Figure 9. Typical Preapplication Sketch

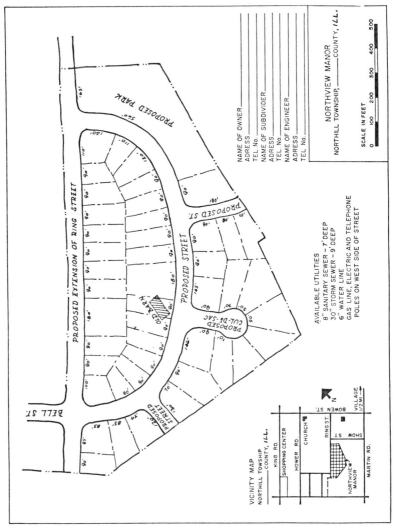

Source: Model Subdivision Regulation, Ohio Department of Development, July 1971, as reprinted in *Illinois Citizen's Guide to Subdivision Regulation*, 1977.

clarify the regulations as they apply to the particular parcel and proposed subdivision. It helps avoid misunderstandings and substantial investment in surveys and drafting for a concept that will not be accepted under the requirements. The sketch may be freehand, but drawn to approximate scale. It is suggested to include:

- A location map showing the site in relation to the entire jurisdiction.
- A sketch plan on a topographic survey map showing general layout, streets, major drainage ways, and other features. Surrounding land ownership would be shown, including the entire holdings of the subdivider.
- General information on the uses of lots, probable covenants, and types of utility systems to be used. (See figure 9.)

At this informal review the subdivider should be informed of any zoning matters or requirements that may apply, the òther local and state agencies whose review will be required, and whether there are floodplain or soil limitations of which he should be aware. The subdivider should be generally advised as to how well the sketch plan conforms to the specific requirements and intent of the subdivision regulations and should be provided with information on the procedure to follow to obtain approval.

Many of these are courtesies intended to prevent misunderstanding and conflict and potentially open the way for negotiation of the fine points of design of the subdivision. In most cases, the discussion will occur with the subdivider's agent—a land surveyor, engineer or occasionally a landscape architect or site planner.

Minor subdivisions as defined in the regulations will proceed to final plat review. Major subdivisions will proceed to preliminary plat review.

Preliminary Plat Review

Following review of the sketch plat, the subdivider submits a preliminary plat for review by the planning board and all other relevant parties. The plat is submitted in the number of copies and form specified in the regulations. At a minimum, the county or state health agency or, where sewer and water systems will be used, the city or village or special district expected to provide them will be included in the review. Others might include the county or village engineer, the public works or road department, and the private utility companies.

All required improvements and easements should be shown on the plat documents. It is at this stage that approval of the subdivision is really given. The requirements for sanitation should be met at preliminary plat review before planning commission approval is given, and it should be assured that all necessary utility extensions or street extensions have been arranged.

If all substantive requirements have been met to the satisfaction of the planning board or other approving body, approval is given. Or if the approving body is not satisfied that the subdivision meets the regulations, the application can be denied and reasons specified in writing.

Conditions are generally recorded on the face of the plat to avoid misunderstanding and confusion. It is possible to require resubmission of a conditionally approved plat before proceeding to final plat review to assure that the conditions are met. When a plat has been given preliminary approval, the subdivider may proceed to install improvements. The installation of improvements or provision of a bond (or other cash assurance that improvements will be completed as discussed above), is required before final plat approval can occur, the lots be recorded, building permits issued, and lots sold. The locality must be prepared to inspect improvements as they are made to assure conformance with the approved plat. (See figures 10 and 11).

Final Plat Review

The final plat, prepared to the specifications in the regulations, should reflect the conditions imposed on the preliminary plat, if any. Final plats are not approved or recorded until improvements are installed or arrangements made to guarantee their installation as indicated above. After improvements are assured, the plat can be recorded with the county register or recorder of deeds and building permits can be issued. Evidence

Figure 10. Typical Preliminary Subdivision Plat

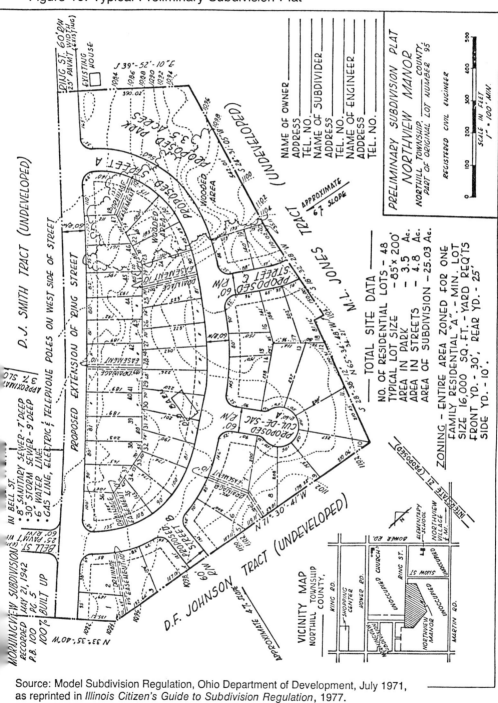

Source: Model Subdivision Regulation, Ohio Department of Development, July 1971, as reprinted in *Illinois Citizen's Guide to Subdivision Regulation*, 1977.

Figure 11. FORM 1. Preliminary Plat Checklist

Date_____   Application No._____

Subdivision_____

The following item(s) (does, does not) conform with the requirements of the _____ (City, County) Subdivision Regulations. Those items not conforming are explained on the final page.

	Does	Does Not	Item
1.	_____	_____	Name of Subdivision (no duplication permitted)
2.	_____	_____	Locational Description
3.	_____	_____	Name and address of owner, subdivider, surveyor and engineer
4.	_____	_____	Proper scale
5.	_____	_____	Date and North point
6.	_____	_____	Names of adjacent subdivisions and owners
7.	_____	_____	Zoning classification of all major parcels and proposed changes
8.	_____	_____	Location, width, and names of existing streets, right-of-ways, easements
9.	_____	_____	Corporation, township, range, section lines
10.	_____	_____	Location of existing utilities including sewers, water lines, and communication lines or poles
11.	_____	_____	Layout, names and widths of proposed streets or easements and proper dedications
12.	_____	_____	Layout and approximate dimensions of all lots
13.	_____	_____	Building setback lines
14.	_____	_____	Other information as specified by Chapter 5

Date_____   _____ Title or Position

_____

Signature

Source: *Wyoming Model Subdivision Regulations*, June 1976.

of clear title must be presented or title insurance provided to protect both subsequent purchasers and the locality. All covenants, easements, dedications and other substantive requirements must be met and appropriate documentation provided at this point.

What occurs at preliminary as opposed to final plat review is worth further discussion. Freilich and Levi (p. 41), for example, provide for endorsement of health authorities at final plat approval. This is too late for rural areas. The subdivider should satisfy himself and the health authorities that sanitary requirements for septic tanks can be met for the subdivision before too much is invested in the preparation and review of the plats, that is, at preliminary plat review. While a knowledgeable subdivider should do this as a matter of course, it is reasonable to require it to avoid any possible misunderstanding. (See figures 12 and 13).

Development of the subdivision in stages also presents special review problems. Many rural and small town subdivisions will be small and developed all at once. Large subdivisions are commonly phased to spread the front end costs of improvements and preparation of final plats. This also allows for changes in the plat if housing market conditions change, even though changes may require a return to preliminary plat review. Generally, the entire subdivision is shown at preliminary plat stage and the approval is valid for one year. The planning commission may give permission for staged submission of the final plat and as a practical matter can provide that the preliminary plat approval is valid for a longer period. Another approach (Freilich and Levi, p. 43), requires that the entire final plat be submitted to the planning commission, but allows it to be recorded in stages.

Getting the Most Out of Subdivision Regulation

Some of the objectives of subdivision regulation relate only to what occurs in a particular development and the subdivider's obligations in constructing the development. Other objectives are concerned with the relationship of the subdivision to the

Figure 12. Typical Final Subdivision Plat

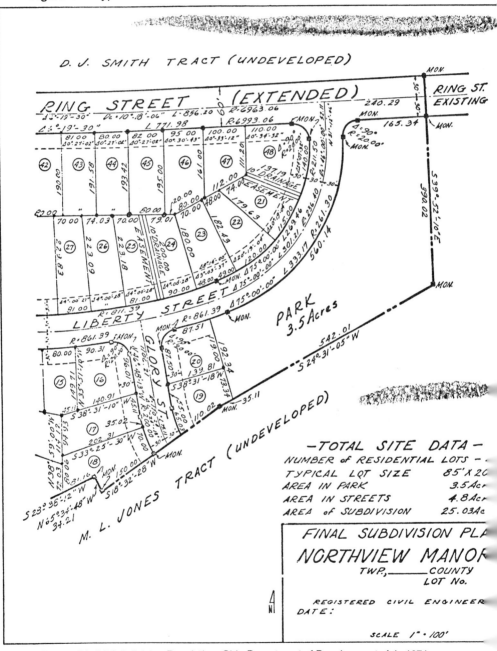

Source: Model Subdivision Regulation, Ohio Department of Development, July 1971,
as reprinted in *Illinois Citizen's Guide to Subdivision Regulation*, 1977.

Figure 13. FORM 2. Final Plat Checklist

Date_____   Application No._____

Subdivision_____

The following item(s) (does, does not) conform with the requirements of the
_____ (County, City) Subdivision Regulations. Those items not
conforming are explained on the final page.

	Does	Does Not	Item
1.	_____	_____	Submitted within 12 months of preliminary approval
2.	_____	_____	Conforms to preliminary plat and incorporates suggested changes
3.	_____	_____	Name of subdivision
4.	_____	_____	Proper scale
5.	_____	_____	Date and North point
6.	_____	_____	Locational Description
7.	_____	_____	Name and address of owner, surveyor, and engineer
8.	_____	_____	Accurate survey data—seconds; lineal dimensions to hundredths of feet; radii; internal angles; points of curvature; tangent bearing; lengths of arcs; lengths of cords
9.	_____	_____	Bearings and distances to permanent monuments
10.	_____	_____	Name, location, width, and centerline of streets
11.	_____	_____	Lot numbers and dimensions
12.	_____	_____	Location and description of monuments
13.	_____	_____	Building setback lines
14.	_____	_____	Parks and open spaces and proper dedications
15.	_____	_____	Final improvement plans
16.	_____	_____	Installation or guarantee of installation of improvements
17.	_____	_____	Required final certifications

Date_____   _____ Title or Position

community in general. Of particular concern are the relationship to the overall plan of the community; development in areas of natural or health hazards; treatment of unique topography; plans for major streets, parks and public water and sewer facilities; and the relative financial responsibilities of the subdivider and the locality. The general policy statement provided by Freilich and Levi in their *Model Subdivision Regulations* highlights these concerns:

1.2 Policy.

(1) It is hereby declared to be the policy of the municipality to consider the subdivision of the land and the subsequent development of the subdivided plat as subject to the control of the municipality pursuant to the official master plan of the municipality for the orderly, planned, efficient, and economical development of the municipality.

(2) Land to be subdivided shall be of such character that it can be used safely for building purposes without danger to health or peril from fire, flood, or other menace, and land shall not be subdivided until available public facilities and improvements exist and proper provision has been made for drainage, water, sewerage, and capital improvements such as schools, parks, recreation facilities, transportation facilities, and improvements.

(3) The existing and proposed public improvements shall conform to and be properly related to the proposals shown in the Master Plan, Official Map, and the capital budget and program of the municipality, and it is intended that these regulations shall supplement and facilitate the enforcement of the provisions and standards contained in building and housing codes, zoning ordinances, Master Plan, Official Map and land-use plan, and capital budget and program of the municipality.

Basically, as Freilich and Levi indicate, subdivision regulation operates best within the framework of a land-use plan and zoning ordinance.

Chapter VI
Infrastructure Planning

Section I—Underlying Concepts

Introduction

Provision of clean water and removal of both waterborne and solid wastes has been a responsibility of urban governments since at least the Roman times. In the past and in many developing nations today, it has been handled through "scavenging" more than by a highly organized refuse removal process. Within the United States today, water supply systems are planned to supply every citizen with roughly 100 gallons of water per day, sewerage systems are planned to be capable of removing that 100 gallons from the household as wastewater, and solid waste disposal systems are planned to remove and dispose of roughly five and one-half pounds of solid waste generated per capita per day in an environmentally acceptable manner.

Environmental decisions that were once the sole responsibility of the local community or of the individual property owner are now considered to be broader social concerns. Frequently they are the subject of federal regulation. Within just more than a decade we have seen the passage of the Solid Waste Disposal Act of 1965 (PL 89-272), the Resource Conservation Recovery Act (RCRA) of 1970 (PL-512), the Federal Water Pollution Control Act of 1972 and 1977 (PL 92-500), and the Safe Drinking Water Act of 1974 (PL 93-523). With the passage of each piece of legislation, the requirements of the local government have shifted from complete autonomy to operation within federal and state guidelines. With each change, the role of the planner has evolved from back seat to driver's seat in the generation of projections and criteria upon which to base decisions on investment in infrastructure. To accept this role requires that the planner be aware of the physical constraints, the economic tradeoffs, and the significant secondary impacts of extensive infrastructure development in the area of wastewater management, solid waste management, and provision of water supply.

The purpose of this section is to introduce the planner to the concepts and criteria used in the design and construction of infrastructure systems, focusing on those areas in which the skills of the planner will be most in demand where he or she can exercise the greatest leverage. It first discusses the planning information and tools common to all three infrastructure systems: service area definition, population projection, and financial analysis. The section then discusses the physical and land-use parameters of each of the three services, focusing attention on those aspects of each over which the planner has maximum leverage. It is clear that no chapter of this length can provide full information for the design and planning of such systems; but this chapter seeks to present the accepted criteria and coefficients for planning, the special problems and methods of financing for major infrastructure facilities, and a sound understanding of the complexities of the issues of infrastructure planning. Throughout the text an effort has been made to refer to the basic working volumes which can be of use to the planners as they deal with more complex issues of water supply, wastewater, and solid waste management.

In some sections this chapter will present estimates of the costs of capital facilities and operation. These are presented as indications of average relative costs at a given point in time. Caution in their use is advised: first, they are averages and as with all measures of central tendency only poorly represent the actual range of values which would apply to specific applications; second, the figures presented are for one point in time. The cost of providing environmental infrastructure has been increasing dramatically as have most construction costs; therefore, recent editions of those sources referenced should be consulted for up-to-date "average" figures.

The author would like to express his appreciation to Dr. James Hudson of Urban Systems Research and Engineering and Mr. Clark Binkley of Yale University for their critical comment on earlier drafts of this chapter.

A glossary of terms used in infrastructure planning can be found at the end of the chapter.

General Considerations

Many of the design criteria for infrastructure investments have been reduced to engineering "rules of thumb" and to standard "off the shelf" designs for purification systems, sewage treatment plants, and solid waste disposal facilities. While many of these rules have led to the simplification of design choices for engineering firms, they may have removed planners and city officials from an active part in the decision process. An examination of the initial design parameters for water, wastewater and solid waste disposal systems (projections of future population and selection and planning of service area), shows them to be more within the realm of the planner than that of the design engineer. There are issues of system sizing in which the financial and/or population impacts on a given community may be severe. System sizing for wastewater facilities has been shown in numerous studies to be a significant factor in directing the growth of the communities and the suburbanization and urbanization of rural areas. (Real Estate Research Corporation, 1974; Binkley, *el al.*, 1975; and Tabors, Shapiro and Rogers, 1976).

Three design parameters determine to a large extent the sizing of any infrastructure facility: ultimate extent of the service area, ultimate service area population, and the projected per capita service level requirements. While the third parameter may fall more within the purview of the engineer than the planner, responsibility for estimation of the first two parameters lies directly with the planner or planning board within the community. Even though it is frequently argued that one is better "safe than sorry" in sizing infrastructure facilities, conservatism carries with it a cost in excess capacity which may place an unreasonable payment burden upon initial system users, or, in the case of excess interceptor sewer capacity, may allow for unplanned sprawl or expansive development along the lines of the interceptor systems not "planned for" as a portion of the growth path of the community. This unplanned growth frequently costs the community more in terms of increased service requirements of new arrivals (in demand for schools, for example) than increased property tax base can support.

While there is no perfect solution to the sizing issue which may be applied across all communities, only a thorough understanding of the mechanisms which enter into sizing a system can guarantee a planner the confidence and expertise required to present a strong case for controlled development and planned facility expansion. The remainder of this section highlights the significant decision parameters associated with sizing of centralized infrastructure: definition of service area, projection of population, and estimation of per capita consumption/generation; later sections will discuss parameters of on-lot or decentralized disposal systems.

Geographic Service Areas

Choice of service area for water supply, sewerage, and solid waste varies considerably. Water supply service areas are highly dependent upon availability of sufficient quantities of potable water within a reasonable distance of the point of demand. For small towns or rural areas this may mean little or no long distance transport as water may be supplied from deep wells, free-running streams, or lakes in close proximity to the community. In contrast, water for urban areas in arid zones regardless of size frequently is transported over great distances.

Water

Because clean water is a basic requirement for public health and because with increased density there is increased possibility of contamination of on-site water supplies with on-site wastewater disposal facilities (septic tanks and cesspools), public water supplies tend to extend into any area likely to have relatively dense residential developments. All water systems are maintained under pressure; most maintain pressure from a water tower or hill-mounted tank. As a result, water lines do not follow topography as closely as do sewer lines. Water supplies to cities and towns within larger metropolitan regions have tended to be interlinked and to expand as required to cover suburbanizing communities if this can be done within existing supplies. Water supply systems are, within bounds of supplies, expandable to adjacent communities, and are neither significantly topographically bound nor do they usually act as significant contributors to the process of urban sprawl—both characteristics of wastewater collection systems. In arid areas, however, the extension of water systems may have an urbanizing effect. Many communities have developed using public water systems but on-site sewerage disposal (such as septic tanks or cesspools).

Wastewater

Unlike fresh water supplies which must be kept under pressure, centralized wastewater systems are often least expensive and most practical when they can be gravity flow systems. As a result, the most economic means of designing sewerage systems is to have them follow natural drainage basin areas within communities or across communities' boundaries. While the vocabulary of water supply is "metropolitan," the vocabulary of wastewater removal is "basin"-oriented, so that one finds the "Saw Mill Creek Sanitary District," the "Haikey Creek Interceptor Systems," the "Horn Lake Interceptor System," etc. Stream and river basins seldom are coterminous with boundaries between communities.

Recognition of public health hazards associated with high density use of on-site disposal systems, increased land costs (which encourage more concentrated development), and increased awareness of need for water quality improvements have led to expansion of sewerage systems into areas previously served by on-site systems as well as into areas identified for future large-scale moderate density residential development. In recent years, such expansions have been assisted greatly by funding provided by PL 92-500, the Federal Water

Pollution Control Act. Given development pressures for expansion of sewerage systems, the presence of such systems frequently has meant the financial success or failure of land development activities. (Tabors, Shapiro and Rogers, 1976, pp. 152-168). Under these circumstances the delineation of the service area for any sewerage system can become a highly political decision within a community, and an investment once begun cannot be easily diverted from its course.

While sewer districts may be constrained (if they are gravity systems) to follow topographic boundaries, they are neither constrained to service the entire basin, nor to exclude acceptance of wastes from other basin areas if they can be pumped across the basin divides. As a result, the precise delineation of the sewerage district is a significant planning variable for use in encouraging, discouraging, or directing growth within a developing community. Delineation of a sewer district is a tool for land-use planning only at the initial stages. Once in operation within a service area, it is usually considered an individual's right to be connected to the sewer. The sewer district must then provide the expansion in treatment capacity brought about by this additional sewer connection.

Solid Waste

While the service area vocabulary of water supply is most frequently "metropolitan," and that of sewerage, "basin," the vocabulary of solid waste disposal is uniquely "local." While there are examples of successful regional solid waste operations such as those in the San Francisco area, in most other areas of the nation solid waste disposal must be handled and frequently reaches its final disposition within the confines of a local community. The concept of one community (generally rural) being the "sink" or recipient for a region is accepted by all voters except those in the receiving community, with the result that efforts in regional cooperation have frequently ended in stalemate. While the major determinants to cost of solid waste management are frequently the cost of transportation, geographic constraints play a far less significant role in determining the final boundaries of a service area than do local political constraints.

Projection of Population

In planning for water, sewerage, or solid waste disposal systems, no calculation is more important in the sizing of the system than the projection of future "ultimate" population of the community or region. Population size is frequently dependent upon infrastructure development as much as the size of infrastructure investment is upon the size of the population. Particular services act as leading indicators of population growth. Highways have filled this role in the past; now sewers and water supply fill almost the same role of providing the preconditions for development. This section of the chapter is concerned with the projection of population size at some point in the future within a specified service area. While the techniques of demography are well developed for projection of populations of major political or geographic areas, they are poorly developed for the small area population projections required for sewerage system planning. In general, the smaller the geographic area, the more important are the nonbiological determinants of population growth: economic growth and migration. (Tabors, Shapiro and Rogers, 1976, pp. 20-23).

Because of this, population projection for minor areas has become more of an art than a science. All methods used in local projections are necessarily crude and range from an assumption of constant incremental growth—straight line projections—to more complex component methods of projection, which look to economic growth and land-carrying capacity as constraints to total population size. It is important to note that at the local level, methods referred to as "straight lining" frequently produce results nearly as good as those of the more sophisticated demographic models at far less cost and without the need for computational facilities.

The significance of assumptions and methods concerning population growth can be seen in *Interceptor Sewers and Urban Sprawl*, which investigated fifty-two interceptor sewer projects.

> In the majority of the case study projects, there was great uncertainty in the population forecasts. In each case where uncertainty existed, the population projections ultimately used in sizing the interceptors were very high—far in excess of past

growth trends for similar areas. For example, in Fulton County, Georgia, the engineer predicted levels of population well in excess of those predicted by the regional planning agency...In the Horn Lake Creek/Southaven, Tennessee projects, there is a feeling of inevitability about the prospects for growth. The projected figures used in sizing the interceptor were over ten times the current population...Connection fees will finance the project and there will be a great incentive to permit any and all new development. (Binkley, *et al.*, p. 5)

There is a set of standard methods for population projection available to the engineer and planner. The most useful of these techniques are summarized in Figure 1. There are in addition other methods suitable for small area projections which the interested reader might seek out. (Meier, 1972, pp. 883-896). Most traditional sanitary engineering and land-use planning texts and references contain summaries of population projection methods similar to those which follow:

Arithmetic

The arithmetic method is the simplest projection method. It assumes that the population will grow by the same number of people each year. This is also known as linear growth.

Geometric

Geometric growth is growth at a constant rate. It is the same principle as compound interest in a savings account. The growth rate is the percent change in population each year.

Decreasing-Rate-of-Increase

The rate of population growth, particularly in larger cities, is seen to decrease with increasing population. This method allows the planner to set a saturation population based on existing zoning or other information, and project a population growth path which approaches the saturation population at a decreasing rate.

Logistic

The logistic method, in principle, is similar to the decreasing-rate-of-increase method in that population growth is projected to increase at a decreasing rate to a saturation population.

Figure 1. Population Projection Methods and Equations

Method	Basic equation	Definition of terms	Evaluation of constants
Arithmetic	$\dfrac{dP}{dt} = k_a$ $P = k_a t + P_0$	P_0 = initial population (t = 0) P = population at time t t = time k_a = arithmetic growth constant	$k_a = \dfrac{P_2 - P_1}{t_2 - t_1}$
Geometric	$\dfrac{dP}{dt} = k_g P$ $P = S - (S - P)e^{k_d}$	k_g = geometric growth constant	$k_g = \dfrac{\ln(P_2) - \ln(P_1)}{t_2 - t_1}$
Decreasing-rate-of-increase	$\dfrac{dP}{dt} = k_d(S-P)$	S = saturating population k_d = decreasing-rate-of-increase constant	$k_d = \dfrac{-\ln\left[\dfrac{S-P_2}{S-P_1}\right]}{t_2 - t_1}$
Logistic S	$P = \dfrac{S}{1 + me^{bt}}$	S = saturation population m, b = constants P_0, P_1, P_2 = populations at times t_0, t_1, t_2 n = interval between t_0, t_1, t_2 $t = t_x - t_0$ in years	$S = \dfrac{2P_0 P_1 P_2 - P_1^2(P_0 + P_2)}{P_0 P_2 - P_1^2}$ $m = \dfrac{S - P_0}{P_0}$ $b = \dfrac{1}{n}\ln\left[\dfrac{P_0 - (S-P_1)}{P_1 - (S-P_0)}\right]$
Ratio and correlation	$\dfrac{P_2}{P_{2R}} = \dfrac{P_1}{P_{1R}} = k_r$	P_2 = projected population P_{2R} = projected population of a larger region P_1 = population at last census P_{1R} = population of larger region at last census k_r = ratio constant	$k_r = \dfrac{P_1}{P_{1R}}$

Source: Adapted from Metcalf and Eddy, *Wastewater Engineering: Collection, Treatment and Disposal* (New York: McGraw-Hill Book Company, © 1972 by McGraw-Hill Book Company), p. 19. Used with permission of McGraw-Hill Book Company. As used in Richard D. Tabors, Michael H. Shapiro, and Peter P. Rogers, *Land Use and the Pipe: Planning for Sewerage* (Lexington, Mass.: Lexington Books, D. C. Heath and Company, 1976), pp. 22-23.

Unlike the above method, however, the logistic method calculates the saturation population from previous growth data. One specific caution must be applied to use of the logistic method.

The growth rate between t_0 and t_1 must be greater than the growth rate between t_1 and t_2 for this method to yield meaningful results.

Ratio and Correlation

Population projections at the state or regional level are frequently available to the planner. These may be stepped down to local areas by assuming that the local population will remain a fixed proportion of the larger population.

Component

The component method of projection requires detailed information on each of the major components of population growth: births, deaths, and migration. The most commonly used component method is cohort survival with a side calculation for migration. This method requires relatively complex calculations and data frequently not available at the local level.

The art of population projection lies in knowing enough about the local conditions within a region or community to choose the most appropriate projection technique or techniques. Working with a range of techniques and/or a range of population projections frequently allows the planner and the individuals concerned with the evaluation of a system design to identify areas of excess capacity in the system, and therefore areas of potential savings in total system costs.

Financing

This section of the chapter introduces the set of basic concepts which underly the economic evaluation (analysis) of alternative investments in environmental infrastructure. While it is generally not possible to quantify the benefits to be gained from infrastructure investments, it is necessary that there be an analysis of the relative costs of the alternatives. This section will highlight the conceptual framework and methodology for cost comparisons, but will not deal explicitly with alternative costs of development.

The annual cost to a local community of any investment in infrastructure is a combination of three variables: the annualized cost of capital; the cost of operation and maintenance for a given year; and either the annualized value of any once-only capital subsidy raised through another level of government, or the annual subsidy provided through another unit of government (both cost decreasing). Evaluation of these terms is necessary if one is to look at the "life cycle cost" of a set of options rather than only the first cost. There are tradeoffs which one can make between high first costs with low operating and maintenance component. An example of such a tradeoff might be in the purchase of new or used equipment for refuse collection. A community unable to raise sufficient funding to purchase a fleet of new compacting vehicles may be able to purchase these used from adjoining communities. While the first cost may be reasonable, the costs of maintenance will be greater given the age of the equipment being operated.

Federal or state subsidy or grant programs may alter significantly the locally-perceived cost of any given alternative. State or federal grants for capital have the effect of reducing the initial capital costs of a project; an example of such a grant program is PL 92-500, which has provided up to 75 percent federal funding for wastewater projects. Under such circumstances capital becomes relatively inexpensive when viewed from the standpoint of the local community; however, operating subsidies make operation and maintenance appear relatively less expensive to the local community.

Comparative Costing Methodology

All of the discussions which follow assume that an analyst is working in constant dollars, i.e., that there is *no* inflation; these same calculations apply when working in current dollars (with inflation) although generally such calculations do little to clarify the concepts and add an additional variable, inflation, to the calculation.

All financial analyses begin from the conceptual base of "present value" or present dollar worth of an investment. If I were able to be guaranteed a return of five percent ($r = .05$) interest on an investment of $100 which I was about to place in the bank, I would be expecting to have $105 at the end of the year $(1 + .05)($100) = 105. In the second year I would expect a return of an additional five percent of my investment (now $105) or:

$$(1 + .05)(105) = \$110.25$$
or:
$$(1 + .05)(1 + .05)(100) = \$110.25$$
or:
$$(1 + .05)^2(100) = \$110.25$$

Carried out for n years I would be expecting to receive
$$(1 + .05)^n(\$100) = \$$$

In much the same way I can calculate the "present value" of $100 one year from now given an interest rate of 5 percent. An investment of $95.24 today will be equal to $100 ($1.05 \times \$95.24 = \$100$) in the bank one year from today and as a result given that I want $100 in a year I should be indifferent to receiving $95.24 today or receiving $100 one year from today. Hence, the present value of $100 at 5 percent one year from now is $95.24. Again, it is possible to generalize the calculation to any point in the future and any rate of interest.

$$PV = \frac{1}{(1 + r)^n} \cdot K$$

Where   n = years
         r = interest rate 100
         K = future investment in capital

If I am now interested in calculating the total cost of a project over its lifetime, I wish to sum up the present value (PV) of the yearly investments in capital with the present value of the operation and maintenance charges (OM). This total present value can be calculated as:

$$PV_t = K_0 + K_1 \left(\frac{1}{(1+r)^1}\right) + OM_1 \left(\frac{1}{(1+r)^1}\right) +$$

$$K_2 \left(\frac{1}{(1+r)^2}\right) + OM_2 \left(\frac{1}{(1+r)^2}\right) +$$

$$K_n \left(\frac{1}{(1+r)^n}\right) + OM_n \left(\frac{1}{(1+r)^n}\right)$$

PV_t is equal to the present value of all expenditures both in capital and in operating and maintenance costs incurred over the length of a project.

A second and equally useful concept is the annualized cost of a project, i.e., the cost which would have to be paid out each year to exactly equal the costs of capital, interest, and operations and maintenance for the lifetime of the project. This concept is the same in principal as the monthly payments which one makes on a mortgage.

$$\text{Annualized costs} = \frac{(PV)\ (r)}{1 - \frac{1}{1+r}^t}$$

From the concepts and equations presented above it is possible to calculate either the total cost (present value) of any project or the annualized cost of a project as a means of evaluating the cost of an analysis of infrastructure provision. This type of analysis is frequently sufficient when comparing systems which will provide an identical service and as a result there is no difference in "benefits" which would accrue to one as opposed to the other. This analysis is not sufficient to evaluate the cost of systems providing unequal services or benefits, such as a system of solid waste removal which would pick up two days a week as opposed to one which would have collection on only one day. A complete discussion of these concepts of cost-benefit analysis is beyond the scope of this chapter; the interested reader should seek out texts in either public finance or engineering economics for a more complete discussion: (for example, Musgrave and Musgrave, 1973; Mishan, 1971; and Gran and Reson, 1974).

Determinants of Total Costs:

Much of the art of urban and regional planning is incorporated in projections of the future. This chapter has already discussed projections of population, and in the sections which follow will discuss the projections of consumption of water and production of wastes needed to estimate future requirements of infrastructure services. All of our efforts at projection of the future would be but academic were it not for the fact that construction—provision of services—represents a "lumpy" investment. Construction of a plant must be done all at once. If we were able to add a single unit of additional capacity when that unit is required, and if that unit cost the same amount regardless of when it were added *and* how many were added at the same time, there would be little economic advantage to careful projection of the timing and sizing of our investments. This is clearly not the case. Few major investments in services do not contain economies of scale; the average cost (per capita or per unit of service provided) declines as the total size of the facility (sewage treatment plant, water purification plant, incineration facility, or sewerage or water pipes) increases. This occurs for a number of reasons, probably the most significant of which deal with either the basic lumpiness of specific portions of the operation or the capital structure, or because of basic physical properties of the systems themselves.

Most infrastructure facilities require land based operations. To a large extent the quantity of land is not directly related to the capacity of the facility. Thus, doubling the size of a sewerage treatment facility does not require doubling the amount of land. For sewer pipes, water mains or refuse trucks, there are frequently minimum sizes set by law (8 inch pipes) or by manufacturers (16 to 32 cubic yards for a compactor). Given this "lumpiness," the average cost of operation declines until the system reaches capacity. In much the same way the operation and management of a facility do not expand in a straight line with the capacity of the facility. The number of specialized operators required is a set minimum which does not vary as much with the capacity of the plant as it does with the number of shifts worked and the basic indivisibility of the manpower involved. One requires one plant manager per plant regardless of its size, though you may have to pay the manager of the large plant more for his skills in management. Size represents an advantage in supply of required chemicals and other inputs as well. A large water purification plant pays less per unit of chlorine when it receives it by the rail carload at its back door than the smaller plant requiring intermittent deliveries by truck.

A second area of economies of scale is that of the actual size relationships inherent in the facilities themselves. Sewer and water pipes offer an excellent example of this relationship. The volume carried in a given pipe is proportional to the cross-sectional area (r^2) of the pipe while the materials required for construction of the pipe itself are *more nearly* proportional to the circumference of the pipe ($2r$). Trenching costs are even less sensitive to volume carried, as the hole dug for most smaller pipe sizes is most often a function of the equipment used rather than the pipe size.

Economies of scale become particularly important as we consider the trade-offs between investments in large-scale facilities (those that will contain excess capacity for a considerable period in the future) and development of facilities which are smaller, and less costly. Figure 2 graphically and simply presents a linear growth path in total sewage flows for a hypothetical community. The assumption in all service systems is that demand will always be satisfied, i.e., in figure 2 that the system will always expand ahead (above and to the left) of the demand. Given this requirement it is possible to choose an infinite number of different paths to fulfilling demand. As discussed earlier the value of future dollars is less than that of a dollar today. Were there no economies of scale working, path one would be superior to path two.

Small increments to systems are frequently far more costly per unit of service delivered than are large additions to capacity. This is true in water supply and wastewater systems and less true in solid waste systems, where collection system costs tend not to be as subject to economies of scale. In addition, construction of a second, parallel pipe costs more than did the first, as areas have built up along water and sewer lines. In solid waste management, the same phenomenon may be seen

Figure 2. Capacity Expansion Path

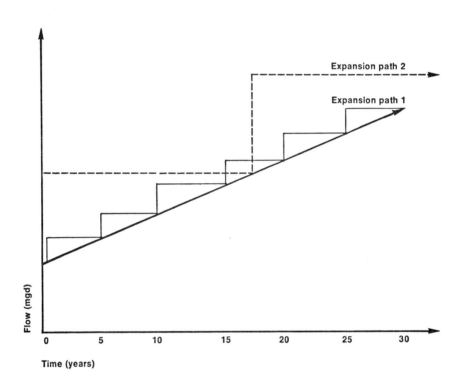

Time (years)

Source: Adapted from R. D. Tabors, M. H. Shapiro, and P. P. Rogers, *Land Use and the Pipe: Planning for Sewerage* (Lexington, Mass.: Lexington Books, D. C. Heath and Company, 1976), p. 80. As used in *The Practice of Local Government Planning* (Washington, D.C.: International City Management Association, 1979), p. 191.

in the cost of additional land-filling capacity. While in the short run it may be less expensive to maintain a land-fill site with limited capacity, in the long run owning a larger site will reduce the cost—and may allow for the existence of a land-fill operation—whose location more nearly minimizes total transport costs.

The final area in which economies of scale play a significant role in the development of environmental infrastructure is in the decision to develop regional facilities. Through the capital funding which has been guaranteed with PL 92-500, and through mandatory regional considerations (Section 208) of the Act for wastewater facilities, a number of small and medium sized communities have found regional wastewater solutions to their economic advantage. The trade-offs for decisions to construct one regional or a set of local facilities for wastewater, for water supply, or for solid waste disposal are those between savings in capital through economies of scale and costs in operation (or additional capital) required to transport water or wastes over a greater distance. In the case of wastewater facilities the trade-off is between capital costs in treatment plant and the cost of interceptor sewers to connect together the two service areas to a single plant. In the case of water supply the concerns are roughly the same. In solid waste management the regionalization issue from an economic vantage is again the trade-off between capital savings in a larger disposal facility and operating costs of a greater haul to the disposal site. At a more practical level the issues related to regionalization of solid waste are more closely related to location of the disposal facility/site than to economics. The concept of the "sink" community is one that has been discussed in the literature; even though the economics may be persuasive for a regional solid waste disposal facility, the sociology and politics are more difficult to predict.

The purpose of the three sections which follow is to make the reader a more informed critic of the processes of design, sizing, and investment criteria of infrastructure. No portion of a chapter can begin to develop a reader's technical design expertise; it can only hope to focus attention on those specific questions not covered earlier in this chapter which are of concern to the planner in understanding the design process, or are decision variables over which he or she has some control. Each of the sections which follow focuses upon the issue of per capita generation of wastes (or demand for water), upon the technical design criteria required for understanding of the total system, and upon identifying the specific points in the planning/decision process over which the planner, by virtue of training, has the greatest leverage.

Section II—Water Supply

A uniform and protected supply of drinking water has been a necessity since populations began to come together in large groups. While man consumes an estimated .42 gallons of water per day for drinking purposes, our total need may be as much as 100 to 125 gallons per capita per day. This section is divided into three parts: the first briefly discusses the primary issues in water supply planning, the second introduces the engineering design criteria for centralized water supply systems, and the third looks briefly at the design and safety requirements for small-scale on-site water supply systems.

The majority of the materials presented in the sections on water and wastewater have been derived from a set of basic texts on water and wastewater engineering. The most complete of these are: Fair, Geyer and Okun, 1965; Hardenburgh and Rodie, 1960; and Metcalf and Eddy, 1972. While these books are useful detailed references, they are written for the engineering student, not for the planner. There are a number of publications on rural water supply and sanitation prepared by the United States Department of Public Health and the Agricultural Extension Service. Tabors, Shapiro and Rogers, 1976, have attempted to bring together a number of the major issues associated with wastewater planning. Their discussion of projection techniques, financing, and land use, however, is of importance beyond simply sewerage planning

Major Issues in Water Supply

How Much Water to Whom?

Community water systems supply far more than the drinking and bathing needs of the citizenry. Within the United States roughly 43 percent of the water supplies in cities of over 25,000 goes to residential uses, while 19 percent goes to commercial, 25 percent to industrial, and 13 percent goes to public and other uses. Requirements for fire protection affect both the average consumption of urban water, and more significantly, the planned system capacity.

> For instance in a city of 10,000 population with an average consumption of 1,250,000 gpcd,† the total consumption is 1,250,000 gpd or about 875 gpm, while the required fire flow is 3,000 gpm

(as set by the National Board of Fire Underwriters). Therefore, the fire rate determines the sizes of water mains and pumps, if used, and the reservoir capacity in small cities. (Hardenburg and Dodie, 1960, p. 45).

As shown in table 1, the population must increase by a factor of four for the fire supply requirements to double and by a factor of ten for the requirements to treble.

Table 1. Fire Flow Required by National Board of Fire Underwriters*

Population	Required Fire Flow in Average City (gpm)	Population	Required Fire Flow in Average City (gpm)
1,000	1,000	28,000	5,000
2,000	1,500	40,000	6,000
4,000	2,000	60,000	7,000
6,000	2,500	80,000	8,000
10,000	3,000	100,000	9,000
13,000	3,500	125,000	10,000
17,000	4,000	150,000	11,000
22,000	4,500	200,000	12,000

Source: W. A. Hardenbergh and E. R. Rodie, *Water Supply and Waste Disposal* (Scranton, PA: International Textbook Company, 1961), p. 45.

While for planning purposes average daily water requirements per capita range between 100 and 200 gpcd (depending on non-residential requirements), most flows, particularly those to residences, are not smooth through the day. Figure 3 shows the peaked nature of water use in residences. The result is that the peak demand for water—and the requirements for the carrying off of the wastewater—is considerably greater than the hourly average.

While this is significant in the design of water systems, the fact that they are under pressure allows for the delivery of increased quantities with little increase in pipe size above the minimum. It does, however, require that supplies be available to the system at such periods of high demand. Local reservoirs

---

†Definitions: GPCD = Gallons per capita per day;

GPD = Gallons per day;

GPM = Gallons per minute.

Figure 3. Time of Day Daily Household Water Use

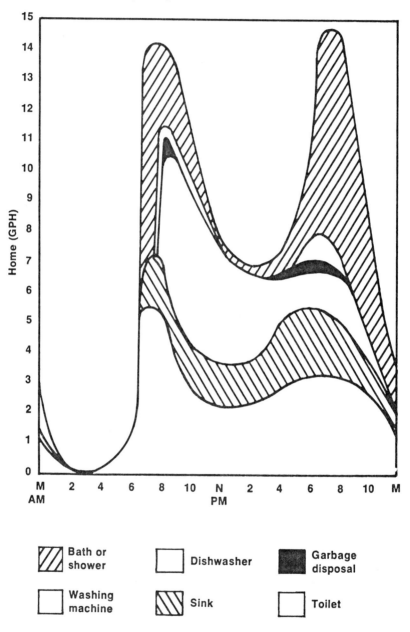

Source: J. F. Kreissel, "Rural Wastewater Research" (unpublished mimeo). As used in *The Practice of Local Government Planning* (Washington, D.C.: International City Management Association, 1979), p. 194.

or water tanks are generally available with roughly one full day's capacity to maintain both pressure and quantity during peak periods.

When to Provide Public Supplies and Why?

Within the United States, centralized water supply systems exist in nearly all cities, towns, and most villages or unincorporated places down to systems serving a small set of households. Despite this, however, a significant number of rural areas and small communities are supplied by individual wells. As these areas grow they must face the decision of provision of centralized water supplies or protection and monitoring of individual systems. The decision to extend or to create centralized water systems is based upon a series of factors. The most significant have always been and will continue to be fire protection and public health. "Water supplies must be wholesome and palatable...attractive to the senses of sight, taste and smell...(and)...free from disease organisms, poisonous substances, and excessive amounts of mineral and organic matter." (Fair, Geyer and Okun, pp. 1-8). Public water supplies are provided when densities increase in suburban areas to an extent that it is no longer possible to provide both on-site water supply and on-site sewage disposal, or when there is a danger of contamination of water supply from sewerage disposal systems, and as is implied above, when requirements for fire fighting necessitate a reliable high pressure water system.

How to Provide and Protect Potable Water Supplies

The source of all potable water is initially the same—rainwater which may be collected for use, allowed to run off, then collected (river/stream intake systems), stored in a natural or man-made reservoir, allowed to infiltrate into the ground from which it may be pumped (a well), or from which it once again emerges (a spring). While collection of rain water is seldom used for major water requirements, in areas where groundwater is brackish or scarce, this may offer the only option. More common systems of water supply rely on combinations of river flows, storage reservoirs, and wells.

The majority of the centralized water supplies are from surface water, either from continuous draft (or selective draft) systems or from impoundage systems. Continuous draft or selective draft systems remove quantities of water from flowing-water bodies such as rivers and streams, as well as from ponds or lakes whose capacities are sufficient to allow for year-round fresh supplies. Because such continuous water sources are frequently also used for either industrial or sanitary waste removal from upstream communities, they frequently require major purification works.

In areas in which continuous draft water supply systems are not possible, communities have traditionally maintained protected impoundments at a distance from the community and carried clean water through aqueducts to the community. There has been a long standing tradition of protection of upland watersheds to prevent contamination and thus, to obviate any need for purification other than chlorination. This desire for impoundment protection has virtually eliminated the use of reservoirs as recreational sites and has, in many areas, isolated their associated watersheds from hiking and camping. This condition, which increased information concerning potential dangers, may be ended by the Federal Safe Drinking Water Act (PL 93-523).

The final source of potable water available to some communities is groundwater. Where water tables are sufficiently close to the surface and where infiltration rates are sufficiently great to insure recharge with a minimum of drawdown, or where potable surface water is not available, groundwater may offer a viable water supply or augmentation source for communities. Memphis, Tennessee is supplied entirely from 30 wells, while there are a number of other communities that derive a portion of their water requirements from well water.

The source of potable water is a major concern in all areas of the country. Costs of providing water vary greatly depending on the combination of protected source, transport requirements, and purification works. While well water is generally clean, it frequently contains minerals in solution which make it hard, discolored, or flavored. Protected watersheds located in areas at a distance from the demand point require high capital expenditures and land costs in impoundments and easements for aqueducts. Investments in water supplies have become exceedingly high as communities or groups of communities are forced to go further or deeper for adequate supplies, or are required to treat extensively water sources not previously used as potable water. All of these factors point toward conservation as a significant economic concern.

How to Purify Water

The Safe Drinking Water Act of 1974 (PL 93-523) for the first time charged the U.S. Environmental Protection Agency with the setting of primary drinking water regulations. These regulations, in preliminary form, were set in December 1975 and finalized in 1977 to establish maximum contamination levels for 10 inorganic constitutents, turbidity, coliform organisms, six pesticides, and radionuclides. With the passage of PL 93-523 the federal government accepted the regulatory responsibility for guaranteeing safe drinking water to all citizens, and included within the jurisdiction of the Environmental Protection Agency not only the setting of standards, but the development and dissemination of information concerning the methods of treatment available for removal of major water supply contaminants. For many communities the passage of the act dramatically affected their treatment procedures, requiring purification of water from impounded 'safe' systems. The secondary impacts of this law will be discussed in greater detail under land-use and recreational considerations.

Filters have been used for water purification since the early 1800's as made clear by John Gibb at Paisley, Scotland in 1804 and James Simpson in 1829 in Chelsea. Traditional purification works were one or a combination of the following three:

1. Filtration plants that remove objectionable color, turbidity, and bacteria as well as other potentially harmful organisms by filtration through sand and other granular substances after necessary preparation of the water by coagulation and sedimentation.

2. Deferrization and demanganization plants that remove excessive amounts of iron and manganese by oxidizing the dissolved metals and converting them into insoluble flocs removable by sedimentation and filtration.

3. Softening plants that remove excessive amounts of scale-form-
ing, soap-consuming ingredients, chiefly calcium and magnesium ions (a) by the addition of lime and soda ash which
precipitate calcium as a carbonate and magnesium as a hy-
drate, or (b) by passage of the water through purification-ex-
change media that substitute sodium for calcium and magnesium ions and are themselves regenerated by brine. (Fair,
Geyer and Okun, pp. 2-15).

For more detailed information on treatment requirements
and estimated costs for purification works required under PL
93-523, and its subsequent amendments, readers should refer
to such volumes as the *Manual of Treatment Techniques for
Meeting the Interim Primary Drinking Water Regulations*
prepared by the Environmental Protection Agency.

Water Conservation

A final issue not being fully addressed in the literature to
date is that of water conservation. Many portions of the country are now water-poor, and to them conservation appears as a
potential 'source' of additional supplies. Conservation is only a
partial solution to water supply problems. As table 2 indicates,
simple water conservation devices such as water-saving toilets,
shower heads, and faucet aerators can make a dramatic difference in total consumption accounting for, at the average,
(assuming consumption of 100 gallons per capita per day),
roughly 25% savings in consumption using these three devices
alone. Combining water-conserving use as shown in Figure 5
with other behavioral changes, such as curtailment of lawn
watering and car washing can account for savings in particular
seasons and geographic areas well above the 25% reported
above. Modification in basic structures and design is required
for additional savings. Certainly recycling of 'grey' water
(water used in washing) is one such option, but an option
requiring extensive investment in dual piping systems and
storage of water. Appliance standards which encourage more
water—and energy—efficient appliances will be another structural change which will have a significant impact on water
supply requirements and indeed on wastewater flows as well.
The final solution in water conservation may be behavioral
changes causing the consumer to use less water in many of his
daily activities. One jokingly remembers the bumper sticker

"Save Water, Shower with a Friend" which might rightly be replaced with "Save Water, Take a Quick Shower with a Water-Saving Shower Head (and a Friend)."

Table 2. Water Saving Devices for Homes

	Consumption per unit (gallons)	Annual savings per person per year
Standard Toilet	5-7 gal.	
Water Saving Toilet	3.5 gal.	1950-6390
Standard Shower Head	8-10 gpm	
Flow Restricting Shower Head	3.5 gpm	3280-5930
Faucet Aerators	Save 25% of faucet flow	

Source: Man L. Chan, *et al., Household Water Conservation and Wastewater Flow Reductionn*, prepared for the U.S. Environmental Protection Agency, Office of Water Planning and Standards (Cambridge, Mass.: Energy Resources Co., Inc., July 1976), pp. 19-21.

Design of Water Supply Systems

Centralized

A complete water supply system, for simplicity, may be thought to contain four elements: a source, an aqueduct or conduit from the source to the purification plant, a purification plant, and a distribution system. Both the source of supply and the method and requirements of purification have been discussed in the issues section above. The material which follows covers primarily the concerns of sizing and of configuration of conduits and water distribution systems.

Aqueducts from the source to the storage point within the community or to the purification plant may be force systems or gravity flow systems. These pipes are generally designed to carry roughly 50% more than the average daily requirements of the community to allow for rapid drawdown by fire, or excessive demand from summer usages such as sprinkling or air conditioning. Such large pipes tend to follow the shortest distance principle constrained only by access to right of way and natural impediments such as major water courses or difficult terrain.

Distribution systems within a community are generally classed as one of two types (figure 4). The preferred system is the 'gridiron' system in which any point on the system may be fed from more than one supply source. In larger systems the gridiron pattern is frequently nested such that the principal mains themselves feed from more than one direction within the inner loop or central business district area. The less preferred distribution system is the 'dead end' system designed in a dendritic or tree-branching pattern with increasingly smaller branches leading away from the main supply lines.

The gridiron pattern is preferred over the dead end system for several reasons. Most importantly, in the gridiron, water is supplied from more than one direction to any user, minimizing the potential for interruption in the case of line breakage or other repair requirements. In addition, the dead end system leaves a large number of ending points at which water can stagnate and as a result develop undesired odor, taste, coloration, or bacterial or algae growth. Inability to design for a perfect gridiron system requires utility access to end points that can be opened to prevent excessive stagnation.

As was discussed in the introduction to this section, water supplies are required for fire use nearly as much as they are for public health. To a limited extent fire requirements determine the dimensions of the system itself. While "a 4-in. pipe will carry enough water for the domestic needs of about 1,000 people (it)... will barely supply a single fire hose... Moreover, the cost of laying 6-in. or even 8-in. pipe is not materially greater." (Hardenburgh and Rodie, pp. 133-134). As a result, it is argued that a 6-inch pipe should only be used when there is a good reason to do so and that otherwise an 8-inch pipe should always be chosen. Given the number of individuals in residences served by a 4-inch pipe, an 8-inch will service 6.28 times as many. This suggests that most residential systems have sufficient access capacity in the water system to allow for considerable additions to the residential stock without putting

Figure 4. Major Types of Water Distribution Systems

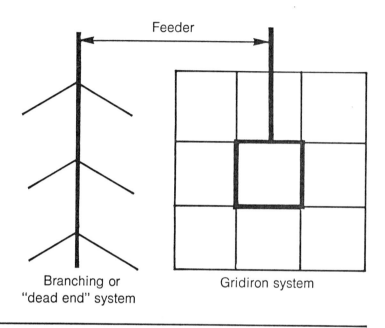

Branching or "dead end" system

Gridiron system

Source: Fair, Geyer and Okun, *Water and Wastewater Engineering* (New York, John Wiley & Sons, 1965), p. 2-24. As used in *The Practice of Local Government Planning* (Washington, D.C.: International City Management Association, 1979), p. 199.

undue pressure on the distribution system. Note, however, that this calculation says nothing about either large increases in the service *nor* about the availability of increased supplies.

Decentralized

Virtually all rural homesteads and most small community individual homes are supplied from on-site sources or from sources which are shared by a finite number of neighbors. These systems are generally wells with no treatment facilities. The depth of draw and the hardness of the water are a function of the groundwater condition and the material through which the water flows to the well itself. These methods of supply are adequate to all individual needs to the point at which the density of habitation increases to cause actual or potential interference between on-site water supply systems and on-site sewage disposal systems. The specific technologies available for provision of water vary from area to area. Information concerning technologies is available from farmers' bulletins of the Department of Agriculture as well as from state, federal, and local health departments. Where regulations apply for separation of water supply from wastewater system locations, these are local ordinances based upon public health criteria.

Summary

Planning issues associated with supply of fresh water within major urban areas are focused more heavily upon supply than upon distribution. Distribution networks are largely fixed by public safety (fire) requirements on the smaller end and by a relatively fixed central business/high density demand pattern on the upper end. The more critical issues of water supply today and in the future are those associated first with the number of inhabitants and the location and adequacy of supply to serve the projected population, and second with the new requirements for extensive treatment of municipal water supplies which make the maintenance of protected watersheds and impoundments less attractive finally and less necessary for public health. Use of water supply reservoirs and use of water supply watersheds are likely to be the major water supply issues facing planners in the decade ahead.

Section III—Wastewater

While the provision of centralized sewage collection and treatment facilities has long been recognized as one of many factors influencing suburbanization, the increased awareness of environmental quality has now made the provision of sewerage a major investment required for development. This preeminence, combined with the large federal grants program under PL 92-500, has brought the possibility for large-scale sewerage development into virtually every small community in the United States, and with it a challenge to local planners to see provisions of sewerage as a potential tool for the guidance and direction of land use within a community. Where sewerage planning has traditionally been the responsibility of the civil and sanitary engineer, the planner must now assume a significant role in this process if phased and directed growth is to occur at the urban fringe.

The role of the planner is strongest early in the sewerage system design process and diminishes as the process becomes closer to the final system design. The planner's role is particularly important in issues of service area definition and population projections. It begins to diminish in overall contribution as issues of per capita flows and allowances for "peak to average" flow are decided. The role of the planner is minimal in system sizing and in selection of type or design of treatment facility. The discussion which follows focuses first on centralized, then on decentralized systems.

Thorough discussions of the engineering criteria for design of wastewater systems may be found in Metcalf and Eddy, Inc., & Fair, Geyer & Okun. A nontechnical discussion of the engineering criteria may also be found in Tabors, Shapiro and Rogers, 1976.

Major Issues in Sewerage

How Much Sewerage is Generated

Planned system capacity depends critically on the assumed number of gallons per capita per day (gpcd) generated; errors in estimation contribute significantly to excess capacity (conservatism in system design). Such excess capacity frequently allows for "unplanned" developments within the community and/or creates unreasonable financial burdens on the existing population. Existing estimates and rules of thumb for per capita daily waste flow generation vary widely. In areas with metered public water supplies, sewerage flows have been shown to be between 60 and 80 percent of metered water. Values for average water use vary as a function of the season of the year due to water uses not entering the sewage system—watering of lawns and washing of automobiles during the summer months and running taps to prevent freezing water lines in the northern areas of the United States during the cold months. Other inaccuracies in projection of water use per capita are generated when per capita flows are set equal to total water dispatched divided by population. In this calculation, losses due to leakage, fire flow and unmetered usage are attributed to the average household. In addition, when homes with public water systems are on septic tanks, past experience has shown that when they are sewered there is a tendency for water use to increase with acquisition of new water-using appliances. As a result, even for communities in which there has been public water supply, estimates of future sewerage flows from present water use may be low. In areas in which there are no available records on water use, engineers fall back upon comparative figures for similar communities or upon generalized rules. Though a number of survey methods are available to the planner, few net truly accurate results, forcing one back to the literature or to rules of thumb.

One hundred gallons per capita per day is a figure generally accepted by the EPA for sizing of interceptor sewer systems. Two studies, one in 1960 and one in 1976, raise questions concerning the rationality of assuming per capita flows as high as 100 gpcd. In 1960 the Public Health Service, in a report to the Senate Select Committee on Natural Resources, estimated residential water use to be 60 gpcd with wastewater roughly 42 gpcd. No authoritative study has been conducted since that time, but in 1976, Tabors, Shapiro and Rogers attempted to estimate wastewater generation on the basis of work done by Ligman *et al.* (1974) to analyze the composition of waste flows. By building a worst case (assuming maximum water use by appliance type) Tabors *et al.* arrived at a figure of only 89 gpcd as a maximum per capita generation. (Tabors, Shapiro and Rogers, p. 29). Given present trends in increased appliance and plumbing efficiency, it is unlikely that it would be possible to generate on average the estimated 89 gpcd, less so the 100 gpcd suggested as standards by EPA. While higher values of per capita flows insure sufficient capacity into the future, that capacity may encourage either additional unplanned population increase or will cause an unnecessary burden in debt support on the part of the present users of the system.

The design flow for a sewerage system is generally calculated as:

$$Q = (GPCD) \times \frac{(Population) \times}{(Peaking\ Factor)}$$

Given this relationship it is possible to see that any errors or overestimates of the variables on the right hand side of the equation are multiplicative to quantity Q, such that an error of say X% in population creates an error greater than X% in Q.

The Decision to Sewer

There are a number of strong forces at work pushing communities, particularly rural or suburban communities, toward major investments in sewerage facilities. Probably the strongest force in this direction was the passage of PL 92-500, the amendments to the Clean Waters Act. PL 92-500 provided for both a standard of quality in treatment by 1977 and a sizeable purse of federal funding to develop both the collection systems and the treament facilities required to improve water quality nationally.

The decision to sewer or not to sewer depends to a large extent upon the alternatives available within any specific community and geographic/geological environment. In areas in which development has occurred using on-site systems in which soil and ground water conditions cannot support on-site disposal, the decision is frequently mandated by the Board of Health, although the precise specifications of the decision may be open to negotiation. In areas of new development the requirement that lots be roughly ¼ acre for the development to be financially successful necessitates some form of sewerage facility off-site. In areas in which homes presently are being served by on-site systems operating relatively well, and where future development is anticipated to be higher priced single family dwellings only, it is possible to maintain environmental quality without requiring large-scale sewerage faciliites (through large lot zoning combined with organized inspection and maintenance of on-site systems). Such "non-structural alternatives" to development of large-scale sewerage facilities are now being considered by many communities which can afford dispersed development, as well as by selected other communities who are able to combine small package treatment facilities with monitored on-site systems. Each community is different in its needs and options. That there are options in each instance must be kept firmly in mind as centralized treatment facilities may create more problems—even for water quality—than they solve.

Treatment Alternatives

While it is beyond the scope of this chapter to discuss fully the alternatives for sewerage treatment, it is significant to identify the three major groupings of treatment facilities.

Primary Treatment: Primary treatment refers to the removal of between 30 and 35 percent of the organic pollutants and up to one-half of the suspended solids. Generally, the processes involved are a screening process for removal of heavy solids, a skimming process which removes floating solids, and a settling period to remove heavier suspended materials. The cost is generally between $0.05 and $.25 per 1,000 gallons treated.

Secondary Treatment: Secondary treatment removes between 80 and 90 percent of the organic materials and over 80 percent of the suspended solids. It generally requires a multi-step process involving one biological process and one or more processes for settling of suspended solids. Biological processes include activated sludge, stabilization ponds, and trickling filters. The objective of all of the steps in the secondary treatment process is to increase the amount of both organic and suspended matter which is removed. The cost is generally between $0.10 and $0.70 per 1,000 gallons treated.

Tertiary Treatment: Because of the large quantities of synthetic organic compounds and inorganic ions in the waste stream, many localities are being asked to extend their treatment processes. Tertiary or advanced waste treatment adds additional steps to primary and secondary treatment in order to provide additional removal of standard organic pollutants or to remove one or more specific organic compounds or inorganic ions from the stream. Common pollutants removed are phosphate and nitrate. The actual process chosen depends upon the ions or synthetic organic compounds to be removed. Phosphorus removal costs an additional $0.10 to $0.20 per 1,000 gallons treated. (See definitions in Tabors, Shapiro, and Rogers, p. 16).

Potential Land Use Impacts

There are three essential elements in the process of suburbanization and development within the United States: highways, water supply, and sewerage. To a large extent, highways have been completed with the final linkages in the interstate system and with a partial halt to new construction around many of the major urban areas. As was discussed in the last section, water systems are seen as essential to public health, and as a result tend to be available when required. In addition, managers of water supply systems frequently see themselves as utilities actively seeking new customers. Sewers are different: they are expensive and are public goods provided by tax dollars. As a result, at present, the battle over land use and land-use planning is centering on the extension of sewerage facilities before large-scale, moderate density, single family housing developments—frequently described as sprawl—can begin.

Examples of the land-use impact of sewer extensions may be seen documented in the three case studies in Tabors, Shapiro and Rogers, 1976, and in *The Cost of Sprawl*, 1974.

Where suburbanization and increasing land values once were said to follow the major feeder highways into the rural countryside, now the trends appear to follow the extensions of interceptor sewers. The primary impacts are relatively clear: increased development of single family dwellings on ¼ acre lots and the potential for multiple dwelling units and commercial "strips." The secondary environmental impacts are less easily identified, although these frequently are: decreased water quality through non point source pollution—fertilizer and highway runoff, lower air quality from increased automotive emissions, and lowered visual quality through intensive development. Many of these impacts can be either lessened or avoided with more attention to the use of sewerage development as a tool for land-use planning. The summary to this portion of the chapter discusses in greater detail the alternatives for positive land-use impacts from sewerage development.

Alternatives to Sewers

The alternatives to large-scale sewerage systems are frequently not well articulated in the sewerage planning process. While they cannot apply to all applications, they offer points of economic and environmental comparison to the large sewerage systems. In many existing rural communities in which on-site systems are used extensively, consideration of extension of sewers is made on the basis of septic tank failures. While there are areas where soil characteristics are not suitable for septic systems, the more normal problem is poor maintenance and insufficiently frequent pumping. Where the alternative exists, establishment of an enforced septic tank inspection, maintenance, and pumping program can offer a cost-effective alternative to sewer extension as can actual ownership of on-site systems by municipal institutions (such as sewerage authorities). In such areas there may be the need for a septage treatment facility, land disposal site, or specific arrangements made with adjoining communities with sewage treatment facilities to handle the septage.

A second alternative to large-scale sewerage systems is the "package treatment plant," a small scale, frequently prefabricated, secondary treatment facility which can be readily installed, easily maintained, and cost effective for groups of homes or small commercial or institutional establishments. To date, package treatment facilities have received insufficient attention to evaluate their long-run reliability. They require both a means of disposing of the effluent from the plant as well as systematic disposal of the sludge. Effluent disposal can be to a flowing water body or, in some instances, to the ground in large leaching fields. Sludge disposal requires the same precautions and concerns for these small plants as for the larger treatment plants. Package systems are designed to operate with minimum supervision, though some states require full-time operators, making the economics of operation less advantageous.

While there are two major alternatives to large sewerage systems, there are others ranging from large holding tanks to on-site tertiary treatment facilities. The significance of any of the alternatives is to allow the planner the opportunity of comparing, on the basis of cost, performance and risk, a set of alternative strategies for accomplishing the same objective.

Design of Sewerage Systems

Centralized

Wastewater treatment systems are made up of three components: a collection system, a treatment facility, and a disposal system. Wastewater is generated from a number of sources which, when summed, equal the total flow of the systems. These are wastes from residences and commercial establishments, wastes from industrial establishments, storm waters—in combined systems—and infiltration (or exfiltration) depending upon the groundwater regime and the quality of the jointing between sections of interceptor and/or collector piping. To project the quantity of wastewater which will be collected and processed (for sanitary sewers only) requires an estimation of residential population to be within the service area multiplied by their average daily production. The calculation for commercial areas generally takes into consideration the population of the service area multiplied by a coefficient to represent an average number of stores, offices, etc. Projection of industrial wastewater loads must be done on a community-by-community, industry-by-industry basis for any large-scale wastewater-producing firms, and is again frequently estimated as "population equivalents" for smaller non-water-using firms. The last component of sewerage flow is the estimation of infiltration into the pipes from surrounding groundwater or exfiltration (leakage) to the surrounding soil.

The carrying capacity of the sewers (pipes) within a sewerage system must be planned to accommodate the peak flows. As was seen in figure 2, the ratio of maximum to minimum flows can be more than an order of magnitude. For small residential systems these peaks can be great, although as a system grows the peaks tend to smooth out, both as a function of different use patterns—the addition of industrial flows or commercial flows—and the greater distances over which sewage must flow within the pipes themselves. There is a clear time dimension to sewage flows just as there is to traffic flows within a city. It takes longer for traffic to travel from the rural areas than from the central suburbs, and the impact of the additional car arriving at any point is diminished as the road system increases in size. This is roughly analogous to the distance smoothing effect within a large sewerage system.

In general the requirements for sizing of the pipes within a sewerage system vary with the size of the "upstream" population. The smaller the population the larger should be the ratio of peak to average flow. The same logic holds for minimum to average flows as well. While the planner has less control over the determination of the appropriate value of peak or minimum to average flow, it is necessary that he be aware of the relative range. As can be seen in figure 5 for small populations, the minimum to average flow ratio is 0.3, with the peak to average 4.0; for larger systems the ratio is from 0.8 to 1.25%.

Additional details may be found in such sources as Tabors, Shapiro and Rogers, 1976, or Metcalf and Eddy, 1972.

From the perspective of the rural and small community planner, the most significant engineering variable is that of minimum pipe size generally set by state law. The minimum diameter for street laterals and downstream collectors is set at 8 inches for most states with house connections of either 4 or 6-inch minimum size. At 100 gpcd an 8-inch pipe in moderately sloping terrain can service roughly 60 acres of ¼ acre-lot development before reaching capacity, thus for many sewer systems built in suburban areas the vast majority of the system is frequently made up of the minimum size pipe—8 inches in diameter.

Figure 5.

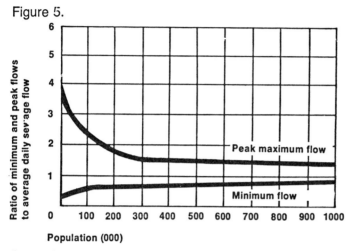

Source: Adapted from R. D. Tabors, M. H. Shapiro, and P. P. Rogers, *Land Use and the Pipe: Planning for Sewerage*, (Lexington, Mass.: Lexington Books, D.C. Heath and Company, 1976), p. 32. As used in *The Practice of Local Government Planning* (Washington, D.C.: International City Management Association, 1979), p. 205.

The remaining engineering criteria for sewerage system design center on the exact location of the system and upon the material from which the system is constructed. Because sewage is waterborne, it is most economically collected with a gravity system. Discussion of two other systems, force mains and pressure systems, is beyond the scope of this chapter. Gravity systems must maintain a minimum flow within the pipes which is sufficient to prevent sedimentation in pipes while not being fast enough to cause erosion in the pipes. As a result, for gravity systems, the slope of the pipes is calculated such that the flow is between 2 feet and 10 feet per second. While there are frequent tradeoffs between cost of system components which are exceedingly smooth and not subject to erosion, the most common piping systems are concrete with a rubber or synthetic gasket between sections of pipe.

Decentralized

Decentralized wastewater systems fall into two categories, those designed for individual homes and those designed for groups of homes. Increased environmental awareness has directed most communities toward policing of on-site disposal systems, and frequently toward small treatment facilities which can service a set of homes, a school or hospital complex, a shopping center, or a rural industrial park. The small systems called package plants can be purchased essentially "off of the shelf' and installed by the vendor in a relatively short period of time.

As described by Tabors *et al.* a package plant is a small treatment plant which is partially or completely preassembled to a manufacturer and shipped to the designated location. Although a package plant may provide primary, secondary, or tertiary treatment, most being manufactured today are secondary treatment units. Package treatment plants are available in a range of sizes, from units designed to serve a single dwelling to modular units capable of handling one million gallons per day (mgd). They are used extensively to serve isolated facilities and subdivisions because, over the applicable range of sizes, they are much less expensive than comparable facilities constructed in place. Package treatment plants are designed to operate with a minimum of supervision, though some state and local governments require that an operator be on duty at all times. Such requirements may effectively preclude the use of small package plants, because the operating costs become excessive.

Individual on-site sewerage disposal systems are generally only acceptable when the soil conditions within a given area are such that the effluent, the liquid from the system, can percolate into the soil without contamination of the groundwater and without surfacing to create areas of dense, green, damp lawn. The percolation test required for acceptability of soils and/or specific locations for lots for septic systems varies from state to state but generally requires the absorption or percolation of a fixed quantity of water out of a hole of specified depth within a fixed period of time. (See figures 6 and 7). Constraints upon the success of the perk test are brought about by rocky soil, by ledges which do not have sufficient soil covering, by high water tables such that the perk test hole "strikes water", and by extremely porous soil conditions which virtually guarantee that the wastewater will reach the ground water table.

Figure 6.

How to Make a Percolation Test.

1. Dig six or more test holes four to twelve inches in diameter and about as deep as you plan to make the trenches or seepage bed. Space the holes uniformly over the proposed absorption field. (See Figure 3 for a diagram of a test hole and test hole distribution. Roughen the sides of each hole to remove any smeared or slickened surface that could interfere with water entering the soil. Remove loose dirt from the bottom of the holes and add two inches of sand or fine gravel to prevent sealing.

2. Pour at least twelve inches of water in each hole. Add water as needed to keep the water level twelve inches above the gravel for at least four hours—preferably overnight during dry periods. (If percolation tests are made during a dry season, the soil must be thoroughly wetted to simulate its condition during the wettest season of the year. The results should then be the same regardless of the season.)

3. If water is to remain in the test holes overnight, adjust the water level to about six inches above the gravel. Measure the drop in water level over a thirty-minute period. Multiply that by two to get inches per hour. This is the percolation rate. After getting the percolation rate for all the test holes, figure the average and use that as the percolation rate.

4. If no water remains in the test holes overnight, add water to bring the depth to six inches. Measure the drop in water level every thirty minutes to four hours. Add water as often as needed to keep it at the six-inch level. Use the drop in water level that occurs during the final thirty minutes to calculate the percolation rate.

5. In sandy soils, where water seeps rapidly, reduce the time interval between measurements to ten minutes, and run the test for only one hour. Use the drop that occurs during the final thirty minutes to calculate the percolation rate.

6. Percolation tests for seepage pits are made in the same way except that each contrasting layer of soil needs to be tested. Use a weighted average of the results in figuring the size pit you need.

Source: Goldstein and Moberg, Jr., *Wastewater Treatment Systems for Rural Communities* (Commission on Rural Water, National Demonstration Water Project, Washington, D.C., 1973), p. 16.

Figure 7.

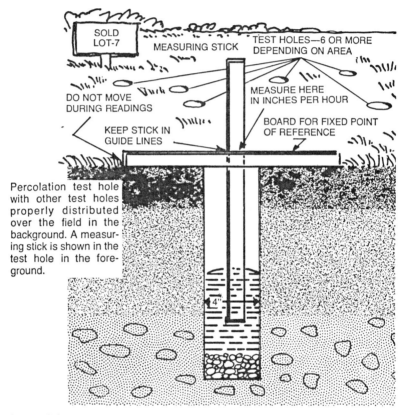

SOLD LOT-7

MEASURING STICK

TEST HOLES—6 OR MORE DEPENDING ON AREA

DO NOT MOVE DURING READINGS

MEASURE HERE IN INCHES PER HOUR

KEEP STICK IN GUIDE LINES

BOARD FOR FIXED POINT OF REFERENCE

4"

Percolation test hole with other test holes properly distributed over the field in the background. A measuring stick is shown in the test hole in the foreground.

Source: USDA, Soil Conservation Service

The two most common on-site disposal systems are cesspools and septic tanks.

A cesspool is a large, porous cistern into which all of the residential wastewater flows. Solids remain in the cistern, while the effluent, or liquid portion, seeps out through the walls into the surrounding ground. Because little biological action takes place in the cesspool, the solids must be removed by frequent pumping. Cesspools cost between $300 and $400 to install. (Tabors *et al.*)

A septic tank system operates on a different principle from a cesspool. It is made up of two major components: the septic tank and the drainage field. A concrete or steel septic tank receives waste from the home and provides a period of settling, during which a significant portion of the suspended particulate matter settles out. The solids accumulate at the bottom of the tank and are gradually decomposed by bacteria. The drainage field is usually composed of lengths of clay pipe placed at shallow depth. The pipe is spaced or perforated to allow the sewage to flow into the soil, where microorganisms and absorption complete the purification of the waste. A well-designed and well-constructed septic system is an ecologically sound treatment device; it returns purified water to the aquifer and recycles nutrients to the soil. Moreover, relatively little maintenance is required: only periodic inspection and occasional (about once every two to three years) pumping-out of partially decomposed sludge from the tank. Installation of a septic tank system, including tank and leaching field, generally costs between $1,000 and $2,500, depending on soil types. (Tabors *et al.*)

In addition to cesspools and septic tanks there are specific systems which are usable in certain areas. When soil conditions do not allow for standard septic systems, there are now available at relatively high cost small-scale tertiary treatment plants which can be used for individual homes. The discharges from such systems are nearly potable water. For extremely dry zones, particularly those with large rock outcroppings and sparse population, it is possible to design systems in which the sewage is spread on the soil for evaporation and desiccation. Other systems which are again expensive relative to septic systems involve incinerating toilets, composting toilets, digesting toilets, and chemical toilets. In each instance the waterborne waste component is held to a minimum. While the traditional "privy" has been seen as a health hazard in any built-up areas, in rural zones this may still offer the required protection to both the environment and the health of the user and surrounding community though only under highly controlled situations.

Summary

Through the majority of the discussion of planning for sewerage, the focus has been upon the planning criteria and the hardware. This final portion of the discussion of wastewater management summarizes the potential for use of infrastructure investment as an active tool for land-use planning. Chapter 2 of this volume discusses the options and techniques available for land-use planning. Here we are concerned only with the potential use to which sewerage policies may be placed in land-use planning. Figure 8 summarizes the policy options using the provision of infrastructure, in particular sewerage, for land-use control. These policies have been divided along two axes, the first by mode of action, either restrictive or incentive, and the second by means of operation, either physical or financial. As can be seen, the majority of the policy options exercised to date have been restrictive and physical, ranging from refusal to sewer and sewer moratoria to policies of carefully delimited expansion through staging of investments. In addition, there have been capital subsidies for construction provided by both state and federal governments to encourage the development of large-scale wastewater systems to accommodate existing and planned growth and development. Such capital grants carry with them restrictions as to the criteria for system design and review through the National Environmental Policy Act (NEPA). In addition, PL 92-500 provides planners with probably their most focused opportunity for input into the sewerage planning process through sections 208, 209 and 303, which provide for states to develop comprehensive plans for water quality maintenance through an ongoing planning process.

Sewerage planning has traditionally been the realm of the engineer, not the planner. What has become increasingly apparent over the past few years is that the planner must be involved in the decisions surrounding construction of such systems if the systems are to complement the development activities of the communities, rather than themselves determining the directions and extent of community development.

Figure 8. Sewerage/Land Use Policies

Policy	Principal Mechanisms	Governmental Level	Time Horizon for Planning	Actual or Proposed Applications
Sewer Moratorium	Ban or quota on new sewers, connections, building permits, subdivision approval, rezoning	State or local	Usually less than two years	Over 200, concentrated primarily in N.J., Fla., Cal., Ohio
Refusal to sewer	Rural fringe and community refuses to provide sewerages	Local, may be overridden by state		Massachusetts
NEPA review	Mandatory agency and public review of federally funded projects to encourage consideration of secondary impacts	Federal; all levels involved in review process	Up to 50 years	Rockland County, N.Y. Delaware
Facility design	Select physical options to encourage certain types of land use, e.g., force mains, smaller treatment plants	County/regional	20-50 years	Sewerage plan for York County, Pa.
Facility sizing	Limit excess capacity in projects to preserve future land use options	Local, county/regional	10-20 years	California
Service area	Establish "urban service area" within which public services will be provided	County/regional	10-20 years	Lexington, Ky., Prince George's County, Toronto, Canada
Staging Policy	Staging of individual facilities to promote certain development patterns	County/regional	5 years	Minneapolis-St. Paul, Minn. Ramapo, N.Y.

Section IV—Solid Waste Management

As with both water supply and wastewater management, in
solid waste planning the role of the planner occurs early and
is critical in developing facilities which lead rather than follow the demand created by the expansion of urban areas.
Throughout this section, two major issues will arise numerous times. The first is the question of land use and land
values associated with sanitary land fills or other final disposal
sites for solid wastes. The second is the question of the costs
and alternatives available for disposal of solid wastes by any
given community.

Major Issues in Solid Waste

Not in My Backyard You Don't

Major land use issues in solid waste management as with
sewage treatment plants have most frequently been associated
with the stigma of having a major solid waste facility in the
neighborhood. "They are fine, but not in my backyard." This
general attitude toward solid waste facilities may be based on
the fact that these facilities can be both hazardous and an
eyesore if improperly run. On the other hand, this general
image of an open dump—with frequent burning of refuse,
blowing of paper, and severe rodent problems—is an image
more attached to the solid waste situation of the fifties (the
dump) and earlier than it is of today (the sanitary landfill).

The development of regional solid waste management facilities brings another set of concerns. Regionalization of solid
waste facilities may offer the only economically acceptable
alternative for communities forced to higher cost solutions
such as more advanced waste processing systems (i.e., incineration). The attitude of "not in my backyard" has extended to
one of "not in my community" for many more suburban or
even rural communities facing the possibility of becoming the
"sink" community for a regional solid waste system. There are
innumerable examples of both public officials and of citizen
groups lying down in front of refuse trucks as they are about
to enter the community.

Land values in proximity to solid waste facilities have traditionally been depressed. The question of whether the facility's location was based on already low land values or whether the value lowered as a result has never been fully documented. Unlike either sewers or water supply, however, solid waste removal and transfer requires trucking, any large quantity of which will cause environmental problems through noise and litter.

A significant planning issue in very rural areas may be the inverse of "not in my backyard" with individual on-site dumps. The control of such activities is likely to be difficult or may not even be desirable. The decision concerning the "closing" of such activities is likely to be that of the health department and is likely to be for health or stream pollution reasons. Small dumps in and of themselves are only hazardous if food wastes are included, but given the composting systems employed by most rural households this ceases to be a problem. Burning and/or blowing papers and rodents can be a hazard but can also be controlled on-site.

Land Use

Easily the most important portion of solid waste planning from the viewpoint of the long-range interest of the community as a whole is the operation and utilization of the landfill site. While in many communities the landfill site was operated as an open and burning dump, and was kept open for large periods of time, new local regulations in most communities prohibit burning of dumps and enforce nightly covering of the waste with a minimum of six inches of soil. The resulting impact has been filling sites more rapidly and creating both the demand for new sites and, significantly, a resource for development at the now completed site. Careful advanced planning of final disposition of landfilling sites has the advantage of preparing a neighborhood or a community for a resource—after the filling has been completed—and thereby making the filling itself somewhat more palatable.

Planning for final disposal has taken on a different appearance over the past several years. Whether the development is for a university, as was the case with the new Boston Campus of the

University of Massachusetts, or for a sledding/tobogganing/ski-
ing slope—Mt. Trashmore—or for golf courses and playing
fields, proper planning in advance will allow for improved attitudes on the part of neighbors, and will allow for the smooth
transition from potential liability to a land-based asset.

Increasing Cost of Disposal

Increasing costs brought about by exhaustion of inexpensive
disposal sites, increased regulation by either state or federal
agencies, or inability of communities to achieve an agreement
over the site of regional facilities for either landfilling or for
resource recovery and/or advanced processing have been a
major issue in solid waste management. The choice of system
for final disposal generates the greatest interest on the part of
the citizens and political leaders but represents only a relatively small portion of the total cost of the overall system
(between 70% and 85% of costs are in collection). Collection
costs are perceived as fixed, yet the method of collection, the
point of pickup, the frequency of collection, truck size and
type, size of district, and bags vs. cans contribute significantly
to overall system cost.

How Much Must Be Removed?

The discussion of solid waste disposal which follows focuses
on four major issues: the major components of solid waste
quantity and collection, transportation, processing (if required), and disposal. Figure 9 represents a flow diagram of
the choices to be made and the basic steps through which the
analysis must proceed in designing and/or evaluating a solid
waste disposal system. (Office of Solid Waste Management
Programs, 1976). This is an excellent source of detailed technical and economic data.

The generation of solid waste is seasonal and it is a function of
the affluence of the individual. Christmas cleanup, spring clean-
ing, fall leaves, heavy months of moving such as June and July
bring slightly higher than average quantities per capita of solid
wastes. In general, however, total (residential, commercial and
industrial) solid waste generation per capita has been increasing from roughly 2.75 pounds per capita per day in 1920 to 5.3
in 1968 (Greenberg, *et al.* 1976, p. 8).

Figure 9. Solid Waste Management Decision Alternatives

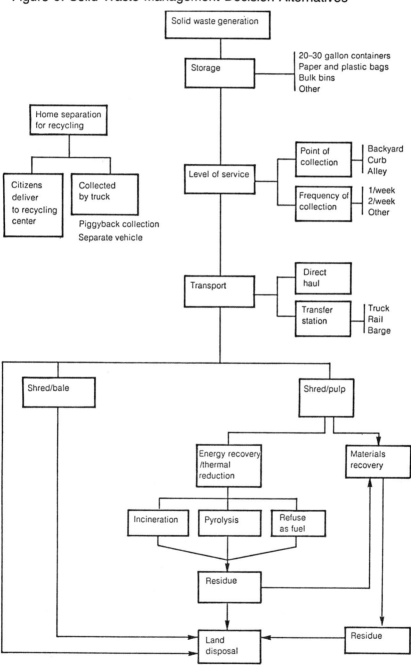

Source: Environmental Protection Agency, *Decision Makers Guide in Solid Waste Management*, EPA Publication SW 500 (Washington, D.C.: U.S. Government Printing Office, EPA 1976), p. ix. As used in *The Practice of Local Government Planning*, (Washington, D.C.: International City Management Association, 1979), p. 209.

What Gets Picked Up, How Often, and in What Type of Vehicle?

Most communities provide for collection of solid waste on a regular basis. The decision of the point of collection and the material to be collected may determine many of the costs of service. Many communities formerly collected garbage (food wastes) separately from rubbish (paper and other combustible and noncombustible wastes), necessitating collection directly from the backyard or alley. Labor now represents the largest component of collection costs and as a result most communities have shifted away from backyard collection and separate collection of garbage and refuse to combined curbside pick-up from standard containers or from plastic bags. The question of how frequently refuse will be collected is again one of cost. There are tradeoffs in operating equipment, routes taken, and crews associated with once-weekly or biweekly collection which require analysis for each community (Act System, Inc., 1974). In general, however, the cost of weekly collection is between 13% and 39% less than biweekly.

One of the most interesting issues in solid waste management has become recycling. While the economics of recycling facilities which separate at the "sink" are marginal, recycling via separation at the source appears far more favorable. The actual economics of such a program depend to a large extent on local conditions and on the means of collection. A number of communities have begun source separation/collection schemes involving collection equipment with special bins for separated materials (glass, aluminum, newspaper) distinct from the compactor, into which all other rubbish is thrown. The analysis completed to date on source separation schemes is interesting in that it shows that participation in the program tends to increase over time. Throughout, however, there is a need to generate and to maintain citizen interest (SCS Engineers, Spring 1974).

Collection vehicles for residential systems range in size from 13 to 41 cubic yards and may be either open or compacting. Because of both length of haul and litter from noncompacting vehicles, compactors are by far the most common today. As indicated in table 3 below, there is considerable range in quantity and cost, though the 20 cubic yard rear loader is nearly ubiquitous on solid waste routes today.

Table 3. Typical Packer Truck Prices 1975

Standard Sizes (cubic yards)	Prices
Rear Loader	16–25 (now 32)
*20	25,000–32,000
Side Loaders 16–37	20,000–38,000
Front Loaders 24–41	35,000–50,000
Roll–off: 35,000 lbs to 75,000 lbs.	30,000–45,000

*Most common size

Source: Environmental Protection Agency, *Decision Maker's Guide in Solid Waste Management*, EPA Publication SW 500 (Washington, D.C.: U.S. Government Printing Office, EPA, 1976), p. 51.

Transportation

After collection of solid waste there are a number of options for transportation to the point of final disposal or processing. These options depend largely on the relative costs of equipment and labor associated with each. In the case of a community controlling a convenient landfill or disposal facility, it is likely that the collection vehicles and their crews will deliver the waste to the site. In communities in which there is a considerable distance between the collection point and the point of final disposal, there is frequently a transfer station in the system which allows for the aggregation of the contents of a number of smaller collection vehicles into a large specifically designed, frequently compressing tractor-trailer vehicle which then transports the materials to their points of disposition.

Disposal

As can be seen from figure 10, there are few options as to the final disposition of solid waste and in all instances the final repository for at least a portion of the material will be in sanitary landfills. The options for final disposal may be grouped into three general categories: a) marginal volume reduction on site, b) baling, and shredding for volume reduction, and c) resource recovery combined with one or both of the above. Landfilling is always the preferred method of disposal.

Only when legal or other constraints prevent it should other methods be used. Landfilling operations are traditionally supervised by state boards of health who mandate operating rules. In general, however, operation with a required daily cover and with compacting tractors allows for efficient operation. *A Decision Maker's Guide to Solid Waste Management* offers more detailed information on planning and operation of sanitary landfills than is possible in this chapter.

Resource Recovery

Resources recovered from urban solid wastes have become an attractive possibility for recycling metals and, significantly for both saving energy—aluminum from existing aluminum requires 5% of the energy required for production of aluminum from bauxite—and for generation of heat through controlled incineration of wastes. Two primary forces have maintained these programs at lower levels than had been predicted by their proponents. First, recovering materials from solid wastes at the "sink" is expensive and the market for recycled materials is highly variable, making the operations of such systems subject to high risk. Second, because most resource recovery systems depend at least in part upon incineration for volume reduction and solids separation, the solid waste operation interfaces directly with the air quality regulations controlling both particulates and emissions of combustion products of plastics, rubbers and heavy metals. Given the uncertainties associated with both the setting and the regulation of federal clean air requirements, processes involving incineration of solid wastes within air quality control regions have become highly uncertain. As was stated earlier, the most inexpensive means of recovering resources for recycling is at the source before they become intermingled. Be it cans, bottles, or newspapers, these are most conveniently collected separately through independent pick-ups or through the use of combined pick-up vehicles designed specifically for the purpose. While this requires active participation on the part of the citizenry, the cost in operations and capital on the tax dollar appears to more than make up for this inconvenience.

Figure 10. Comparative Economics and Feasibility of Major Resource Recovery and Disposal Options

Alternative	Feasibility	Net operating cost per ton*	Alternative	Feasibility	Net operating cost per ton*
Sanitary landfill	Institutional—there may be active citizen opposition to potential locations. Technical—depends on geological characteristics of the land. Economic—decided savings in cost per ton if facility handles over 100 tons per day.	$1.50-$8	Heat recovery to generate steam	Technical—1,000-ton-per-day plant is in shakedown operation in Baltimore. Air pollution problems have been encountered. Economic—markets for steam are limited.	$4-$8
Conventional incineration	Technical—feasible. Economic—cannot economically meet new air pollution standards.	$8-$15	Materials recovery:		
Small incinerator	Technical—feasible. Economic—varies with particular case.	$8-$15	Newsprint, corrugated, and mixed office papers	Technical—separate collection, possibly with baling, is required. Economic—markets are variable; when paper prices are high, recovery can be profitable.	
Steam generation from waterwall incinerators	Technical—several incinerators are in operation, only 2 are marketing the steam produced. Economic—markets for steam are limited.	$4-$10	Mixed paper fibers	Technical—technology has been demonstrated at 150-ton-per-day plant in Franklin, Ohio. Economic—fiber quality from Franklin plant is low, suitable only for construction uses.	$7-$13
Solid waste as fuel in utility or industrial boiler	Institutional—owner/operator must contract with utility for sale of electricity. Technical—combustion in utility boiler as supplement to coal has been demonstrated in St. Louis. Economic—practical feasibility depends on cooperation of local utility or user industry.	$6-$10	Glass and aluminum	Quality can be upgraded by further processing. Technical—technology being developed. Economic—market potential is adequate but system economics uncertain as yet.	
Pyrolysis: Solid waste converted into combustible gas and oil	Technical—has been demonstrated at 200-ton-per-day pilot plant. Economic—transportability and quality of the fuel produced are primary factors. Ability to store and transport fuel offers broad market application.	$4-$12			

*Includes amortization of capital equipment.

Source: Environmental Protection Agency, *Decision Makers Guide in Solid Waste Management*, EPA Publication SW 500 (Washington, D.C.: U.S. Government Printing Office, EPA 1976), pp. xii-xiii.

Summary: Infrastructure Planning

Infrastructure planning is a new area of concern for the professional planner in small communities and rural areas. It is an area traditionally controlled by civil and sanitary engineers, but one in which there is increasing need for integration with the more traditional areas of planning if infrastructure is to complement rather than lead the development of communities. The four sections in this chapter have attempted to point to the areas in which planners are likely to have the maximum leverage—those areas early in the facilities development process when locations are being considered and when such significant parameters as population projections and future land use and density patterns are being discussed. As the process of infrastructure development continues, the planner's role diminishes. In design of systems, as in operation, the planner's input is small. With the exception of solid waste planning, in which a significant role occurs at the end—when the landfill site is ready for redevelopment—the role of the planner may be relegated to trying to work around an infrastructure which has been inherited, or which has been allowed to develop without his or her direct participation. The technical information concerning the design and construction of infrastructure facilities contained in this chapter will not make the reader an engineer. It should, however, offer the first steps in making him or her an informed consumer of consulting engineering reports.

Definitions

WATER SUPPLY

Impoundment: A reservoir used to collect and hold rain water and runoff. Generally a natural watershed which has been dammed.

Aqueduct: A large conduit for carrying water generally from an impoundment or reservoir to a purification plant or a distribution system.

Stand Pipe: A small storage facility into which water is pumped to maintain system pressure. A stand pipe differs from a water tower in having vertical sides.

Water Tower: An elevated storage facility, generally spherical in shape, into which water is pumped to maintain system pressure.

Water Main: One of the major distribution pipes for water, generally covering all pipes except house connections within distribution system.

WASTEWATER*

Sewage: Sewage refers to the wastewater flow from residential, commercial, and industrial establishments which flows through the pipes to a treatment plant.

Sewerage: Sewerage refers to the system of sewers, and physical facilities employed to transport, treat and discharge sewage.

Sewer: Sewer refers to the pipe, conduit, or other physical facility used to carry off wastewater (see figure 11).

Sewer or Sanitary District: A sewer district is either a semiautonomous governmental unit whose purpose is the provision of sewerage or a spe-

---

*Source: Definitions taken from *Decision Maker's Guide to Solid Waste Management*, pp. 75, 79, 84 and Commonwealth of Massachusetts, Department of Public Works, Solid Waste Disposal, *How to Plan, Engineer and Operate a Sanitary Landfill* (Boston: State Printing Office, No. 6223), pp. 3, 4.

Figure 11.

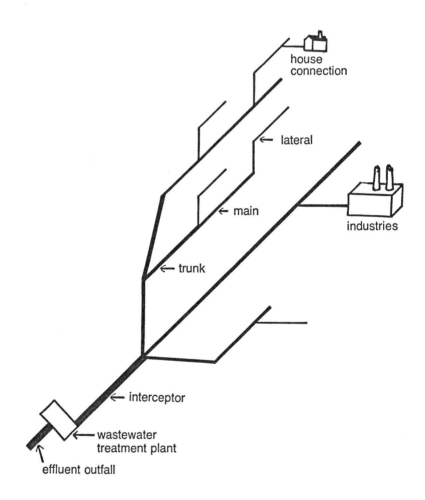

Source: Tabors, Shapiro and Rogers, *Land Use and the Pipe: Planning for Sewerage*. (Lexington, Mass: D.C. Heath and Company, 1976), p. 23.

	cial assessment district within which sewerage facilities are provided to residents.
House Connection:	Sometimes referred to as house laterals, house connections are the points of contact between the individual dwelling unit and the sewerage system.
Lateral:	A lateral is the pipe to which individual houses and business establishments attach. If one considers the analogy of a tree, the laterals represent twigs.
Main/Submain:	The word main is frequently used loosely to indicate a large pipe which is not a lateral and not an interceptor. Like a trunk, a main or submain frequently forms one of the large branches of a complex collection system.
Trunk:	A trunk sewer is one of a set of large pipes which form the branches of the sewerage system. In many communities it would be the pipe which collects sewage from a large portion of a community and then discharges it into an interceptor.
Interceptor:	Interceptor sewers derive their name from their original design purpose in older cities in which they intercepted the flow of smaller trunk sewers that were going directly and untreated into a river or a stream and carried that flow to a downstream treatment facility. Interceptor now refers to any pipe, regardless of size, that carries wastewater to the treatment plant.
Sewer Outfalls:	Sewer outfalls, or effluent outfalls, are interceptor-sized pipes which transport, after treatment, the effluent of the sewage treatment plant to the final receiving body.
Force Mains:	All of the pipes discussed above are portions of gravity-flow sewerage systems. Force mains are used to remove wastewater under pressure against the force of gravity, allowing for transfer of sewer between natural

drainage basins for conveyance of waste-water at minimal slopes over relatively long distances. Force mains have the advantage over gravity sewers of having a greater capacity relative to the diameter of the pipe. They have the disadvantage of requiring capital investments and operating expenses for pumping stations, and the advantage or disadvantage, depending on the perspective of the individual, of not allowing inexpensive tapping-in of additional inflow points. Unlike a gravity system, a force main requires a relatively sophisticated pumping system for the tapping-in of a new connecting line.

Pressure Sewer Systems:

A relatively new development in American sewerage practice is the use of pressurized collection systems. In these systems, each connection has a combustion grinder-pump device which forces the sewage into a network of pressurized collectors. Because the sewage flows under pressure, the collection network can be placed at minimum depth, essentially independent of topography. Thus, considerable savings in capital costs are possible, particularly in terrain which is unfavorable for gravity networks. Cost savings are also possible because the pipe sizes employed in pressurized systems are significantly smaller than those for corresponding gravity collectors. A disadvantage of the pressurized system is the high energy and maintenance costs associated with its operation. However, many communities appear to be willing to incur these costs in exchange for considerable capital cost savings.

SOLID WASTE*

Garbage:	The animal, vegetable, or other organic waste resulting from the handling, preparing, cooking, or consumption of food.
Refuse:	Putrescible and nonputrescible solid wastes, except body wastes, and consisting of all combustible and noncombustible solid wastes including garbage and rubbish.
Rubbish:	Combustible and noncombustible solid waste material except garbage, which includes but is not limited to such material as paper, rags, cartons, boxes, wood, excelsior, rubber, leather, tree branches, yard trimmings, grass clippings, tin cans, metals, mineral matter, glass, dust, and the residue from the burning of wood, coal, coke and other combustible materials.
Baling:	A method of reducing the volume of solid waste. It has the potential to achieve cost savings when transfer and long haul are necessary prior to disposal and when land disposal is at a premium. It also has an added benefit in that baling makes the waste potentially easier to handle and transfer.
Shredding:	Reduces the volume of solid waste and turns it into a relatively homogeneous material. This is a generic term for all similar size-reduction processes, including pulverization, milling, hammermilling, grinding, and comminution. It has been found that shredded waste did not attract vectors, support combustion, have an objectional odor, or lead to littering—problems often associated with the disposal of solid waste on land. The most attractive feature is the bulk reduction achieved.

---

*Source: Tabors, Shapiro and Rogers, *Land Use and the Pipe: Planning for Sewerage*, pp. 13, 15, 16.

Sanitary Land Fill:	A method of disposing of solid wastes on land in such a manner as will protect the public health, safety, comfort, and convenience and prevent a nuisance or a danger to the public health by reason of odor, dust, fires, smoke, the breeding or harboring of rodents, flies or vermin, or other cause. Such operation shall utilize the principles of scientific and engineering planning and control to confine the solid wastes to the smallest practical area, to compact and reduce it to the smallest practical volume, and to cover it with a layer of earth at the conclusion of each day's operation or at more frequent intervals as may be necessary.
Incineration:	The controlled burning of solid, liquid, or gaseous wastes. Reductions of 80 to 90 percent of the total volume of municipal solid waste, and 98 to 99 percent by weight, of the combustible portion are possible through incineration. There are end products of municipal incineration, however, that require further processing or disposal; these include the particulate matter carried by the gas stream, incinerator residue, grate siftings, and process water. Incinerator residue consists of noncombustible materials such as metal and glass, as well as incompletely burned combustible materials.
Transfer Station:	A terminus at which collection vehicles unload into larger vehicles which transport solid wastes to final disposal site.
Compactor:	One of a set of vehicles used at a sanitary landfill designed with additional weight; vehicle both moves solid wastes and reduces volume.

Chapter VII
Rural Public Transportation:
Problems and Possibilities

Rural transportation problems are no longer restricted primarily to poor, handicapped, and older persons: the escalating prices of fuel and automobile operation have caused increasing numbers of rural residents to experience a transportation problem. In addition, the decrease in self-sufficient households, and the replacement of local stores and business districts with regional centers, have caused more rural people without cars to face serious problems satisfying basic day-to-day needs. The problem will probably worsen. Noting that rural households appear to spend more of their income on transportation than do urban households, the Economic Research Service of the Department of Agriculture predicted that if inflation and energy problems continue, more rural people will become transportation-disadvantaged. This group might even contain members of higher-income households that are forced to reduce multiple-car ownership (1975, p. 173).

Mobility is essential for the one-third of the U.S. population that lives in non-metropolitan and rural areas. Not only do these people need access to work, shopping, medical care, recreation, etc., but the goods and labor markets in rural areas would benefit from the increased mobility of rural residents. Businesses could serve wider markets, and workers would have more choice in employment (Economic Research Service, 1975, pp. 173-174). Since the majority of rural residents are dependent on non-farm activities for their income, and displaced farmworkers must often commute to distant employment centers (Barnett, 1976, p. 38), inter-rural area transportation is also a critical need.

The following sections, summarizing the transportation characteristics and problems in small towns and rural areas, suggest that the major problem confronting these areas is personal mobility. Thus the bulk of this chapter will be devoted to an analysis of the alternative ways to meet the mobility needs of persons in small towns and rural areas.

This chapter is intended to provide an overview of rural transportation problems and alternatives, and to this end takes the form of a resource guide. Many references are provided throughout the text, and complete citations may be found in the Bibliography. The typical reader may not use most of the references; rather, the references are provided so that the reader may follow-up on those topics in which he or she needs more detailed information.

We cannot overlook the other transportation problems in these areas. Although we will not concentrate on them, they include the abandonment of some rail lines, unfavorable freight rates, an inability to take advantage of economies of scale, and the need to rely on a single mode of transportation. There are also the problems of deteriorated road surfaces, narrow and unsound bridges, unprotected railroad crossings, inadequate lane widths, and lack of emergency medical care transportation (Coates, 1974, pp. 58-61; National Area Development Institute, 1975, pp. 246-264; and Stocker, 1977). Which of these many problems can be addressed locally, and which should be tackled first, are questions which must be asked by the small town and rural planner.

Rural Transportation Characteristics

Basic statistics about the transportation characteristics of small towns immediately suggest the primacy of the personal automobile. Since at least 90 percent of all trips in small cities are made by automobile, and since public transit typically does not exist or is constrained to limited routes and schedules and old equipment (Macy, *et al.*, 1968, p. 3), the person or family without access to an automobile has serious problems. The U.S. Census shows that over 80 percent of the families in rural areas and small towns have access to an automobile, and this has sometimes caused the mobility problem to be dismissed. In some small cities and rural areas, however, up to 25 percent of the households do not have an automobile (Macy, *et al.*, 1968, p. 22). Actual mobility is probably less than reported mobility because some households indicate auto ownership when their auto is inoperable (National Area Development Institute, 1975, p. 281). In addition, some persons who have a means of transportation, for example, obtain rides from friends or relatives, pay dearly for those services (Gerald, *et al.*, 1977, p. 136). The problem does not stop here. Even in households with a functioning vehicle, some members may be "transportation handicapped" since the family breadwinner often takes that vehicle to work, leaving the balance of the household stranded (Subcommittee on Rural Development, 1974, p. 2).

The extent of the dependence on the automobile in rural areas is only too clear when we examine automobile ownership among the poor. In 1972, almost 70 percent of all low-income rural people (household income less than $5,000) owned a private vehicle, compared with 40 percent of the urban poor. Almost all nonmetropolitan households with incomes of $5,000 or more owned a vehicle. Fewer older persons own vehicles, as would be expected both because of their lower incomes and because health problems prevent them from driving. Forty percent of households with a head 65 or older do not have a vehicle (Economic Research Service, 1975, pp. 175-178).

The percentage of carless households increases with the size of an urban area, but public transit is also more available the larger the urban area. The carless have consistently indicated a desire to travel more frequently than they do, and they would prefer to make those trips by car (Tardiff, *et al.*, 1977, pp. 4-7). A study conducted to determine whether the carless are more transit-oriented than persons with cars concluded that they were not. Most of the respondents had

driven in the past and intended to purchase an auto in the
near future, when they felt they would be able to afford one
(Kidder and Saltzman, 1972).

Rural residents make more and longer auto trips than urban
residents, and people in unincorporated areas and small incorporated areas (5,000 to 24,999 population) make the most
trips per day of all Americans. Residents of towns under 5,000
use cars the least because they are able to walk to many
places. Work trips in unincorporated areas are longer than
those in urban areas (Economic Research Service, 1975, p.
174). Except in retirement communities, the work trip accounts for almost half of the home-based trips, followed by
personal business, social and recreational, and shopping trips.
The smaller the city, the greater the percentage of trips to the
central business district (Macy, *et al.*, 1968, p. 25).

Many rural residents must own cars at the expense of other
basic needs. There is little carpooling in these areas, and
apparently little encouragement for it has been given by employers or local officials. Overt efforts to increase carpooling
have not been very successful. The aversion to carpooling
seems to be greater in towns under 25,000 in population,
perhaps because drivers take more trips in these places and
the destinations are widely scattered. Coates and Weiss feel
that it is a myth that small town people help one another with
rides (1975, p. 27).

Although comprehensive data on the topic do not exist,
mobility problems associated with carlessness are probably
more severe in nonmetropolitan areas for a number of perhaps
obvious reasons. Public transit usually does not exist in these
areas, and where it does it may be limited in frequency and
coverage, and may serve only certain designated groups. Furthermore, taxi service may not exist, and persons without
telephones may have difficulty arranging for ride sharing. Convenience shopping may not be within walking distance, and to
obtain the full range of services rural residents may have to
travel to several towns (Tardiff, *et al.*, 1977, pp. 7-8).

The private automobile is likely to remain the dominant
transportation mode in small towns and rural areas for the
same reasons it will remain so in larger urban areas: it is the

most convenient and fastest mode. Furthermore, it becomes the least expensive mode if the value of one's time is considered as a cost when comparing alternative ways to travel. This is especially true in a rural area (except for low-income groups) because of the circuitous routing needed to obtain high seat capacity (Rupprecht, 1977, pp. 116-117). Rupprecht has argued that public transit in rural areas could be both fruitless and wasteful because people will continue to rely upon the auto which, even in the face of higher energy costs, will be more economical to operate there. He feels that the only people opting for transit will be those with physical and income limitations (1977, pp. 117-118).

Even in small cities where transit service is available, it carries a much smaller percentage of total trips than does bus service in larger cities (Macy, *et al.*, 1968, p. 22), it may not serve outlying areas, and it may not provide evening or weekend service. Taxi service sometimes fills this void, but the transportation-dependent segment of the population often cannot afford the fare.

Public Transit

If auto users in small towns and rural areas cannot be convinced to give up their vehicles for public transit, there remains, nonetheless, a need for public transit. This need exists for transit both within towns and between them. Unfortunately, very few small towns have public transit systems because of low demand and high operating costs (Coates and Weiss, 1975, p. 2). Intercity bus service is more common, more than 95 percent of towns between 2,500 and 5,000 in population being served. But many towns are facing reduced service (Coates and Weiss, 1975, p. 17), and the number of transit systems serving nonmetropolitan areas is gradually dwindling (National Area Development Institute, 1975, p. 280). Rail and air passenger service to these towns is almost nonexistent. Only 4 percent of towns between 2,500 and 5,000 in population have rail service; 12 percent have direct air service (Levine, 1977, p. 118). Yet many people in these rural areas need to get from one town to another to obtain specialized services that they cannot obtain in their own town. Unfortunately, the absence of concentrations of users and captive riders found in larger urban areas makes rural bus service, both intra- and intercity, expensive to provide.

Buses have historically provided service among small cities and between them and larger urban areas. They have been able to provide the service for lower rates than other modes because the bus was able to use the existing road network and obtain a low cost-per-seat mile by adapting to the demand characteristics of rural areas. But by being able to respond quickly to demand, particularly decreasing demand, bus systems have been able to cut back and eliminate service. Although some cities have taken over failing private bus systems, the smaller the city the less likely the ability to do so. Since the cost per bus mile is lower in smaller cities because of lower wage rates, the heart of the problem is clearly the decline in passenger volume, including passengers-per-bus mile, per-seat, and per-vehicle. The decline has been attributed to many factors, including a lack of innovation in scheduling, routing, and equipment size, combined with the increased use of the private auto. Not to be overlooked is the classic cycle of cutbacks leading to further reduced demand and revenues (Economic Research Service, 1975, p. 185). The evidence seems to be overwhelmingly against the small town being able to support an economically self-sufficient mass transit system (Coates, 1974, p. 63).

Some small towns that cannot generate enough traffic to justify service themselves are fortunate enough to be located along intercity bus routes. The importance of intercity bus service is staggering. Approximately 15,000 cities and towns are served by intercity bus service, and for 14,000 of them it is the only form of public transit available, except for taxi service (Webb, 1976, pp. 154-155). Unfortunately, regularly-scheduled service to these areas has deteriorated in recent years and the trend is expected to continue (Levine, 1977, p. 120).

Intercity bus companies that stress express service between major cities, and those that have added package delivery to their services, would often rather not serve small towns, which cut into their ability to provide timely service. The Economic

Research Service has suggested that small towns may be able to retain intercity bus service if signaling devices and bus shelters were provided on expressway ramps to reduce pickup time (1975, p. 186).

In Michigan, intercity bus services are provided by private carriers under contract to the state. Towns of 2,000 to 4,000 in population which have not had service for 30 years are now being served. State assistance is provided to make up the shortfall when fare box revenues fail to meet operating costs (Webb, 1978, p. 155).

Solving the problem of intercity bus service may be out of the hands of the local planner, although states and localities may move to subsidize intercity bus service. Direct federal financial assistance to offset operating deficits of the intercity bus industry has been called "the alternative of last resort," (Levine, 1977, p. 120).

Faced with an assumed need for an alternative to the private auto for a portion of the residents in small towns and rural areas, and faced with either a bankrupt private bus system or no service whatsoever, what are the alternatives? Intercity transit, as noted above, has the capability of serving only a small portion of the needs of a small town. The alternative adopted by many communities is paratransit—the use of bus-like vehicles, often run by nontraditional transit operators, and usually providing demand-responsive service. Experience with these systems has grown in recent years. Launching such a system means dealing with the estimation of need and demand, vehicle selection, systems management, financing, etc.

Transit Need Versus Demand

The issues of need and demand can spark a heated argument among transportation planners, local officials, politicians and service providers. The "need" for rural public transit has been documented (National Area Development Institute, 1975, pp. 277-279), and it is relatively easy to prove such need for poor and elderly rural persons. Approximately 10 percent of the households in the Old West Region, for example, do not own an automobile, and approximately 60 percent have one car, which when taken to work by the breadwinner, often leaves them with no means of transportation. However, in economist's terms, "demand" for bus service has been too low to justify service. Since "demand" is measured in terms of willingness and ability to pay for bus service, the demand for rural transit will be very low, although need may be high. Would-be planners of rural transit systems have been warned about this by the Department of Transportation: "Regardless of how much hardship may be created by the lack of such service, there are few people, especially the potential riders, who are willing *and able* to pay for it," (Office of Policy and Plans Development, 1974, p. 5). The department interpreted this to mean that any transit provided must not exceed the objective it was designed to meet, that the service must be carefully tailored to serve specific types of trips, and that its cost must be kept as low as possible (1974, p. 7). This distinction between need and demand has been challenged because it has been seen as a way to avoid a commitment to serving isolated persons. One observer has argued that the fare box is not an appropriate indicator: "A societal decision to provide mobility-assistance for its isolated people by way of revenue sharing funds, tax revenues, and other devices could provide the initiative for transportation demand to approach transportation need," (Kay, 1976, p. 25).

This argument aside, the design of a rural public transit system requires an estimate of the type and frequency of trip by origin and destination. Estimating demand for rural service remains somewhat undeveloped. Traditional techniques such as surveys, which are expensive, have failed to measure latent demand and to yield accurate information about potential riders. On the other hand, demonstration projects have given probably the best information, but they yield the information only after at least six months of service (Economic Research Service, 1975, p. 187).

Certainly to be avoided are those techniques that rely upon subjective estimates of demand drawn from what are believed to be the trip-making needs of local persons. Another unacceptable subjective technique is gap analysis, where demand is calculated as the difference between the number of trips now being taken by a specific group and the number they "should" be taking. These methods are not likely to produce results based on reality.

Alternative demand estimation techniques include the testing of systems through implementation and continuous surveillance. This option is recommended for small communities where the feasible alternatives are limited and the cost of testing the service would not be great. Another possibility would be to use the demand rates from areas where similar systems are in use, adjusting them on the basis of a small-scale survey in the subject area. Other analysts have tried to estimate the trip frequency for geographical and social segments of the population (Tardiff, *et al.*, 1977, pp. 19-22).

It is essential that accurate demand estimates be made. Perhaps the most devastating thing that can happen to a new transit system is to purchase too many vehicles and hire too many drivers. Several papers describing recent attempts to estimate demand may be found in the *Proceedings of the First National Conference on Rural Public Transportation*. Burkhardt argues that aggregated estimate techniques and simulation produce the best results.

Aggregated estimates are produced under the assumption that per capita ridership is roughly the same for all rural areas. Of course, variation exists among areas. Thus the estimates derived from this technique have ranged from 0.01 to 3.0 trips per person per year. Burkhardt believes that most of the variation is between 0.10 and 0.70 trips per person per year, based on the total population of the area (1976, pp. 70-72). Most people seem to be surprised when they apply these rates, since they usually produce a lower ridership than expected. Burkhardt extends a warning to people who are inclined not to believe the lower-than-expected estimates, "Most rural transportation systems do not serve more than 5,000 riders per month, and many serve less than 1,000." (1976, p. 74).

Instead of calculating trip-generation for total households alone, it can be computed for categories of households with various characteristics that might be related to the use of public transit, for example, auto ownership and household size or income. The cross-classification model operates in this matter (Colangelo and Glaze, 1977). Demand is estimated by using the observed relationships between two or more variables. For example, auto ownership and household size might be classified to determine the number of trips by transit per day taken by households of various size, with differing degrees of auto ownership (Byrne and Neumann, 1976, pp. 77-78). Of course these data would have to be computed in an area where public transit is available.

The trip-generation model using borrowed rates was successfully applied in northwest Wisconsin to estimate rural transit demand. Potential ridership groups within the service area were identified and expected rates of transit use per person were obtained from operating experience in similar areas. Demand was then estimated for each target group, (target groups might include the elderly and non-elderly low income persons). The demand computed in this manner was then adjusted upward by a factor which accounted for the proportion of all trips made by the target groups (Peterson and Smith, 1976, pp. 90-102). In the same study, estimating trip-making by applying an average trip-making rate to the proportion of the population using transit was shown to be unreliable. Similarly, computing trip-making from a conception of the number of trips people should make in order to achieve certain nontransportation or societal goals (such as obtaining certain levels of health services, social contact or nutrition) did not produce accurate results (pp. 95-99).

A similar demand-forecasting model that uses trip rate data from other cities and does not require a local survey has been successfully used in New York State (Kulka and Sampson, 1978). Average trip rates, stratified by population age group and sex for a given mode and fare level, were used to produce mode-specific demand estimates.

Mathematical models that simulate the demand for service are judged to be the most accurate techniques, although they too predict a wide range of use. The advantages of this technique include permitting experimentation with the components of the system, and seeing how the changes would affect ridership and costs (Burkhardt, 1976, p. 72). *Methods of Predicting Rural Transit Demand* by Burkhardt and Lago should be consulted before actual demand estimates are made.

Other researchers have been experimenting with a variety of mathematical models to estimate trip-making. Accessibility models attempt to predict trip-making based on one's distance or travel time from a key destination, and regression models are being used to estimate trip rates from a variety of social and economic characteristics (Byrne and Neumann, 1976, p. 78).

When estimating demand several characteristics of paratransit should be kept in mind. First, these systems often are not designed to provide for the home-to-work trip. It is sometimes assumed that workers are able to provide for their own transportation, and often the systems are targeted at the elderly, handicapped persons, special education students and other special groups. Furthermore, many of these systems simply could not handle the peak demand of work trips. The level of service of these systems is also sometimes limited to one round trip per day, and in some cases to even as little as two trips per week.

Clearly there is no single way to estimate demand. A jurisdiction must do the best it can with the money, time, and skills at its command. One can obtain a rough estimate by applying trip-generation rates per household obtained from similar areas. If the data are available, these estimates could be made for various segments of the population. When the skills are available, mathematical models might be used to simulate demand. Perhaps the safest route to take would involve beginning a small system and adding additional service as demand is determined through actual experience. As the case studies reported later show, it often takes considerable time for ridership to develop. For example, one system which covered 70 percent of the state highways in a county plus 90 percent of the villages and offered fixed-route six-day-a-week service operated for a full week before picking up its first passenger, even though the system had been promoted on the local media.

Paratransit service could be provided by a unit of government, local or state. On the other hand, if a municipality or county did not desire to operate the system, it could contract for service with a private firm, such as a local taxi service or a private transit service. If transit is already being provided by a community organization or agency, that group might be willing to expand its service.

Alternatives

Assuming that both a need and demand for public transportation exist, the question arises as to what type of system should be provided. The answer depends, of course, upon the population to be served, the density of population, the distribution of trip-generating activities, etc. The fixed-route-system—the type of system found in larger cities—is used when potential riders are located along major routes and the demand and density are such that buses can pass fixed pickup points at regular intervals. This system works well in high-density areas and when people are travelling to a few activity centers. It does not work well for physically handicapped persons and in areas where distances make it difficult for persons to walk to pickup points.

In contrast, a demand-responsive system is routed in response to the requests of users. Typically involving minibuses or vans, door-to-door service is provided to persons who call for a ride. Usually the calls are received in advance at a central location and routes are established so that passengers are picked up as others are being taken to their destinations. Demand-responsive systems have the advantage of greater flexibility in destinations, door-to-door service, the elimination of the need to transfer, and the ability to more easily serve physically handicapped persons. On the other hand, demand-responsive systems may be less reliable since travel times can be affected by the demand on the system, variation in routing, delays in waiting for passengers, etc. Most rural transit systems are demand-responsive, in whole or in part (Transportation Systems Center, 1976a).

In Merrill, Wisconsin a "point-deviation system" (only the second major system of its kind) combines the fixed-route and demand-responsive methods. Buses travel between fixed pickup points, but are free to pick up riders along the way. This type of system apparently is able to provide broader coverage than fixed-route systems while achieving the capacity levels of fixed-route systems. Riders pay various amounts, depending upon whether they were picked up at their doors or at pickup points (Flusberg, 1978).

School buses have sometimes been proposed, and also used, for rural transit. Since the vehicles sit idle part of the day, it would seem logical to use them for this purpose. However, they tend not to serve well because they do not meet adult comfort standards nor safety standards for general transportation (Barnett, 1976, p. 39). When they are the only transportation available, school buses have apparently proved acceptable (Administration on Aging, 1975, pp. 66-88; and Economic Research Service, 1975, pp. 188-189). Some states, however, prohibit the use of school buses for nonschool use. (Administration on Aging, 1975, p. 67).

Postal vehicles have been used to transport people in Great Britain, and a similar experiment is being conducted in West Virginia (Wolfe, 1976, p. 212). In Great Britain people either call the post office or signal with their mailboxes that they need transportation. Carriers pick up passengers on their way to the post office and return them later in the day (Economic Research Service, 1975, p. 189).

Taxis and jitneys are modes that might be considered, but unsubsidized taxi costs tend to be too high for most rural transit users and the density needed for efficient operation of both taxis and jitneys is available only in the larger towns in rural areas. Subsidized taxi service for older persons has been provided in a number of communities, including Missoula, Montana. However, these efforts encountered some problems (Administration on Aging, 1975, pp. 27-43), and the experience should be reviewed before being attempted as the sole source of public transit.

A more important issue in the use of taxis involves the threat of unfair competition if a demand-responsive system is established where taxi service is available. Section 13(c) of the Urban Mass Transportation Act is intended to protect employees of a transit system that is taken over, replaced, or affected by a service supported by federal funds. Several transit projects have been forced to close by court order for violating the franchises of private operators. In two California counties dial-a-ride service was established but the local taxi companies were not included; the companies brought suit and won, and the transit district was ordered to buy out the taxi companies (Hart, 1976, p. 128). Although the decision is applicable only to transit districts, a locality considering a demand-responsive service should determine whether a local taxi service might be willing and able to provide the service. In the long run this may be less expensive than establishing a new service, especially when management and technical experience is not available. Should the existing taxi service appear to be a viable alternative, the experiences of others in development and arrangement should be examined (Crain and Associates, 1977; and Hart, 1976). Recent transit legislation gives the Secretary of Labor permission to waive Section 13(c) for rural areas and small towns.

Sources of Funding and Assistance

Ingenious funding arrangements have been devised to support rural transit services. Many of the early systems and some even today are largely voluntary operations. Often a single van is provided at cost or donated by a local organization and volunteer drivers and dispatchers operate the system. In recent years, funds for rural transit have been provided through a number of federal programs, including Titles III and VII of the Older Americans Act and Titles XIX and XX of the Social Security Act and the Rehabilitation Act of 1973. Transportation to community and social services has been financed through programs of the Office of Economic Opportunity (now the U.S. Community Services Administration). The Office of Human Development Services of the Department of Health, Education and Welfare is also supporting several projects aimed at demonstrating and evaluating the coordination of existing transportation systems supported under various agencies of HEW, DOT, Community Services Administration, Department of Labor, and ACTION (1977). More than 90 federal programs either provide for or permit transportation support for social service programs.

Although urban areas were provided limited federal aid to transportation systems by the 1964 Urban Mass Transportation Act, it was not until 1973 that rural areas were provided financial assistance for transit systems. Section 147 of the 1973 Federal Aid Highway Act, administered jointly by the Urban Mass Transportation Administration and the Federal Highway Administration, authorized the Rural Highway Public Transportation Demonstration Program and established the rural transit demonstration program which began in fiscal year 1975. This one-time funding was awarded to 102 projects in 48 states. Projects range from one-bus, fixed-route projects to a multi-county service by a regional transportation authority, offering fixed-route, demand-responsive, and contract service.

Urban Mass Transportation demonstration and capital grants have also been used in the provision of transit services in small urban and rural areas under 50,000 in population. In 1974, $500 million of UMTA Section 3 funds (capital assistance program for public agencies) were set aside to provide transit assistance in nonurbanized areas from 1975 through October of 1980. (Prior to 1975 these funds had been available for locally-initiated requests, but few requests had been made).

Other types of transit assistance are available through UMTA, including planning assistance (Section 9) to state departments of transportation and other state agencies. These funds may be used to finance technical studies or transit development programs that are needed to qualify for UMTA capital grant programs.

Under Section 16(b)2, the capital assistance program for private nonprofit organizations, funds are made available by formula to state agencies that assist private nonprofit organizations to provide transit for elderly and handicapped persons. The states are responsible for submitting a consolidated application to UMTA.

UMTA also funds a service and methods demonstration (Section 6) to test innovative transportation services of national importance. Unlike other UMTA support, these funds can be spent on operation as well as capital facilities.

In addition to these funding sources, rural public transit systems have used dozens of other sources on a single project, including fares, fees from charter service, revenue sharing, Emergency Employment Act funds, Regional Commission funds, CETA, and in-kind funds. Two of the major problems which have faced these systems, however, are the financing of operating deficit and the continuation of funding.

Responding to the growing recognition of a need for resources to support rural transit, Congress approved, as part of the Federal Public Transportation Act of 1978, funds for operating and capital assistance for public transportation in small towns and rural areas. These amendments to the Urban Mass Transportation Act of 1964 provide each state with three-year funding in proportion to its share of the total U.S. nonurbanized population. Funds will be permitted for providing local transportation service directly or under contract, and federal funds can be used to subsidize up to 50 percent of operating expenses.

Costs and Subsidies

The cost of providing rural transportation service can vary widely, depending upon the size and nature of the system, whether paid workers or volunteers are used, and whether administrative costs are included. Table 1 presents the costs of operating selected systems, chosen to illustrate the types of small town and rural projects funded by a variety of sources. Brief descriptions and references for each system conclude the chapter.

The costs presented in table 1 were taken or computed from published data. However, since the raw data were not collected systematically, the computed figures are only rough estimates of the indicated measure. Furthermore, the data have not been adjusted for inflation nor regional differences. Thus the data that are five to ten years old should be read with caution.

Table 1. Costs for Paratransit Systems

	Data Base Year	Service Area Population	Demand/Capita/Year	Annual Operating Cost	Passengers/Mile	Cost/Passenger Trip	Cost/Vehicle Mile	Primary Funding Source
AORTA Appalachian Ohio Regional Transit Association	1976	84,629	1.78	$125,976	.67	$1.13	$.75	Many Sources City Funds ARC & Sec. 147
Merrill, Wisconsin	1976	9,500	7.7	$84,600	NA	$.99	$.78	State
Merced, California	1975	30,000	2.40	$80,000	NA	$.84	NA	State
Northwest Wisconsin CAP Transit System	1975	6,859	3.65-7.59	$31,900*	.47-.39	$.92-$1.43*	$.43-$.56*	CAP
Pennsylvania Rural Transit	1973	778,568	.01-.03	$59,900	.02-.06	$4.78-$26.02	$.27-$.59	State Dept. of Welfare
Montgomery County, Illinois	1973	8,218	.54-.77	$11,160	.32	$1.76-$2.52	$.56-$.80	AOA, Title III
Jackson County, Oregon	1973	49,800	1.93	$84,000	.59	$.88	$.45	OEO
Raleigh County, West Virginia	1969	66,000	.78	$44,400	.42	$.90	$.36	OEO

NA = Not Available
* Excludes insurance and administrative expenses

Note: Data are not adjusted for inflation or for regional price differences.

For each nonvolunteer system the major expense was the salaries for drivers and administrators—typically over 50 percent of project costs. Data provided by the Federal Highway Administration for current Section 147 projects indicate that drivers' wages still account for slightly more than half of the operating costs. The cost per passenger trip of current Section 147 projects ranges from $1.54 to $10.47, with an average of $3.25, slightly greater than that of the eight cases illustrated in figure 0. The cost per vehicle mile for the Section 147 projects is $.59, quite close to the cost of most of the sample projects.

None of the projects is self-supporting. Even when volunteers are used, most systems will require some degree of subsidy (Coates, 1974, p. 63; and Economic Research Service, 1975, p. 187). For example, fares in the current Section 147 projects average only 20 percent of operating and administrative costs. The decision whether to subsidize would depend upon local factors, including the availability of federal, state, and local assistance.

There are economic as well as philosophical reasons both for and against subsidies. On the one hand, the subsidy does not allow for a full accounting of costs and benefits, and the benefits are not fully compensated for by the costs to the recipient. In addition, the subsidy prevents the system from achieving equilibrium and may hide inefficiencies. The counter argument is that the system should be subsidized because it gives individuals freedom of choice, and as such is a useful social investment that permits disadvantaged persons to obtain needed services (Tardiff, *et al.*, 1977, p. 29). Furthermore, if the goal of a rural transit system is to provide service to the carless, then it is unlikely that these people will be able to pay the full cost of such a service.

Arguments have been advanced for charging some fare, including avoiding the stigma of "welfare buses." Partial fares would also reduce the amount of subsidy required, and would tend to prevent "overutilization" of the system (Tardiff, *et al.*, 1977, p. 26). In some cases, though, fares may not be charged to avoid time-consuming public hearings and lawyer fees involved in settling fares, schedules, and routes

with a public service commission. Donations might be encouraged (Peterson and Smith, 1976, p. 91). One agency
successfully argued that since it was a public nonprofit organization, not a service for hire or a common carrier, that it was
not subject to the state's Public Utilities Commission Regulation (McKelvey, 1977).

If fares are charged, they could be established to make up the
shortfall between the subsidy and operating costs, or they might
be set in relation to the amount being paid for comparable
service in adjacent areas. Other guides might include taxi rates
and donations given to neighbors and friends for shared rides. A
general rule is to avoid setting fares too low at first so that riders
will not be irritated by an increase shortly after the system
opens for service. Fares have ranged from two-to-five cents per
passenger mile or from $.25 to $1.00 or more per trip (Kidder,
1976; and Department of Transportation, 1976a).

Not to be overlooked is the need to provide insurance for
the transit system. Costs appear to vary widely among states
and types of transit services. Special provisions must be made
to protect volunteers, should they be involved in an accident.

The Planning Process

Planning rural transit service ideally should take place as part
of the transportation element of the comprehensive planning
process, since transportation needs are so closely related to
population density, land use patterns, economic activity, etc.
Information about transportation planning for small towns and
rural areas is available in a number of documents. A nontechnical overview of problems and possible solutions is available in
a report prepared for the U.S. Department of Housing and
Urban Development (Macy, *et al.*, 1968). Technical reports
which analyze alternative techniques and procedures for small
area transportation planning are also available (Grecco, *et al.*,
1976; and Transportation Research Board, 1977).

This focus upon transit does not mean to imply that small
towns and rural regions have no other transportation problems. On the contrary, many towns could benefit from a

redesign of the major street system, construction of railroad grade separations, improved signalization and channelization, resurfacing, bridge replacement, etc. These needs should be identified through the general planning process and assistance should be obtained from relevant agencies. Possible sources of assistance include municipal and county engineering departments, local road commissions, state departments of transportation, etc. These organizations may also be able to provide transit planning assistance. The following publications should also be studied: *Rural Passenger Transportation: State-of-the-Art Overview* by the Transportation Systems Center; *Demand-Responsive Transportation* by the Transportation Systems Center; and *Para-Transit: Neglected Options for Urban Mobility* by Kirby, *et al.*, of the Urban Institute; *Paratransit*, a newsletter published by the Transportation Research Board, 2101 Constitution Avenue, N.W., Washington, D.C. 20418.

Planning public transit service is an iterative process; changing circumstances and new knowledge gained during the planning process may demand that earlier decisions be modified. The major steps in that process, and the questions to be addressed at each step are sketched below. A procedure for planning and implementing a rural transportation system is also provided in *Rural Passenger Transportation: State-of-the-Art Overview*, pp. 27-41, and the U.S. Department of Agriculture is in the process of preparing *Rural Rides: A Practical Handbook for Starting and Operating a Rural Public Transportation System* for eventual widespread distribution. The first step in the process might well be to conduct a preplanning reconnaissance.

1. *Preplanning.* Is a public transit service a new idea? Have earlier attempts been made? Are there old proposals that can be analyzed? Who has supported and opposed similar proposals in the past? Do such systems exist in nearby areas? Is planning assistance available from the state department of transportation or the highway department? Is help available through local universities or the agricultural extension service? What data bases are available? This would also be a good time to contact the Federal Highway Administration and the

Urban Mass Transportation Administration. Both are at 400 7th Street, S.W., Washington, D.C. 20590. For the FHWA, phone (202) 426-0677. UMTA is (202) 426-4043.

If you are planning to offer public transit in an area where service is already being provided, perhaps to a specific target group, you may be required to coordinate service. For example, the Administration on Aging and the Department of Transportation have an agreement to coordinate transit services for the elderly and handicapped.

In order to get people to think about transit options, you may want to show a half-hour film that describes what four small cities have done and how local residents feel. "Transit Options for Small Communities" describes a fixed-route system, dial-a-ride service, route deviation and subsidized taxi service. It may be borrowed from the Broadcast/Audio Visual Division, Office of the Secretary (OST) (S-83), Department of Transportation, Washington, D.C. 20590.

It would probably be useful to establish a planning committee at this time.

2. *Estimating Need and Demand.* These data may already be available in studies and plans made by other agencies, or you may have to generate them from census data, from studies for similar areas, and from other sources. Recall the demand-estimation problems discussed above. Is there local political support for transit service as well as need and demand?

The following publications can help you begin to estimate demand: *Small City Transit Characteristics: An Overview; Small City Transit, Merced, California*; and *Small City Transit, Merrill, Wisconsin*, each by the Transportation Systems Center; *Demand-Responsive Transportation Systems Planning Guidelines* by the Mitre Corporation; *Methods of Predicting Rural Transit Demand* by Burkhardt and Lago; "Analytic Model for Predicting Dial-a-Ride System Performance," in *Transportation Research Board Special Report No. 147*, by Lerman and Wilson; and *Transportation Planning Techniques for Small Communities: Transportation Research Record 638* by the Transportation Research Board.

If your transit system is expected to attract a substantial number of older persons, you will want to consult the following reports: *Transportation and Aging: Selected Issues* by Cantilli and Shmelzer; *Transportation for the Elderly: the State of the Art* by the Administration on Aging; *Guidelines and Considerations in Planning and Operating Transportation Systems for Older Americans* by McKelvey; and *Transportation Services for the Elderly—Planning Handbook* by the Administration on Aging. You might also contact UMTA's Office of Technology Development and Deployment, Bus and Paratransit Division, (202) 426-4035.

3. *Determining Type of Service.* Is a fixed-route or demand-responsive system needed? This will depend upon the size of your area, the population density, location of trip-generating activities, and a comparison of costs. Will the service be restricted to a target population? What do citizens desire? What would be an acceptable level of service? What types of vehicles will be needed?

Sources of information include: *Small Transit Vehicle Survey* by Flusberg, Kullman and Casey; and *A Directory of Vehicles and Related System Components for the Elderly and Handicapped* by the U.S. Department of Transportation. If you are considering taxi-operated paratransit, see *Establishing Innovative Taxicab Services: A Guidebook* by Gilbert, Garber and Foerster; and "User-Side Subsidy on a Shared-Ride Taxi Service for Handicapped and Elderly" by Crain and Associates.

Information about the latest developments in buses and taxis can be obtained from UMTA's Office of Technology Development and Deployment, Bus and Paratransit Division, (202) 426-4035.

4. *Estimating Costs.* This task requires making assumptions about demand, routing, management, vehicle size, wages, etc. Can costs be reduced by using volunteers? It is useful to separate fixed costs and variable costs (those costs that vary depending upon the amount of service provided).

Fixed costs would include salaries for managers, secretaries and dispatchers, the purchase or lease of vehicles for the basic fleet, wages for the basic fleet operators, taxes and insurance, and office rent and supplies. Variable costs would include wages of additional drivers, fuel, vehicle maintenance and repairs.

Demand-Responsive Transportation Systems Planning Guidelines by the Mitre Corporation; *Rural Passenger Transportation: State-of-the-Art Overview* by the Transportation Systems Center; and *Small City Transit,* also by the Transportation Systems Center would provide help at this point, but you will have to produce much of the data based upon local policy decisions. UMTA's Office of Technology Development and Deployment may be able to refer you to the latest financial data.

5. *Determining Financing.* How can the service be funded? If it is to serve a target group, special funding may be available. For example, transportation services have been provided through both Title III and Title VII of the Older Americans Act administered by the Administration on Aging. Other sources include Title XX of the Social Security Act, Title XIX of the Medicaid Program, CETA, and the Community Services Administration. What programs are available from UMTA, FHWA, the state? Remember, these sources often fund one-time-only projects. Will a fare be charged? How much?

The experiences of other cities and regions will be instructive. For the ways in which four transit services have pooled their resources see: *Evaluating Rural Public Transportation* by McKelvey.

6. *Implementing the System.* Who will operate and manage the system? Should local government offer the service? Is there a private transit system which might agree to provide the service? How will vehicle maintenance and service be provided? Many of the reports cited earlier would again be useful, including *Rural Passenger Transportation: State-of-the-Art Overview;* and *Demand-Responsive Transportation: State-of-the-Art Overview.*

7. *Evaluating the System.* If a system is launched, what data should be collected? For what purposes will they be used? Who will keep the records? What will drivers be required to record? A good source of information about recordkeeping is *Evalutation Methodology for the Rural Highway Public Transportation Demonstration Program* prepared by Burkhardt and Lago for the FHWA and UMTA; or *Evaluating Rural Public Transportation,* prepared by McKelvey for the U.S. Department of Transportation.

Case Examples

Rural transportation projects have been developed across the country, and they provide useful insights into the problems of establishing and operating a paratransit system. Eight projects which illustrate the variety in the scope, cost, area-coverage and funding of projects are summarized below. The particular projects were selected because information about them is available through public sources and because data were available from which we could compute demand per capita, passengers per mile, cost per trip and cost per miles. Additional case studies may be found in the publications from which these examples were drawn.

Raleigh County, West Virginia (1969)

The Raleigh County Community Action Association in Beckley, West Virginia operated a free transportation service from 1967 to 1969 (Resource Management Corporation, 1969). The service, funded by an OEO demonstration grant, was to serve the rural poor in Raleigh County, population 66,000 in 1968. Initially nine vans were operated over eighteen routes, each route receiving daily service. However, ridership was not sufficient to demand this level of service. The operation was trimmed to five vans, but the eighteen routes were maintained, and service was reduced. Only two routes received daily service. The service was used primarily for shopping, attending community meetings and trips to the doctor.

Drivers kept the vans at their homes overnight, picked people up according to a fixed schedule, and took them to Buckley, the major population center in the county. Buses returned to the outlying areas when fully loaded or when all the inbound passengers returned. Seventy-three percent of the riders were picked up at their homes and 23 percent walked a mile or less to catch the bus.

Service during the life of the project varied considerably, making operation estimates difficult. After the initial startup problems had been overcome, and several record-keeping problems were resolved, the system was carrying 494 round-trip passengers per week, making 175 round trips per month, and covering 24,700 miles per vehicle per year. This converts to 51,324 one-way passenger trips per year and 123,500 vehicle miles per year. The system cost $44,400 per year to operate, or $.36 per vehicle mile or $.90 per passenger trip. Drivers' wages, averaging $.20 per vehicle mile, comprised the bulk of the project costs.

The project terminated when OEO funding ran out. An attempt was made to have families contribute $1.50 per month for service but that failed. Later, in order to provide some service, drivers were allowed to operate the buses over specified territories and collect donations. This eventually collapsed, although one or two drivers were able to make a modest wage.

Jackson County, Oregon: Operation Transport (1973)

Operation Transport, an arm of the Jackson County Community Action Agency, contracted with a private for-profit local bus company for transit service (Committee on Agriculture and Forestry, Subcommittee on Rural Development, 1974, pp. 39-41). The private company, Rogue Valley Stage Lines (RVSL), provided scheduled and fixed-route service to the Bear Creek area of Jackson County. RVSL provided service on four primarily intercity routes connecting five towns in the area with populations ranging from under 2,500 to over 28,000. All vehicles were modified vans, except for one 35-passenger bus. One shuttle service was provided in the largest city. Each route had a nominal schedule and fixed route (varying from 11.5 to 31 miles round trip), but buses deviated from these routes to pick up approximately 10 percent of the system's passengers. Drivers were contacted by two-way radio when people called in for a pick-up. Radio contact was also used to coordinate transfers.

In 1973 the system was carrying more than 8,000 passengers per month and operating approximately 164,000 vehicle-miles per year. Costs were averaging slightly more than $7,000 per month, for a cost of $.45 per vehicle-mile and $.88 per passenger trip. The contract rate between Operation Transport and RVSL ranged from $.32 to $.35 per vehicle-mile, with revenues averaging from $.22 to $.26 per vehicle-mile. The system's deficits varied from $.09 to $.16 per vehicle-mile or from $.19 to $.34 per passenger trip. The major expenses were drivers' salaries (50 percent) and office wages (19 percent). Initially the deficits were covered by the Community Action Agency (CAA) through an OEO grant. Later, the subsidy was covered by a combination of sources, including the largest city in the area, the state, and county funds through the CAA.

Operation Transit provided service primarily for shopping and medical trips for elderly and poor persons. Efforts to provide service for work-trips failed.

Montgomery County, Illinois (1973)

A minibus system was installed in this rural county in late 1972 as a pilot program to test the effectiveness of this type of transportation (Patton, et al., 1975) A seven-county Economic Opportunity Corporation operated the service with Title III funds from the Administration on Aging. During the pilot phase one eleven-passenger van provided free bus service to persons 55 years of age or older in one of the seven counties. The service was later expanded to twelve minibuses serving the seven counties.

The minibus operated from a senior citizens' center in the county seat five days per week, and served various parts of the county on different days. There were 8,218 eligible users—persons aged 55 or above. Users were served on a first-call-first-served basis by calling the senior citizens' center or various locations throughout the county. These field dispatchers would relay the calls to the center to avoid toll calls for the users. Rides were to be booked one day in advance. Both drivers and dispatchers served on a volunteer basis.

Because the service was staffed by volunteers, the annual project cost of the pilot phase was only $7,550, including van operating expenses and telephone costs. Assuming that drivers had been paid (to make the costs of this service comparable to the others reported here), the annual cost would have been approximately $11,150. Based on a twelve month total of 4,431 passenger trips and 14,028 vehicle miles, the pilot project cost $2.52 per passenger trip or $.80 per vehicle mile. However, if these costs are recomputed on an annual basis but excluding the five-month start up period, the figures drop to approximately $1.76 per passenger trip or $.56 per vehicle mile. During this part of the project, the bus averaged 527 passenger trips per month, with an average one-way trip of 3.2 miles. More than half of the trips were for shopping, followed by social trips, and visits to the doctor.

Pennsylvania Rural Transit (1973)

The Pennsylvania Department of Agriculture developed and operated the Rural Transportation Program under contract to the Pennsylvania Department of Public Welfare. Twenty-five percent of the funds were provided by the Department of Agriculture (Pennsylvania Department of Agriculture, 1973). Service was provided for a nine-month period from October 1972 through June 1973 to a four-county area with a population of 778,568. People needing transportation called a toll-free number to reserve a ride on a future date, preferably a week in advance.

Three leased vehicles were placed in each of the four counties—six vans and six sedans. Lack of demand from the most rural county caused the service to be cut back to ten vehicles. Routes were established so as not to conflict with existing carriers. Unemployed persons were hired as drivers, and they took the vehicles home with them to avoid the travel time to, and costs of, a central motor pool.

Approximately $59,900 was spent for the nine months of transportation service. Additional funds were allocated for planning and evaluation. During the beginning of the project the cost per rider was high, $26.02, and the average cost per mile was $.59. An average of 1.3 people per day rode in each vehicle, and the average trip was 44 miles. As more riders were attracted to the service, more efficient routing could be devised. This caused the average trip length per person to be reduced to 18 miles, and the vehicle cost per mile declined to $.27. The cost per passenger trip declined to $4.78. Driver wages comprised 25 percent of the cost of service, and the salaries of the field supervision and dispatchers came to an additional 34 percent. Had the service been continued and had it maintained the ridership level of its last months, approximately 9,000 persons per year would have been transported.

Northwest Wisconsin CAP Transit System (1975)

Transit service is provided to rural and small town residents in parts of two counties in northern Wisconsin (Peterson and Smith, 1976). Since October of 1974 school bus type vehicles have been providing fixed-route service in each county. One line is 10 miles in length, the other 26 miles. Each line provides service to the central city in the region and each terminates at an Indian reservation. Three round trips per day are made, five days per week. No fare is charged, but donations are accepted.

Together the two lines serve an area with a combined population of 6,850. The service is used by both young and old, and for work and shopping trips. During 1975 approximately $31,900 was spent to operate the system. The operating cost per passenger trip was $.92 on one line and $1.43 on the second. This converts to $.43 and $.56 per vehicle mile (exclusive of insurance and administrative expenses). Driver wages comprised 67 percent of the cost of operating one line and 59 percent of operating the second.

Merced, California Dial-A-Ride (1975)

After an unsuccessful attempt to have the local taxi service provide a dial-a-ride service, the city of Merced established such a system with state funds provided through SB325 (Transportation Systems Center, 1976c). The city contracted for planning and development of the system under a "turn-key" arrangement, with a consulting firm submitting the low bid for the planning and development of the system. Door-to-door service is now provided to any point within the city limits for a flat fee of $.25. Children under six ride free when accompanying a fee-paying passenger. Four vans cruise within the city five days per week and are dispatched from a central control room to which people desiring rides phone. In addition, subscription service for regularly scheduled trips is provided.

Ridership increased steadily during the first year of service, from 138 riders per day to 330 (near the capacity of the system). Fares cover more than one-fourth of operating costs. In 1975 operating costs were $80,000, and passenger trips averaged $.84. Data about vehicle mileage and cost per mile are not available. Driver wages amount to 39 percent of the operating costs.

Merrill, Wisconsin Point Deviation (1976)

Through a grant from the Wisconsin Department of Transportation, Merrill, Wisconsin was able to institute a point-deviation service to replace a city-subsidized taxi operation and an electric dial-a-ride service for the elderly and handicapped (Flusberg, 1978; and Transportation Systems Center, 1976d). The point-deviation system was planned and designed by a consultant and began operation in 1975.

The system operates two 23-passenger buses at half-hour headways. The buses generally follow a direct route between ten checkpoints, but they are free to respond to requests for doorstep pickups and dropoffs. Drivers are radioed by a dispatcher who receives telephone calls from persons who want to be picked up.

Fares are $.25 for trips between checkpoints with an additional $.15 charge for the first deviation and $.10 for the second. A door-to-door trip costs $.50. Annual operating costs for the year under study were $84,600, and the system required a subsidy of $.73 per passenger. The operating cost per vehicle mile was $.78; the cost per passenger trip was $.99. Driver wages amounted to 42 percent of the operating cost.

Appalachian Ohio Regional Transit Association (1976)

The Appalachian Ohio Regional Transit Association (AORTA) provides transportation service to four counties in southeastern Ohio (McKelvey, 1977). The counties are sparsely populated, contain small urban areas isolated from one another, each urban area serving surrounding small towns and villages. There is no dominant metropolitan area. The automobile is the predominant mode of transportation, but over 17 percent of the households do not own a vehicle and 28 percent do not have a telephone. More than 40 percent of the households in the area have annual incomes of less than $6,000.

Because of the need to provide low-cost access throughout the region to health, social services, and employment, a three-county Community Action Agency established a rural transportation demonstration project. Service began late in 1971 with a 1963 school bus serving Hocking County. In early 1973 the CAA began the Athens Transit Company to serve Athens County and 26 communities in the county. In mid-1973 the CAA received a grant from the Appalachian Regional Commission (ARC) to renew support of the existing system and to expand it to Perry County. Low ridership caused this service to be cut back. In 1974 the three-county bus system was incorporated as the Appalachian Ohio Regional Transit Association, and AORTA contracted with the city of Athens for special service which now consists of three routes.

Service to the City of Athens accounted for over half of the system's total operating time and 80 percent of total ridership in 1976. The shortfall between fares and operating costs is covered by general revenue sharing funds from the city and Ohio's Elderly Bus Fare Assistance program.

Service in Vinton County was developed through that county's Commission on Aging to provide transportation to meal sites, clinics, etc. Ridership is also sought from the general public.

In late 1976 AORTA established "Reserve-a-Ride," a demand-responsive system in Athens County, requiring two-day advance reservations for the door-to-door service. This service allowed AORTA to eliminate some low demand fixed-route service.

AORTA operates ten vehicles with capacities ranging from twelve to forty passengers. The Athens, Hocking and Vinton County systems each operate one bus on different routes on various days of the week. AORTA also operates three routes in the city of Athens and the demand-responsive system in Athens County. Expanded service, to be provided through a Section 147 grant, will require the addition of seven buses.

This project is of interest because of its history of incremental growth and the variety of sources from which funds have been obtained. Financial support, in addition to fares, contract services, charter services, advertising revenues and leasing, has been derived from the U.S. DOT (Section 147), the Appalachian Regional Commission, the Office of Economic Opportunity, and the Ohio Department of Economic and Community Development. County and city funds include those from CAA agencies, Title VII, city and county revenue sharing, the Emergency Employment Act, CETA and Title XX.

Figures available for 1976 show that the system carried 156,834 passengers (including 5,981 charter passengers) within Athens, Hocking and Vinton Counties. These three counties have a combined population of 84,629. Total system costs amounted to $176,477 for an average cost per passenger of $1.13 and an average cost per mile of $.75. Earned revenues (including contracted service with the city of Athens paid from revenue sharing funds) cover 61 percent of the system's costs. Federal funds (ARC support and Section 147) cover 23 percent of the system's costs. The balance, 16 percent, is local subsidy. The largest single source of support is from contract service with the city of Athens. The second largest source is the ARC subsidy.

Conclusion

Rural planners tackling transportation issues will be faced with a potpourri of problems and obstacles. The problems do not stop at the town or village boundary, and many of them are regional in scope. Some transportation problems, such as the abandonment of rail lines or the transportation of grain, are part of a nationwide problem. If this were not enough, transportation problems are often interrelated with those of housing and community services. Solutions in one area depend upon solutions in another.

Even when the capital costs of public transit are covered, operating and maintenance costs may be prohibitive. In sparsely settled rural areas there are simply too few persons over whom to spread total costs. Rural paratransit systems, while modest in cost when compared with other ways to increase rural mobility, typically require subsidies. Furthermore, costs are high during the early stages of these systems, whether measured as cost per rider, cost per mile, or cost per trip. Success often comes slowly, and it may take many months to develop a clientele, to establish an efficient routing system and to make a visible impact on the lives of rural residents. These lessons indicate the importance of clearly identifying the costs and benefits expected throughout the implementation period.

Recent case examples also show the need for patience. Time is needed for a system to mature (to attract repeat clients, to train a reliable staff, and to develop standard operating procedures). Furthermore, aborted programs disappoint dependent individuals and spoil the chances for the success of future projects.

Chapter VIII
Rural Housing and Community Services

Problems in the areas of housing and community services are often more difficult to address in rural areas because the population is dispersed, often isolated, and tends to be older and poorer. Furthermore, the physical facilities in rural areas are more often substandard, and financial resources are often lacking. Some governmental units have not developed basic devices for dealing with these problems. In the housing area, for example, the absence of building codes in a number of locales has permitted the *construction* of substandard housing. Some communities do not have a capital improvements program and consequently are unprepared to finance the development of community facilities. Nevertheless, it is possible for communities to devise plans and programs to provide needed services, although the limitations of time and money often require hard decisions to be made about which programs to launch first.

Few planning staffs in rural areas contain specialists. Thus, the burden of analysis falls upon generalists with divergent backgrounds and capabilities. Furthermore, problems and priorities vary among locales. Consequently the following sections about housing and community services each begin with an overview of the problem, followed by an identification of planning guidelines and possible solutions. Case examples are cited where possible to illustrate problems, principles, and solutions, and basic references are provided for persons who intend to develop a particular program or service.

Throughout this chapter we will be referring to housing and community services in rural areas and small towns. Unfortunately, the term "rural" is defined differently among various researchers and agencies. In some cases "rural" means settlements of less than 2,500 population. In yet other instances the size of the town may be as great as 10,000, or even 50,000 in population. The term "nonmetropolitan" is also used to describe rural and small town America. This term generally refers to those parts of America under 50,000 in population not located in a Standard Metropolitan Statistical Area.

Section I: Housing

Rural communities, for the most part, have relied upon the private market for the construction of housing, the government helping to construct 19 percent of nonmetropolitan housing during the 1960's and approximately one-quarter of it during the 1970's. In many rural areas, though, the private market has not been able to produce a satisfactory residential environment due to conflicting social and economic trends. The modest commitment from federal and state governments, although contributing to improvements in housing, has not significantly lessened the housing deprivation of many rural households. The housing programs created under the Federal Housing Administration (FHA) and the Farmers Home Administration (FmHA) have helped encourage the operation of the private market since 1930. The agencies, by insuring mortgages and providing security on loans, showed private financial institutions that they had confidence in rural people's ability to repay their loans.

Even though there has been progress in reducing substandard housing in rural American (Bird and Kampe, 1975), there remain many problems. Housing problems in most nonmetropolitan or rural areas are as great as those in urban areas. In many sections of the country they are worse. While 3 percent of metropolitan housing is substandard, 10 percent of nonmetropolitan housing falls into this category (U.S. Department of Agriculture, 1977, p. 22). Based on U.S. Census data, almost one-half of the nation's occupied substandard units are located in nonmetropolitan areas, but these areas contain only one-third of the households (Bird and Kampe, 1977, p. 9). Under census definitions, a dwelling unit is substandard if it is dilapidated or lacks one or more plumbing facilities such as hot running water, a flush toilet, or bathtub or shower for private use. This definition generates a conservative estimate of poor housing conditions in rural areas, since factors such as overcrowding, the lack of heat, and a large payment for housing expenses are overlooked.

The age and income of households bear upon the ability of rural areas to sustain a suitable housing supply. Households on fixed or retirement incomes often do not have the financial capacity to provide upkeep or periodic repairs to a unit. In rural areas 23 percent of the households are headed by a person aged 65 or older (Bird and Kampe, 1977, p. 14), while in urban areas 19 percent of households are so headed. The trend for retirement households to locate in rural counties, particularly those which have recreational amenities, is likely to continue and may actually accelerate (Beale, 1975, p. 9). Communities experiencing such pressure may have to undertake new financing programs and related institutional activities to assure adequate housing for these households.

The impact on rural areas of households in poverty is also pronounced. In 1974, 20 percent of elderly persons living in rural areas were in poverty, as opposed to 15 percent of the elderly living in central cities and 11 percent of those living in suburbs (Department of Agriculture, 1977, p. 62). For all households in poverty, 44 percent are located in nonmetropolitan areas (Greendale and Knock, p. 115). Most of these households live in severely inadequate housing.

The Housing Analysis Process

In order to determine housing needs in small towns and rural areas, and then to develop policies and plans that respond to these needs, the local planner may have to conduct a general housing analysis and a more specific housing market analysis.

The planner should first collect and analyze data that describe the current condition of housing and the demographic and economic characteristics of households in the community. After developing an understanding of these key characteristics, a housing market analysis can be performed in order to determine whether an investment in new housing construction should be made. In the following sections of this chapter we outline the types of data that should be collected as part of a general housing analysis, we describe the key components of a housing market analysis, and we identify the types of housing programs available to rural areas as well as sources of assistance.

The main task in housing analysis is to relate housing conditions to household characteristics through a systematic data collection, storage, and analysis process. Typically, the analysis entails the examination of the economic base of the community, the housing characteristics of the area, and the demographic profile of households.

The analysis of local or regional housing and the creation of a usable information base requires a planner to develop an understanding of a large set of variables and the methods for measuring those variables. You should begin the gathering and analysis of the information by identifying the basic units of measurement.

1. *Define the geographic units.* All data should be collected at the smallest workable geographic unit. This might be the county, municipality, zoning district, or neighborhood unit. By first defining the geographic unit of analysis, any information available can be compiled and related to specific locations, thus providing a clue to the particular problems in that area.

2. *Identify sources of information.* Before starting an analysis of local housing and household conditions, a list of existing sources of data should be made, including local public and private agencies, county offices, state housing and community development bureaus, and national departments.

3. *Define relevant categories.* To facilitate the systematic analysis of households and housing units, identifiable

data categories should be created or commonly accepted categories should be used. For example, household characteristics should include the age of the head of the household, total income of the household, number of household members, etc.

4. *Examine the data for potential updating.* Establishing a housing information base demands that data be collected and updated frequently. Attention should be paid to the types of information that are collected and stored and how often that information will be updated.

As these steps are taken, the usable and more relevant types of data can be evaluated and interpreted. To improve the utility and timeliness of the data, you should attempt to identify a smaller set of workable and understandable variables that can be used for spot-checks and quick updating.

There is no easy solution as to which variables and sources of data would be most useful in analyzing housing. Limitations exist in many types of data and their accuracy and utility must be judged as the planner becomes accustomed to the information. In the housing planning process the most important characteristics to examine include:

1. *Housing Costs.* Where rental households are paying 25% or more of their income in housing, an excessive financial burden may exist. For owner-occupied households, excessive costs are assumed if housing expenses multiplied by a factor of 2.5 are greater than yearly income.

2. *Crowding.* Overcrowding is assumed to be present when there are more than 1.01 persons per room. Severe overcrowding is indicated when there are 1.51 or more persons per room.

3. *Income.* A household may have problems with maintenance of a dwelling unit when its income is less than 80 percent of the median income of the area. Those households below 50 percent of the median income level usually cannot afford safe and decent housing.

4. *Vacancy Rates.* A rental vacancy rate of three-to-five percent of the total rental stock will provide sufficient vacant units to permit new renters to enter the market and to allow current renters to move into better units. For owner-occupied

units, a one percent to two percent average vacancy rate during a six-month period permits new households to locate homes to purchase, and enables existing homeowners to move into higher quality units.

5. *Housing Tenure.* Housing types are usually classified as owner-occupied, renter, or other. The dominance of owner-occupied units usually indicates lower household turnover.

6. *Housing Quality.* No single definition of substandard housing exists. Under the Census Bureau definition, substandard housing is any unit lacking some or all plumbing facilities including hot and cold piped water, flush toilet, or bathtub or shower for private use.

These variables should be the central focus of any housing analysis. They provide "benchmarks" against which to measure changes in housing conditions. Finding these indicators will involve a certain amount of trial and error in data collection. Some may have to be collected through a local survey.

Ultimately the planner wants to determine both the supply and demand for various types of housing. This usually takes the form of a market analysis which requires data that can be obtained in a variety of ways. Current data can be collected through at least the four following methods:

1. *Household and Housing Structure Surveys.* This technique provides a quick identification of specific housing problems. Household and housing surveys can be conducted in several ways. Actual field inspections of housing conditions might be made, in-depth telephone or personal interviews could be conducted with residents, or questionnaires might be mailed to households. Surveys, for the most part, do not consist of investigating the entire community and contacting every household. Rather, a sample of households is systematically selected as a representation of the entire community. When properly done, random survey sampling can provide accurate, detailed information for a much smaller cost than a survey of the entire population.

Generally, survey questions should identify the total number of persons in each household, age of the household head, total household income, physical disabilities of household members (if present), structural components in need of repair (i.e., roof, walk, foundation, etc.), and annual housing expenditures. A detailed guide to survey sampling and questionnaire design is the *Household Survey Manual* by the Department of Housing and Urban Development. Although this publication is currently out of print, a copy may be obtained from a HUD regional office or through the interlibrary loan system by requesting your local library to contact a regional library or government depository library. The handbook provides instructions for developing a survey, including steps in questionnaire design and sample selection.

Another useful manual for survey design and administration is *Survey Research Methods* by Earl R. Babbie. This publication provides an introduction to survey research, survey conceptualization, statistical foundations, and data processing and analysis.

2. *Neighborhood Surveys.* A commonly used method for analyzing housing conditions is a residential "windshield" survey. One simply identifies problem areas within the community on a base map. Those neighborhoods which show signs of structural deterioration or general decline (e.g., vacant dwelling units, nonresidential land uses, or a decrease in yard maintenance) may be in need of assistance. After particularly bad areas have been identified, more intensive analysis can be done, including household surveys, interior and exterior inspections, etc. In some cases where the area is small and data needs are great, a block by block detailed "walk through" survey may be necessary. Items to include in such a survey might include:

- general appearance of the neighborhood;
- appearance of individual lawns, shrubs and walkways;
- condition of foundations;
- condition of doors and windows;
- condition of roofs.

Rating scales, such as: excellent, good, fair, and poor, can be used. For an example of this type of survey see "An Interagency Residential Structural Survey" (Adler and Grenell, 1972). Local building inspectors or contractors might help you identify the key structural components to examine.

3. *Tax Assessment Records.* A recent and promising data source is the assessment records of local counties and townships. In most states, assessors are required to maintain detailed land and building records by parcel. They are required to update assessments every few years and appraise all property on a frequent and regular basis. The amount and types of data collected may differ from area to area, but most appraisal data are divided into three categories: land, neighborhood, and structural data.

Appraisal of property for tax purposes, or "mass appraising," is conducted to measure the combined value of land and buildings by parcel. In order to obtain final measures of value, a number of variables have to be examined within each category. For example, under the land category, data are collected on zoning classification, lot size, traffic, street lighting, and other public utilities. The neighborhood section collects data comparing the quality of parcels and dwelling units. Such factors as the predominant land use in the area, landscaping, and external nuisances are usually taken into account. Structural data, in most cases, contain the more useful information. The total number of rooms, the year built, and various quality characteristics are usually recorded. If data are collected consistently and a standardized rating system is adopted, comparisons among neighborhoods may be made.

There are drawbacks to assessment records, including problems of under- and overassessment and infrequent re-appraisals. Such difficulties should be examined before relying on the data. The records may be useful as an initial indicator of substandard areas, but additional analysis is usually necessary.

4. *Interviews.* One final major method for gathering information on housing and households is through personal interviews with long-term residents, local real estate agents, and people generally knowledgeable about the area. Interviews provide valuable information in terms of defining primary issues, reducing the initial cost of analysis, and obtaining unpublished information. For conducting effective interviews see *Interviewing in Social Research* (Hyman, 1975) and *Elite and Specialized Interviewing* (Dexter, 1970).

Housing Market Analysis

In order to determine whether an investment in new housing construction should be made and the types of housing to construct, a market analysis is performed. This is essentially a process of comparing existing and potential housing demand to the existing supply of housing.

On the demand side, we examine the economy, looking at both current employment and the potential for growth. Demand components include:

1. *Per Capita Income.* These data can be derived through surveys of local employers to determine the total number of people employed in each firm and their average income. Personal income statistics are also published by the Bureau of Economic Analysis, which provides income data by industries for Standard Metropolitan Statistical Areas (SMSA's) and counties. Titles to these publications can be found in the *Survey of Current Business.* This information can be combined with the *County Business Patterns,* published by the U.S. Bureau of the Census, which provides first-quarter employment and payroll statistics for states, counties, and SMSA's. *County Business Patterns* lists the number of employees by type of industry and size of firm.

2. *Net Household Formation.* Estimating net household formation is more difficult. A sample survey can be conducted to estimate total population by household sizes. Information on newly formed households can also be obtained from real estate agents. Utility companies may also provide information on recent hookups in the community.

3. *Migration.* Total migration can be acquired by contacting the U.S. Bureau of the Census which publishes current population reports on states and counties. The P-26 Series provides estimates of population, including births, deaths, and changes by states, counties, metropolitan, and nonmetropolitan areas. Check with the Bureau of the Census or a regional office of the Department of Housing and Urban Development for the availability of current population reports.

4. *Cost of Current Housing.* The cost of housing can be estimated by examining the price of new and existing housing in local papers and by sampling households to obtain an estimate of maintenance, utility, and property tax costs.

On the supply side, a planner should inventory the amount of new private and public construction, current demolitions, conversions, and vacancy rates by housing type. The inventory of current housing calls for the analysis of age, quality, and size of existing units and the types of new units being constructed. Supply components include:

1. New construction, including mobile homes;
2. Net additions in housing through remodeling and rehabilitation;
3. Net change in housing vacancies;
4. Net change through demolition and conversion;
5. Net increase in public housing.

Information on new construction can be obtained from the local building department if the community is a permit-issuing area. Assessor's records may also yield data on square footage, value, and type of housing. Data about mobile homes are also sometimes available from the assessor.

Remodeling and rehabilitation usually require building permits or a series of inspections during construction. These permits or inspection reports identify the location and type of rehabilitation. If remodeling is not inspected, assessor's records will often note such changes by type of unit and location.

Vacancies in existing housing units can be obtained through one of at least four ways. The R. L. Polk Company and the Johnson Publishing Company both publish city and county directories. The directories include names, addresses, and a variety of census-type information, including the number of vacant housing units. The surveys are completed primarily for urban areas, counties, or cities which contract with the companies to gather the data. If directories are published for an area, city officials will have copies. Another method is the Postal Vacancy Survey, which is administered one day per year by the U.S. Postal Service. If such a survey has not been done in your area, contact the local postmaster to arrange for one. In areas where there are few housing units, the "windshield" survey mentioned earlier may be a useful method. Finally, utility companies can provide a list of units for which service was recently shut off.

Data on demolition and conversion can be obtained from the local building department or zoning administrator's office. Specific information about the type of unit demolished is also available from the assessor's records.

The number of currently existing public housing units and recent additions to the stock can be obtained from the local or regional public housing authority.

Housing market analysis is useful in providing a point-in-time perspective on the general conditions of the housing market. It measures the relationship among population and income changes, building levels, price shifts, vacancy rates, and a variety of elements which contribute to an understanding of local housing conditions. For a complete detailed guide to housing market analysis see *FHA Techniques of Housing Market Analysis* (Department of Housing and Urban Development, 1970). This publication is currently out of print, but it can be obtained through the interlibrary loan system. Another source would be *Housing Markets: The Complete Guide to Analysis and Strategy for Builders, Lenders, and Other Investors* by Sumichrast and Seldin. This publication provides a guide to housing economics, household decisions, and detailed housing analysis.

Housing market studies are usually undertaken by private developers to analyze the potential for new construction. In rural communities, however, such studies often do not exist because the lower level of construction activity reduces the need for evaluating the market. Housing market analysis provides a systematic way to evaluate the condition of the market and has become one of the tools used by local housing planners.

Armed with an understanding of the condition of housing in your area, the needs and financial abilities of the households, and the way the local housing market operates, you should be able to pinpoint the location of housing problems. For these subareas you should be able to estimate the type and quantity of housing needed, and the ability of households to pay for it. There is also the possibility that you will find there exists an oversupply of housing. More likely, you will find shortages of particular types of units and an absence of housing in certain price ranges. The analysis might also reveal subareas soon to face housing problems, such as deterioration.

The types and quantity of housing needed in the future may be estimated from the market analysis. However, identifying a range of types and quantity may be all that is possible. Estimating the number of new or rehabilitated units required demands a specification of the percentage distribution of all families by income categories. From this data household expenditures for housing can be estimated and then compared to the current selling prices of new and used housing units. Since precise comparisons between housing costs and household incomes are hard to establish, an estimate of the number of units needed involves judgment based on experience with the local area. By determining the number and characteristics of households entering the market each year who cannot afford new or rehabilitated housing, a planner can better identify the types of public and private actions needed to meet this demand.

If the market analysis indicates a need for new construction, you may want to investigate federal and state loan and grant programs. For deteriorating areas, a community self-help program, a code enforcement program, or a local rehabilitation effort might be appropriate. The following sections provide overviews of major programs for funding new construction and efforts aimed at rehabilitating existing properties.

Rural Housing Programs

Few organized efforts to improve housing conditions and to encourage community development have taken place in rural areas and small towns. Because of the low density, dispersed, and isolated nature of much of nonmetropolitan America, housing problems are not always that visible. Some of the worst housing is found in isolated valleys and on seldom-traveled roads. Furthermore, credit in rural areas tends to be limited and there are fewer nonprofit organizations to undertake development activities. There is simply less institutional and financial assistance available to housing and community development in rural areas.

Assistance has been provided primarily through the Farmers Home Administration (FmHA). As part of the Department of Agriculture, FmHA has assumed an increasingly prominent role in the financing and delivery of adequate housing for rural residents. Since its inception in 1946 and the creation of its housing assistance role in the Housing Act of 1949, FmHA has been making grants and loans for construction and rehabilitation of housing and related improvements at a slowly increasing rate. Although FmHA is not the counterpart of the Department of Housing and Urban Development in rural areas, its role has expanded from initially providing assistance only to farmers to making loans and grants to individuals, nonprofit sponsors, and public housing agencies. Grants and loans have included those for nonfarm rural housing, water and sewer construction, recreation projects, and economic development. Most of the available loans and grants are made through a system of county agents located in 1700 offices nationwide. The local FmHA office guides the applicant through the process of acquiring a loan or grant by: (1) determining the applicant's eligibility; (2) reviewing plans and specifications; (3) appraising properties; (4) inspecting homes; and (5) servicing loans. Most applicants must be without adequate housing and be unable to secure credit from another source. The Farmers Home Administration allows families the opportunity to afford a new home with a smaller down payment and often at a lower interest rate than available from private institutions. The agency also is not dependent on the availability of local mortgage credit to provide loans.

Individuals and organizations must seek other sources of funds before applying to FmHA. States or local public agencies that sponsor new housing are exempted from this rule but must insure that they serve only those applicants who would qualify for Public Law citation assistance (Public Law 95-128, October 12, 1977, 42 U.S.C. 1471, Farmers Home Administration, 1977).

As more loan and grant programs have been established, FmHA has gained administrative responsibility over a larger geographic area. Its jurisdiction was once limited to counties in which the largest town was 2,500 in population. It now provides assistance to areas which have towns of 10,000 or fewer people. FmHA also has jurisdiction in non-SMSA areas of 10,000 to 20,000 in population where shortages in mortgage money exist.

The amount of housing FmHA has helped finance in nonmetropolitan areas has increased steadily since 1950 when it assisted with 0.6 percent of nonmetropolitan home construction. In 1976, FmHA assisted in 15 percent of all houses constructed in nonmetropolitan areas. Total government-assisted housing, including the Federal Housing Administration and Veteran's Administration programs, amounted to 27.1 percent of total construction in rural areas in 1976 (Bird and Kampe, 1977, p. 17). The housing loan and grant programs available under the Farmers Home Administration can be classified into six categories. Each category has restrictions on the amount of the loan, size of the interest rate, length of repayment, and eligibility. Most of the Farmers Home Administration efforts are aimed at households without safe and sanitary housing and that are unable to obtain the needed credit from other sources. Limits are placed upon the size of the unit which can be financed and upon the income of the household.

1. *New and Existing Owner-Occupied Housing: Section 502 and 504.* Under Section 502, loans are provided to buy, build, or improve homes; to purchase a building site; to relocate a dwelling; to modernize a dwelling; and to refinance a loan. Interest rates vary depending on household income and size and length of the repayment period. Interest credits are provided for lower-income families. These credits can reduce the interest rate to as low as 1 percent. There are also limitations on the size of the home and the types of amenities allowed.

Section 504, home repair financing, differs from these provisions. This program provides 1 percent interest loans up to $5,000 for minor repairs and to remove safety and health hazards in structures. Funds are provided for repairs to roofs, foundations, plumbing, and other structural components. An eligible applicant is anyone who lacks adequate income to qualify under the 502 program. Grants are available to very low-income households.

2. *Rental Housing: Section 515.* Loans under this section are provided to private nonprofit organizations, state and local

public agencies, and consumer cooperatives that wish to construct new multifamily units or rehabilitate existing ones. Subsidies may reduce the interest rate to as low as 1 percent. The funds can be used not only for the housing units, but for related facilities, community rooms, and other appropriate services. Rent levels are designed so each household pays no more than 25 percent of its adjusted income for housing. Rural rental housing is designed primarily for elderly, handicapped, and low- and moderate-income families. Any nonprofit sponsor that develops rental units must have community representatives on its board.

3. *Mutual Self-help Housing: Section 523 and 524.* Section 523 financing is provided to private or nonprofit sponsors for technical assistance and supervision of low-income families who participate in the organization's "self-help" housing program. Grants and loans are made to sponsors who acquire and develop land, obtain materials, and facilitate the construction or rehabilitation of housing. Future residents of the housing work with the nonprofit sponsor by providing labor during construction.

Section 524 provides loans to nonprofit sponsors that acquire and develop land for housing sites to be sold to households or to private or nonprofit organizations. Loans include funding for the development of roads, utilities, landscaping, closing costs, and a variety of related expenditures. Maximum interest rates are 3 percent.

4. *Farm Labor Housing: Sections 514 and 516.* This program provides financial assistance to nonprofit farmworker organizations, farm owners, nonprofit sponsors, and public agencies. Depending upon the financial condition of the applicant, grants or loans are provided for the construction or repair of housing, for landscaping, to develop community facilities, and to establish related physical facilities that improve the working and living environment of farmworkers. Maximum interest rates are 1 percent with a repayment period of 33 years. Grants, when provided, cover up to 90% of project costs.

5. *Technical and Supervisory Assistance: Section 525.* This category allows FmHA to make grants and loans to public and private nonprofit organizations and agencies planning, adminis-

tering, or coordinating programs to assist low- and moderate-income people. The money is provided prior to construction or the obtaining of other funds. Interest-free loans are provided and may be used as "seed" money to begin an analysis of market needs. Preference is given to organizations sponsored by state, county, municipal or other governmental bodies.

6. *Condominium Housing and Mobile Homes: Section 526 and 527.* The FmHA is authorized under Section 526 to provide direct or insured loans to low- and moderate-income households to aid in the purchase of condominium and mobile home units. In each case, minimum HUD property standards must be adhered to in order to insure the livability and durability of the units.

Sources of Assistance

The above programs are the major sources of housing assistance provided by FmHA. More information about the programs and eligibility requirements may be obtained from your local FmHA representative, who, in most cases, conducts the preliminary analysis and makes a recommendation to the state office on the feasibility and financing of projects.

The primary role of the FmHA in housing assistance is that of a processor of loans. This has raised doubts about the agency's ability to improve housing conditions in rural areas. Leadership philosophy within the agency and the lack of administrative funds apparently have kept it from taking an aggressive role in effort to improve rural housing (Committee on Banking, Housing and Urban Affairs, 1974, pp. 28-29). The Farmers Home Administration relies on public and private initiative to utilize its credit services. This means that individuals and potential sponsors may be unaware of available assistance, and as a result, needed housing may not be built.

Mobile Homes

In recent years, mobile homes have become a major part of the housing market for both low- and moderate-income persons. Mobile homes, as a proportion of all housing in nonmetropolitan areas, have increased from 1 percent in 1950 to 9 percent in 1975. In metropolitan areas the increase was from 1 percent in 1950 to 3 percent in 1975 (Bird and Kampe, 1977, p.7.) The increase was brought about in part by people who were seeking more space per dollar than conventional housing can provide. For example, the cost of mobile homes ranges from $16 to $28 per square foot, while construction costs for new conventional homes may be up to double this amount. Owning a mobile home also compares favorably with the cost of renting a conventional home.

Many people buy mobile homes because of the smaller initial outlay and monthly payments. Low- and moderate-income households often cannot accumulate the downpayment for conventional housing. It is also much easier to buy a mobile home than a conventional house, which involves a property survey, title search, and closing arrangements. The availability of a complete housing package has been shown to be the most important reason for buying a mobile home (Drury, 1972, p. 26).

Whether mobile home living is a permanent arrangement for many households is difficult to determine. A study conducted in 1970 indicated that one-third of mobile home residents planned to reside permanently in their units (Drury, 1972 p. 33). But the largest percentage of new owners tends to be younger families who are temporarily using mobile homes as inexpensive housing while saving for conventional units. These manufactured homes are also attractive to households because of lower maintenance and taxation costs. This is particularly important for both younger and older households with limited and relatively fixed incomes.

The main drawback to mobile homes, especially the most inexpensive models, is their rapid deterioration and depreciation resulting from poor quality construction and site location. If a mobile home site is poorly planned, does not provide amenities, or is located in an area with minimal services, the value of the unit may also depreciate. On the other hand, well-constructed and attractively-located units have retained their original value.

Regulating mobile home parks or individual sites to maintain health and safety standards and insure property values is often difficult. Local building codes do not apply to mobile homes because of problems with inspecting already-constructed housing which is shipped to the site. Codes designed for conventional housing are also difficult to apply to manufactured housing. Some communities have responded by barring mobile homes. However, zoning which excludes mobile homes from a community is unconstitutional; some provision must be made for this style of housing. Often communities require mobile homes to be located within mobile home parks, and these parks are limited to specific residential or commercial zones.

In unincorporated areas, restrictions based on health and safety regulations are often loosely enforced. A local planner can respond to this challenge by establishing minimum property standards in site development through building code ordinances. You should contact the local building inspector or the state division of building code standards for information about state regulations which apply to mobile homes. Some states do require that manufactured housing be approved by the state before it can be sold. Such regulations often preempt local codes. The Department of Housing and Urban Development has also recently established minimum standards for mobile home construction and siting. These minimum standards must be enforced before either FmHA or HUD will provide insurance or loans for the unit or the space which it occupies.

Local Initiative

Increasing the quality and quantity of local housing does not necessarily hinge upon obtaining outside sources of funding and assistance; rather, local initiatives can be taken to encourage private rehabilitation and home maintenance. Integrating these efforts with outside sources of aid could be the key to the development and maintenance of adequate local housing.

Most of the Farmers Home Administration programs aimed at improving local housing conditions rely on a one-time loan or grant to a household or a sponsoring organization. Although this does result in an improvement in quality, a more comprehensive approach may be necessary in order to upgrade the community as a whole. This comprehensive approach might be developed around a housing rehabilitation program. For such programs to be successful, the support of neighborhood associations, technical assistance, concentrated financing, and code enforcement may be required.

Neighborhood associations provide one means to disseminate information about housing assistance. Where possible, a planner should get residents together to discuss problems and the kinds of financing appropriate for their neighborhood. This could both increase the local awareness of housing issues and lead to the tackling of neighborhood problems which no individual property owner could solve. Technical assistance to households may also be necessary. This help might include the provision of rehabilitation specifications, cost estimates, and financial needs analyses.

Housing quality has been both upgraded and maintained through the enforcement of minimum housing standards. These codes typically prescribe minimum construction standards that are intended to insure the safety of inhabitants. They also may define minimum levels of maintenance after construction. Usually these codes are not administered on a community wide basis. While new housing is inspected during construction, older homes might be inspected when improvements are made. Sometimes inspections are made in response to complaints. Without periodic inspection of all units, an increase in housing quality would be difficult to achieve through this technique.

The main problem stems from the question of enforcement. Although states have created enabling legislation for communities to adopt local housing and building codes, local governments have been hard pressed to develop clear, legally defensible definitions of what constitutes a violation. Obtaining an agreement that a severely dilapidated building is a health and safety hazard is relatively easy. Problems arise with the gradual decline in structural integrity. At what point can a person be required to make corrections? Must the structure be severely damaged? Can action be required if the structure does not threaten life and limb? Enforcing standards also depends upon the availability of housing for families required to vacate substandard units.

For code enforcement to be a useful tool, local government must stand behind the program, local private opinion must support enforcement and compliance, and citizens must be aware of the benefits they will receive from the enforcement of codes (Shretter, 1971, pp. 54-55). However, standards are difficult to enforce when households with very low or fixed incomes cannot afford repairs.

lFexible code enforcement may be one way to address this problem (Ahlbrandt, 1976). Under this scheme, code inspectors cooperate with sponsoring organizations to encourage property owners to improve their housing. The sponsoring agency, the argument goes, should be one that can allay the fears of households, can act as an intermediary, and can even assist owners of units in violation to obtain financing for the corrections required. Sponsors have included churches, private nonprofit corporations and housing authorities.

Before financial assistance is provided through FmHA or the Department of Housing and Urban Development, a workable code enforcement program must be developed. Many small towns and rural areas may not have sufficient construction activity to demand a code enforcement program, since at least 100 inspections per year are needed to justify a full-time inspector (Shretter, 1975, p. 160). Of course, a part-time employee could be hired if there were a reasonable level of demand, or inspection services might be contracted from nearby areas.

There are a variety of model ordinances which can be adopted by communities. These models contain detailed standards and procedures for establishing housing and building codes. Information about each of the four nationally-recognized codes can be obtained from the following associations:

American Public Health Association
U.S. Public Health Service
1015 18th St. N. W.
Washington, D.C. 20036

Building Officials and Code Administrators
17926 So. Halsted St.
Homewood, IL 60430

International Conference of Building Officials
5360 S. Workman-Mill Road
Pasedena, CA 91101

Southern Building Code Congress
Brown-Marx Building
Birmingham, AL 35203

For a basic introduction and overview to code enforcement, *The Housing Code Enforcement Study Guide* by Howard A. Schretter is recommended. Another useful publication is *Housing Code Administration and Enforcement* by Spencer D. Parrat. *Flexible Code Enforcement: A Key Ingredient in Neighborhood Preservation Programming* by Roger Ahlbrandt provides an up-to-date presentation of code enforcement systems.

Local Housing Authority

The burden for the initiation, sponsorship, and management of housing remains with the local community. However, staff capabilities, sponsors, and the authority to establish a housing delivery system are lacking in many communities. In addition, many rural residents have a suspicion of federal programs and an unwillingness to acquire a long-term debt obligation (Butler, *et al.* 1976, p. 639).

One response to the absence of a housing delivery system has come from public and private nonprofit organizations. These groups have been able to develop low- and moderate-income housing under FmHA programs, but have been hampered by the lack of technical, advisory, and community support. Furthermore, many nonprofit sponsors are unable to commit the time required to take a project from conceptualization through start-up to completion.

Since the initiative to establish a local nonprofit organization may not exist, the types of activities it would engage in could be undertaken by a local housing authority (LHA). LHAs have been the primary institution for the provision of public housing since their creation by the U.S. Housing Act of 1937. To establish a housing authority, a county, municipality, group of cities, or group of counties must enter into a contract with the Department of Housing and Urban Development to obtain federal subsidies. State enabling legislation provides the authority for localities to create such an agency after local voter approval. A board of commissioners usually governs the size of the rents, eligibility requirements, and related LHA policies. Although the housing authority owns and manages the units, HUD makes an annual payment to amortize construction costs up to a 40 year period, and provides operating subsidies to cover costs which are not met by the rents. Rent must not exceed 25 percent of a household's adjusted income.

In recent years, LHAs have become more involved in providing programs other than public housing. The Housing and Community Development Act of 1974 changed the regulations for local sponsorship. All of the FmHA programs can now be established through any public agency. Where local housing authorities have developed and manage public housing, staff experience and managerial capabilities make them prime candidates for developing other housing programs. LHAs can sponsor rural rental housing projects and farm labor housing under Sections 514 and 516 and can help construct owner-occupied housing under Sections 502 and 504. Financing for rural rental housing under Farmers Home Administration Section 515 allows an authority to own or manage the units by using housing assistance payments from HUD. Housing assistance payments (Section 8 of the Housing and Community Development Act) are a subsidy provided to low and very low-income households whose adjusted income does not exceed 80 percent and 50 percent, respectively, of the median income of the area.

An LHA or sponsoring organization can contract with FmHA or HUD to construct a project that will be eligible for rent supplements. When a project is complete, the LHA or owner of the project is required to rent 30% of the units to very low-income households. The project owner receives a monthly payment equal to the difference between what the family can pay in rent (not to exceed 25% of its adjusted monthly income) and the total rent for the unit.

Rent supplements under Section 8 also apply to existing and rehabilitated units. Households which qualify are free to seek suitable housing in the private market after a local housing authority has provided a rent certificate. Mountain Grove, Missouri was one of the first communities to successfully utilize Section 515 loans and Section 8 housing assistance payments. The LHA helped create a local sponsoring corporation, and administered the Section 8 payments while ownership, maintenance, and management of the project remained with the corporation (Mitchell, 1975, pp. 494-498).

Should a housing development be contemplated, project scale becomes an important consideration. Small projects may not be able to justify a full-time director and staff, and part-time staff may not be able to keep up with maintenance, the collection of rents, and related administrative matters. The minimum number of units for efficient operation is considered to be 100 (Butler, 1976, pp. 640-641). However, some inefficiency may be overcome where cooperative agreements or regional authorities can be developed. Butler recommends the creation of a regional authority in rural areas because it would be able to pay higher salaries and thus attract more competent personnel, provide better service, allow greater fiscal flexibility, improve accounting functions, and conduct a more effective maintenance program (pp. 644-645).

Two county public housing authorities in Pennsylvania established a cooperative agreement and were able to develop new Section 8 housing. One county authority, supported by a larger population, provided staff assistance to the other county. This cooperation also extended into financing and accounting arrangements. The two authorities used a combination of Section 8 financing, local bonding authority, community development funds, grants, private mortgage financing, and a FmHA loan (Heinz, 1978, pp. 167-169).

Most of the small local housing authorities in rural areas could probably benefit from cooperative agreements. Only a small percentage of the smaller LHAs have executed an annual contract to obtain Section 8 housing rental assistance. The local authorities tend to be unfamiliar with the program, do not understand the application procedures, or feel that rental units are not needed in their area (Department of Housing and Urban Development, 1978a, p. 15).

Even where innovative financing and cooperative agreements do exist, other barriers to housing construction are present. Opposition from the community can arise over questions concerning site management, increased traffic, and resident turnover.

Some rural communities have been notably successful in improving local housing conditions, however. Four small towns with a combined population of 11,000 developed a housing consortium in Alabama using community development block grants. The town filed a joint application, for a three-year rehabilitation and code enforcement program. Part of the grant money was used to hire a building inspector and prepare a structural survey. Based on an analysis of the survey, several areas were recommended for redevelopment. The community development grants were combined with low-interest FmHA loans to bring houses up to code. After receiving an estimate of the total cost of rehabilitation, owners sought FmHA loans. The consortium then provided a grant to the homeowner for the amount in excess of the loan needed to recondition the dwelling unit ("Four Rural Communities," 1977, pp. 6-7).

Creating any local housing assistance program demands that a strong administrative and leadership role be taken by the staff of the LHA or sponsoring organization. The staff should identify families needing or desiring new housing, determine the income eligibility requirements of different programs, and examine the quality of existing housing. Building local community support should also start early.

In the past, locally created policies and attitudes on the part of local FmHA staff have delayed the development of housing (American Friends Service Committee, 1971, pp. 6-15). Differences in FmHA local and state policy have also hindered the creation of low-income housing (Myer, 1974,

p. 21). Nonetheless, the role of the FmHA in providing housing in rural areas has grown over the years, and a recent study suggested that the FmHA change from a processor of loans to a more aggressive agency which targets funds to households in need (U. S. Department of Agriculture, 1978, pp. 87-102). FmHA has had difficulty in reducing substandard housing in nonmetropolitan areas because the majority of households in substandard housing were judged to be unable to repay the loans, and therefore were ineligible under program regulations (U. S. Department of Agriculture, 1978, p. 24). The suggested targeting strategy would establish priorities for families with the greatest need based upon an index of housing deficiency. The study also suggests larger homeownership subsidy programs for low-income households.

Additional Assistance

FmHA funds are not the sole source of housing assistance for rural areas and small towns. Private lenders are certainly an important source for households that can qualify for loans. Other housing assistance programs are provided by the Department of Housing and Urban Development. Available assistance is described in the May, 1978 edition of *Programs of HUD*. Questions concerning HUD programs should be addressed to your regional HUD office or to: Communications Services, Office of Public Affairs, Room 9245, HUD, 451 Seventh Street SW, Washington, D.C. 20410.

Another source of funds is the Community Development Block Grant program administered by the Department of Housing and Urban Development. Although certain governmental jurisdictions are entitled to annual grants, most cities of less than 50,000 in population must submit specific proposals to obtain discretionary funds. These discretionary Community Development Block Grant program funds are provided on a state-by-state basis. Local proposals thus compete with other communities within the individual states (Department of Housing and Urban Development, 1978b). Most local governments have been advised of their opportunities under the

Community Development Block Grant program. For additional information contact your HUD regional representative.

In addition to these agencies, several national institutions provide technical and financial assistance to rural communities. The Rural Housing Alliance and The Housing Assistance Council provide information on rural housing programs, conduct research, and publish sourcebooks for the rural planner. These organizations can help you develop a good understanding of government programs. Their addresses are:

Rural Housing Alliance
1346 Connecticut Avenue
Washington, D.C. 20036

Housing Assistance Council
1828 L Street NW
Washington, D.C. 20036

Section II: Community Services

The rural planner may become involved in planning for the delivery of a wide variety of community services. Although the actual development of the service may be undertaken by another organization (for example, a community action agency, a library board, or a park district), you may be involved in estimating the demand for homemaker services, a branch library, or a swimming pool. In the space available it would be impossible to analyze, summarize, or even outline the problems, needs, and solutions for a fraction of the community services provided by local governments. Rather than attempting this, the following is intended to illustrate some of the basic concepts and problems involved in planning for community services, and to identify a number of basic references.

The major issues in community services planning are not greatly dissimilar to those discussed in regard to housing. You will be faced with the problems of estimating need and demand, of determining costs, and of locating funding sources. You will encounter conflicting opinions about priorities, standards, and which unit of government should provide the service. Although procedures for estimating demand and costs for physical services such as water and sewers have been generally agreed upon, this is not the case with services such as health care and rural recreation. For these types of services there may be considerable debate as to what constitutes an adequate level of service and whether existing services are filling the needs of the community.

Satisfaction With Services

For years it has been assumed that community services in small towns and rural areas are inadequate. Observers have pointed to the one-room school house, the absence of a local doctor, the reliance on the county sheriff rather than a local police force, etc. On the other hand, ever since the 1948 Roper poll, Americans have consistently indicated a preference for living in a small town or rural area (Elgin, *et al.*, 1974). However, recent studies have found that, while most Americans prefer to live in a small town or rural area, they also want to live within thirty miles of a central city (Fuguitt and Zuiches, 1972). Thus they can have the best of both worlds: the small town environment and the range of services and facilities offered in metropolitan areas. One explanation of this apparent contradiction is that people are satisfied with the available services in small towns and rural areas, but they desire additional services. This is, in fact, what we found in a study of several small Illinois towns located within commuting distance of a larger central city (Stabler and Patton, 1977).

Residents in four Great Plains states (Nebraska, North and South Dakota and Texas) also reported being satisfied with their basic community services. Asked whether they were receiving their money's worth in a range of services (water, sewage, solid waste, fire, police, education, and health) most rural residents responded affirmatively (Jones and Morgan, 1977, pp. 243-257). The responses ranged from 66.9 percent being satisfied with educational services to 92.9 percent satisfied with water services and 93.4 percent satisfied with sewage service (table 1). Responses for city residents were similar, ranging from 66.1 percent for education to 93.3 percent for sewage and 94.8 percent for water. Although these persons felt they were getting their money's worth, they nonetheless reported having experienced problems with particular services. For example,

43.6 percent of the rural residents experienced some problem with health care, 54.3 percent with education, and 60.0 percent with water. But when asked to identify the problem they would most like to see eliminated, only 29.1 percent of the rural residents identified a health care system problem, 36.2 percent identified a problem in education, and 32.9 percent identified a problem with water. Taking the questioning a step further by asking the persons who identified a problem most in need of elimination whether they would be willing to pay more to see it eliminated, half or less replied affirmatively. For example, among those rural persons identifying a health care service problem that needed to be eliminated, only 16.1 percent were willing to pay more to eliminate it. Twenty-nine percent would pay to eliminate the most serious education problem, and 52 percent would pay more to eliminate the most serious water service problem.

Satisfaction levels in rural areas may not necessarily remain high in the future. In recent reserach in five small towns in rural Illinois we found that the demand for community services increased as the towns experienced growth. The demand came in part from the new residents who brought with themselves expectations of higher service levels. Although they moved to the small towns for their amenities, these persons eventually began to desire some of the urban services they had experienced in the larger urban areas where they had lived previously. The increased demand also came from longer-term residents of these towns who, experiencing increasing incomes, pressure from children, etc., increased their demand for services from the local government. If the small towns and rural areas in the Old West Region were to experience substantial in-migration and economic growth, they too might experience increased demand for community services. On the other hand, where population is declining, the unit cost of providing services is increased because economies of scale are lost (Schreiner, 1976, pp. 25-26). Communities experiencing both increased demand and declining population will be faced with difficult tasks, including setting priorities on services, raising revenue, and stretching the funds that are available. It has been estimated that the resources of rural areas and small towns are generally ade-

Table 1. Most Rural Residents Feel They Are Receiving Their Money's Worth In Community Services

Service	Percent Receiving Money's Worth		Percent Encountering Any Service-Problem		Percent Identifying a Problem Most Needed to be Eliminated		Percent Willing to Pay More to Eliminate The Most Serious Problem in Given Service	
	Rural	City	Rural	City	Rural	City	Rural	City
Water	92.9	94.8	60.0	60.3	32.9	33.5	52.0	39.0
Sewage	93.4	93.3	39.5	33.8	27.9	23.9	23.4	44.5
Solid Waste Disposal	91.6	85.5	20.1	45.6	14.6	23.2	32.7	32.1
Fire Protection	88.4	91.6	23.1	12.1	17.8	10.6	41.9	51.8
Law Enforcement	78.3	83.2	11.9	21.5	10.7	17.2	22.1	6.3
Education	66.9	66.1	54.3	63.5	36.2	44.4	29.0	60.6
Health Care	78.1	83.5	43.6	39.3	29.1	28.6	16.1	25.8

Source: Jones and Morgan, 1977, pp. 245-255.

quate to support expanded services—if the citizens desire them. The difficulty of funding expanded services, instead of being financial, is rooted in legal and constitutional obstacles, administrative problems, undesirable economic effects, etc. (Stocker, 1977, p. 36).

Current data suggest that rural residents are satisfied with the community services they are receiving—at least the seven services probed in the Great Plains study. Although up to two-thirds of all respondents were able to identify problems with particular services, approximately a third or fewer of this subgroup identified problems that they felt were most in need of being eliminated and half or less of this subgroup felt these problems were serious enough to warrant spending funds to eliminate them.

If these data do accurately describe the satisfaction levels of residents in the Great Plains Area, they suggest that relatively few residents in this area will pressure local governments to improve community services. Furthermore, local expenditures are likely to be opposed by taxpayers should governments move to improve services. Of course, part of the rural population is experiencing problems with these services, and for a number of reasons it may be necessary to meet their demands. The authors of the Great Plains survey have also suggested that it is important to analyze the characteristics of the persons who do identify problems (Jones and Morgan, 1977, p. 257). If we are able to identify the target population, solutions will be easier to design, justify, and implement.

High levels of satisfaction notwithstanding, there are indeed people in rural areas who are in need of assistance. The following overview of selected rural problems was developed for the Secretary of Agriculture (U.S. Department of Agriculture, 1977).

Health Care

Relative to persons in urban areas, rural residents have less access to health care because of geographic and transportation barriers. Defects in benefit and reimbursement formulas are encouraging more expensive treatment, such as hospitalization. Environmental conditions, such as inadequate waste treatment and chemicals from field runoff, are also affecting the health of rural persons.

Education
No matter the testing or evaluation system used, rural school children rank lower than urban children, and at least 5.3 percent of all rural school-aged children are not enrolled in school—more than twice the percentage of urban children. Rural adults also tend to have had less schooling than urban adults.

Fire Prevention
Although national data that describe the seriousness of the fire problem in rural areas do not exist, nonmetropolitan residents have far greater fire fatality rates than metropolitan residents. Dollar losses in rural fires are three to four times as great as losses from urban fires. Many rural areas lack the manpower and equipment to fight fires, if they have any fire protection service whatsoever. In addition, rural areas are often threatened by fires in forests and wildlands.

Estimating Need and Demand
Estimating need and demand for community services involves the same problems as estimating transportation and housing need and demand. Demand again refers to the quantity of community services an individual or community is willing (and able) to purchase. Need, on the other hand, refers to the quantity of services a person or community should have regardless of economic considerations (Cordes, 1977, p. 231).

One can find many interesting discussions of the difficulties in estimating need and demand and it would be easy to be overwhelmed by the problems. But when forced to produce an estimate of demand, there are a number of alternative avenues to take, each with its own roadblocks and pitfalls (Bish, 1977; and Deacon, 1977). There are four primary methods of which you should be aware: (1) individual preference, (2) voter behavior, (3) cost-benefit analysis, and (4) the use of standards.

Individual Preference
For services such as water and recreation and to some extent transportation, individual preference can determine demand. People consume as much as they are willing to purchase. (A

major problem involves the inability of poor people who need services to "demand" them in an economic sense.) Of course, this system breaks down for some services that, if left to individual preference, would probably not be purchased—such as national defense or housing code inspection. It also fails in those instances where nonpayers cannot be excluded from the benefits of the service (for example, mosquito abatement). Individual preference works well for privately provided goods and services, but not quite as well for publicly provided services.

Voter Behavior

Since levels of service adequacy are subjective, the group being served might be permitted to determine its demand level. This could be done through a community survey, but the results may be questionable because of unrealistic expectations of the respondents (Hitzhusen and Napier, 1978, p. 140) and their inability to answer preference questions (Dillman, 1977). People may feel they need a particular service, but may not want to pay for it, or may not be willing to forego another service to obtain it. Because of these problems, levels of adequacy are sometimes assumed to be determined by the community's collective willingness to pay for a service, as demonstrated by approving tax increases for desired services and by rejecting taxes for things not desired.

Cost-benefit Analysis

Cost-benefit analysis, a technique used to quantify the advantages and disadvantages of alternative sets of actions, can be used to determine service levels. For example, the benefits to the community from decreased response time, reduction in losses, lower insurance rates, etc. attributable to the construction of a fire substation could be compared with the cost of constructing and operating the substation. The costs and benefits that would be incurred during the expected life of the facility (say thirty years) would be converted to their present value in order to make the comparison. Benefits must at least equal costs to justify the investment. Alternatively, the size of substation could be determined so that its costs equal the expected benefits. For more information see Tweeten and Brinkman, 1976, pp. 355-365; Mishan, 1976; and Musgrave and Musgrave, 1973.

Standards

The most widely used demand-estimation technique is the application of standards. A variety of measures have been used, including units of service per capita, dollars expended per capita, distance measures, time measures, and similar indicators of effort. This technique has been criticized because standards such as physician-client ratios, teacher-student ratios, waiting time, etc. tend to be arbitrary. Even when these standards are established by professionals, they tend to reflect values and personal preferences rather than scientific determinations. Standards also tend to have wide ranges. For example, the suggested number of physicians per 100,000 population ranges from 67 to 133 (Cordes, 1976, p. 69).

Estimates of future demand are sometimes made by projecting past trends (Tweeten and Brinkman, 1976, p. 197). To use this technique, we must have a record of past usage for the subject area, or we must assume that national usage trends or trends for a similar area are applicable. These usage data, usually expressed as units per capita, serve as standards.

A common demand-estimation approach uses data on expenditure patterns for various types of public services (Deacon, 1977, p. 209). These figures, again often expressed on a per capita basis, can be used to estimate present demand. When related to population projections, they also can yield estimates of future demand. To judge whether an area is underserved, local expenditure ratios are often compared with national averages or averages in comparable areas. Rural analysts have experienced some difficulty estimating costs since little data has been reported on areas of less than 50,000 in population (Schreiner, 1976, p. 57). A comparison of unit costs per capita for community services in metropolitan and nonmetropolitan areas may be found in *Micropolitan Development* by Tweeten and Brinkman (pp. 199-225).

The validity of these types of standards has been questioned because there is little evidence that per capita demand is constant among areas of the country or that equal per capita dollar inputs produce equal unit outcomes. Since the provision of community services eventually depends upon the availability of resources, per capita expenditure levels play a central role in planning for community services. However, they must be used with caution.

Per capita expenditure figures do indicate that substantially smaller amounts per resident are being spent on community services in smaller towns and rural areas. Table 2 shows these levels for selected services and selected city sizes. One interpretation of these data has been that, assuming equal output per dollar, smaller areas receive less service than larger areas. However, Stocker has calculated that the lower per capita expenditures are attributable in some cases to lower wage rates in rural areas, not lower levels of service (1977, p. 33). In education, for example, he found that the per capita local expenditures were 5 percent lower in the smallest counties, compared to all counties, but that the earnings of the teachers in these counties were 26 percent lower than the overall average. In rural areas the number of teachers per 10,000 population was 20 percent greater than the national average. Thus, he concludes that rural areas have greater teacher-pupil ratios but pay less for them. Whether there is a difference in teaching quality among the various size areas has not been answered (pp. 33-34). Using the teacher-pupil ratio standard alone overlooks other important measures of education in rural areas. For example, it ignores nonenrollment or sporadic enrollment among children and the lack of schooling among adults.

As another example of the problem with per capita standards, it was found that rural physicians work more hours per week than urban physicians and see more patients per hour as well. Thus the quantity of service is underestimated if only a per capita measure is employed (Cordes, 1977, p. 237). But here again other measures of adequacy must be considered. For example, in some rural counties the infant mortality rate is twice the national average, and a larger number of bed-disability days per person are suffered in nonmetropolitan areas as well.

Although standards have their shortcomings, they are widely used because of the lack of alternative low-cost, easily obtainable information. Using standards is certainly appropriate for making initial estimates of demand and cost. Standards for a number of community services are available in published form and from consultation with professional organizations.

Table 2. Per Capita Community Service Expenditures by Size of Municipality

Population

Service	1,000,000 or more	300,000 to 499,999	25,000 to 49,999	10,000 to 24,999	5,000 to 9,999	2,500 to 4,999	Less than 2,500
Education	125.14	57.89	29.05	13.65	7.74	2.55	3.31
Highways	19.10	20.65	20.15	20.41	19.88	20.49	19.67
Public Welfare	120.43	6.18	2.12	.78	.39	.25	.34
Hospitals	56.48	6.80	10.07	6.45	6.91	3.24	.04
Health	19.60	4.70	1.31	.87	.52	.39	.08
Police	64.57	31.31	21.75	19.82	17.75	16.34	12.20
Fire	27.00	22.07	16.16	11.34	6.81	5.30	1.28
Sewage	16.03	17.85	15.10	14.65	15.36	14.64	2.24
Parks & Recreation	13.21	20.57	10.19	7.71	5.79	4.70	.87
Housing & Urban Renewal	31.81	11.99	4.85	2.13	1.89	1.14	.00
Libraries	6.06	3.99	3.05	2.30	1.65	1.22	.25
All Services	636.38	296.37	188.41	143.92	123.69	114.10	91.92
Local Tax Revenue	292.27	131.15	96.43	71.84	57.73	49.44	40.23
General Revenue (TOTAL)	620.50	296.00	185.98	143.75	120.14	106.38	91.40

Source: U.S. Bureau of the Census, *1972 Census of Governments.*

Health Delivery Standards

Rural Health Services: Organization, Delivery, and Use edited by Hassinger and Whiting discusses the current status of health care in rural areas. Included in the volume are data about the physician-population ratios of metropolitan and nonmetropolitan areas and a comparison of physician-demand standards. It also discusses alternative service-delivery models and the financing of rural health care.

In *Needs Assessment for Medical Services* Sam Cordes distinguishes between need and demand for medical services. He identifies demand as the quantity of medical services an individual or community is able and willing to purchase. Need, he argues, refers to the quantity of medical services an individual or community should have regardless of economic considerations.

Communities that wish to plan and develop primary health care systems should obtain professional assistance. Many of the issues, obstacles and options in primary health care systems development are contained in *Developing Primary Health Care for Rural Areas in North Carolina* by Howard and Ashley, *Building a Rural Health System* by the Bureau of Community Health Services, and *Developing a Rural Primary Health Center* by the Central Pennsylvania Health Council.

A cost analysis of alternative techniques for delivering rural mental health services may be found in "Regional Planning for the Delivery of Community Mental Health/Mental Retardation Services in Texas" by Hartling and Cox.

Rx: For Small Towns Who Need Doctors, by Wood Simpson, gives advice about how to recruit a physician. It contains a list of organizations to contact, advice about how to advertise, and tips on interviewing prospective doctors. How one community obtained a physician through the National Health Corps under the U.S. Attorney General's office can be found in *Recruiting Physicians in a Rural Area: The Role of the National Health Service Corps.* by Webb Smalling. Strategies for attracting physicians are also discussed in *Rural Health Services: Organization, Delivery, and Use* by Hassinger and Whiting.

If the provision of emergency medical services is a need in your area, the following references should be helpful: *Provid-*

ing Emergency Medical Services by the International City Management Association, and the *Delivery of Rural Emergency Services Systems,* by Roth, Mullner and Goldberg.

Human Services

Human Services in the Rural Environment Reader edited by David Bast gives an overview of the problems and techniques of delivering social services to poor, rural agricultural communities with dispersed populations. The eleven cases reported suggest the need to identify clearly the group targeted for service. They also indicate that service delivery is complicated by transportation problems and the lack of community awareness of the services available.

Parks and Recreation Standards

Standards for parks and recreational areas have been developed, but are primarily applicable to urban areas. *How Effective Are Your Community Services* by the Bureau of Outdoor Recreation and *National Park Recreation and Open Space Standards* by Robert Bucchner for the National Recreation and Park Association provide some guidance, but also consult *Rural Environmental Planning* in which Frederic O. Sargent argues that the methods of estimating recreation needs for urban areas are inappropriate for rural areas. Economic demand analysis, trend analysis and planning standards are rejected in favor of a public participation process which relates the recreational potential of an area to costs and to the attitudes of the public (pp. 115-127). Sargent also provides a set of recently developed recreation standards for rural towns (p. 120) and an evaluation system for recreation site development (pp. 196-199).

Other sources that might be helpful when projecting the need for recreation and planning its development include *Forecasting Recreation in The United States* by Cicchetti, *Outdoor Recreation Planning* by Jubenville, and *Urban Recreation Planning* by Gold. Standards for estimating park demand, as well as physical design standards may be found in *Planning Design Criteria* by DeChiara and Koppelman.

Recreational land development, occurring across the country, can be both a stimulus to rural economies or a threat to the environment. If your community is experiencing second home development, (the national average of second homes by region is 3.1 percent), you will want to obtain *Subidividing Rural America* by the American Society of Planning Officials.

Fire Protection

Standards and procedures for fire protection service are available in several publications, including the *Community Fire Protection Master Planning Manual* by the U. S. Department of Commerce, the *Standard Grading Schedule* by the American Insurance Association, and the *Fire Protection Handbook* by the National Fire Protection Association. Several studies dealing with rural areas may be particularly useful. *Economics of Rural Fire Protection in the Great Plains* by Childs and Docksen draws upon data from case studies in Oklahoma. Although not focusing upon a western area, you might examine *Alternatives for Providing Fire Protection Service to Unincorporated Areas in Tennessee* by James, and *Guidebook for Establishing a Rural Fire Department* by the East Tennessee Development District.

Although not a book of standards, *How Effective Are Your Community Services?* by Hatry *et al.* should be consulted when planning community services. The book identifies a range of performance measures and procedures for obtaining the measures. The services discussed include solid waste collection and disposal, recreation and library services, crime control, fire protection, water supply, transportation, and transit.

Delivery Problems

The delivery of community services, especially human services, to those rural people who are not being adequately served will present problems for reasons touched upon in other parts of this book. These services will have to be delivered over large geographic areas with low population densities. The costs of delivering these *additional* services, in contrast to current delivery levels, may be greater on a per capita basis because the most difficult-to-reach persons will have to be served. This may be especially true when transportation costs are included in the cost of delivering a service. Since some persons are not receiving services because they have no way to reach the service, it may be necessary to transport the service to them, or them to the service. A study of rural service delivery indeed found that transportation was the primary obstacle to providing human services such as health care to rural people—especially children and older people (Office of Rural Development, 1976, p. 33).

Many authors have argued that service delivery in rural areas is fragmented, uncoordinated, and fraught with problems because the delivery systems are based on modes appropriate only to urban areas (Rogers and Whiting, 1976, p. iii). Even in rural areas two or more agencies may provide similar services. Furthermore, the quality of rural community services is affected by the absence of population concentrations that permit specialization (Schreiner, 1976, p. 26).

The response to these criticisms has included attempts to integrate service delivery. Agencies with compatible objectives, service elements, and client groups would be linked to provide service delivery in a "coordinated and comprehensive" way (Williams, 1976, p. 203). Experiments in services integration have been conducted. One such experiment involved the use of human resources coordinators in an attempt to get human services to rural people (Jones, Hammer and Forsyth, 1976). In Montana, a services coordinator brought the human-service providers of the target county together for the first time. An agreement to cooperate led to the development of a facility to house all the county human-service agencies.

Other techniques might also be used to increase the effectiveness of rural service delivery. Interjurisdictional agreements can be used to provide services to isolated areas (Vlasin, 1976, p. 386). Another option would be to provide specialized services through a centralized service, but to have circuit riders take the services to smaller towns on a regular basis (Williams, 1976, p. 225).

Financing Community Services

It is likely that nonmetropolitan areas will need assistance with the financing of community services. Rural areas have about 20 percent less fiscal resources to draw upon, compared to urban areas (Stocker, 1976, p. 34), but obviously financial capacity varies among rural areas and small towns. A report by the Office of Rural Development cited lack of community resources among the problems of providing human services to rural areas. "Many local rural governments lack the resources to meet even the basic service needs of their citizens—water and sewerage, education, police and fire protection—let alone the special services needed by vulnerable sub-populations" (Office of Rural Development, 1976, p. 32). This lack of resources was attributed to a flow of capital to urban areas because of the takeover of family-based agriculture production by large urban-based corporations, and to outmigration that has both reduced the population and tax base of rural areas and increased the dependent portion (retirees and children) of the rural population.

Although federal and state funds are sometimes available for community service development and delivery, these services may have to be developed from local sources of revenue. Much has been made of the fact that, on a per capita basis, federal funds for human resources have gone mainly to metropolitan areas. This has been particularly so for those services to low-income families with children, and federal housing funds (Tweeten and Brinkman, 1976, pp. 16-17).

Sources of local revenue are somewhat limited, consisting mainly of user fees, property and income taxes, and contributions. Federal assistance is available through several sources, including revenue sharing, the Rural Development Act, and other assistance programs.

User Charges

User charges are supported by persons who believe there should be a link between benefits and individual payments. The use of this type of charge has grown considerably during recent decades, from 12.9 percent of general revenues collected in 1953 to 24.1 percent in 1971-72. Private provision of user-charge financed services is more common in rural and nonmetropolitan areas (Hitzhusen, 1977, p. 44). However, as mentioned earlier, user fees cannot be relied upon to finance a number of community services.

Property Tax

The property tax is the major source of revenue for rural government. In the Great Plains states it generates approximately 90 percent of all local tax revenue. It is perhaps trite to mention the resistance to increasing this tax. Its elimination, however, would be disastrous for many rural areas, since for some locales there are no alternatives.

Income Taxes

If an area contains substantial wage and salary employment, an income tax (locally withheld or a piggy-back arrangement with the state) would be a source of potential revenue. Local income taxes are usually viewed as a supplement to other revenue sources rather than as a replacement for them. See *Micropolitan Development* by Tweeten and Brinkman for more information about alternative ways to finance private and public development, including the pros and cons of alternative taxes (pp. 365-407).

Contributions

Fund-raisers, bake sales, and other voluntary activities contribute to the support of rural services. Estimates of the dollar value of these contributions suggest that they are often major sources of revenue, especially for smaller towns (Hitzhusen, 1977, p. 45). However, it would seem prudent not to rely upon this method as the basic source of program funding.

Revenue Sharing

General revenue sharing does provide additional options to communities. However, other federal programs provide greater amounts of aid to projects in rural areas, and governmental units may experience year-to-year fluctuations in the amount of revenue sharing received (Farber, 1977, pp. 97-98).

The Rural Development Act.

In addition to funds for rural housing assistance, the Rural Development Act provides community facility loans and funding for fire protection. Section 104 of the Rural Development Act authorizes community facility loans for towns of 10,000 or less in population. The funds can be used for sewer and water service, recreational development, fire and rescue service, etc. Section 401 of the Rural Development Act authorizes the Secretary of Agriculture to provide financial, technical and other assistance for training and equipment of local forces to prevent and control fires in rural areas.

Other Federal Assistance

Because of the number of federal assistance programs that are available for community services, it would not be possible to begin to report about them here. But help is available through the Federal Assistance Programs Retrieval System (FAPRS). This computer-based information system provides data about federal aid programs to inquirers throughout the country. FAPRS is designed to identify specific federal aid programs for which a particular community may be eligible. It contains data about federal domestic assistance programs grouped into eight community facilities categories. It also includes eligibility information on all counties in the nation. After entering the name of the community for which assistance is needed, and the name of the county and state in which the community is located, the computer asks a series of questions about the community and type of aid requested. The computer then prints out by program name and number all the federally-funded programs for which the community is qualified. The inquirer can then examine the *Catalog of Federal Domestic Assistance* to find program details, to identify the most appropriate source of aid, and to obtain information about initiating an application. To arrange to use this service contact your cooperative extension service.

Conclusion

Rural areas and small towns face many problems in the upcoming years, but they may also be able to take advantage of new opportunities. Furthermore, many rural areas and small towns are attacking their problems with vigor and, as this chapter should indicate, assistance is available. An important thing to recognize, though, is the distinction between short-range and long-range solutions. It would be foolhardy to promise to solve the so-called rural doctor shortage or to pledge to eliminate substandard rural housing. Not only are these problems long-standing, but their solutions lie in economic forces and national policy unlikely to be influenced by even the most adroit individual. On the other hand, success might be had in developing a regional health services center, or in devising building codes to assure that only sound housing is constructed.

Even if there is unanimous support for a particular service, for example a housing weatherization program or a mental health clinic, the rural planner will encounter problems when he attempts to estimate need, demand, and costs. In today's parlance, "the bottom line" is almost always cost, perhaps cost per capita, sometimes total cost, but very often the size of the local share of total cost.

Not to be overlooked is the critical need for political support for housing and community services planning. An ample base of support (which takes time to develop) will help assure that programs are not terminated prematurely, that they will be evaluated in both quantitative and qualitative terms, and that funding will be continuing. How to develop political support, discussed in other chapters, will depend upon the nature of the case area, the area's prior success with planning activities, and, of course, the planner's own power of persuasion.

The data presented in this chapter report upon the present state of the art and the current conditions in rural areas. It is always risky to speculate about the future, but one thing appears certain: there will be an increasing demand for higher quality local and regional services in rural areas. Across the country rural residents are demanding services comparable to those in urban areas. This increased demand is being generated not only by the expansion of the tastes of long-time residents, but also by the already-developed tastes of urbanites who are moving to small towns and rural areas. We have found that these migrants, satisfied with the rural life at first, soon begin to crave the urban services they left behind.

Whether money will be forthcoming to meet these increased demands is uncertain. One action would be to press for more rural development funding, but concurrent actions must also be taken. This would include the more efficient expenditure of present resources, the leveraging of private investment through public expenditures, and the sharing among locales of scarce resources such as physicians, recreation areas, libraries, etc.

Both the present and anticipated conditions in rural America demand that expenditures on housing and community services be made both efficiently and equitably. The bulk of this chapter laid out the present practice in these areas, and the background references provide additional substantive and procedural information. But as a concluding point, we should recognize that the planning *process* must not be ignored. Any community service that is launched must be well conceived, must meet the needs of the local population, must be thoroughly analyzed in terms of costs and benefits before being implemented, must be administered deftly and monitored carefully, and must be evaluated and revised as necessary. This process (or parts of it) has too often been overlooked as planners and administrators rush to place a program in operation. Although such a planning and evaluation process takes precious time from direct service delivery, successful projects have attributed their accomplishments to similar endeavors. Information about how to design and conduct demonstrations and experiments is available from several sources (Glass, 1976; Guttentag and Saar, 1977; and Weiss, 1976). The point is not that each rural planner should become an expert policy analyst or evaluation researcher, but rather that any program supported through public funds must be the most efficient and effective alternative, must be able to be judged on its merits, and must be able to be replicated if successful. Scarcity of resources implies that one shot may be all that we receive. It had better be our best shot.

BIBLIOGRAPHY

Chapter II, Policies and Plans

General

Beal, Franklyn M. "Defining Development Objectives." *Principles and Practice of Urban Planning.* Edited by W. I. Goodman and E. C. Freund. Washington, DC: International City Managers Association, 1968.

Black, Alan. "The Comprehensive Plan." *Principles and Practice of Urban Planning.* Edited by W. I. Goodman and E. C. Freund. Washington, DC: International City Managers Association, 1968.

Hasbrouck, Sherman. *Pragmatic Planning: An Alternative to Comprehensive Planning.* Orono, ME: University of Maine, 1974.

Lassey, William R. *Planning in Rural Environments.* New York: McGraw-Hill, 1977.

Levy, Clifford V. *A Primer for Community Research.* San Francisco: Far West Research, Inc., 1972.

Small Towns Institute. *Small Town.* (A monthly newsjournal.) P. O. Box 517, Ellensburg, WA, 98926.

Stuart, Darwin. *Evaluating Alternative Plans: Methods, Problems, Guidelines.* Planning Advisory Service Report No. 336. Chicago: American Planning Association, 1978.

Wyoming, Office of the Chief of State Planning. Department of Economic Planning and Development. *A Planning and*

Management Handbook for Wyoming Local Jurisdictions. Planning Information Series. vol. 3. Denver, CO: Oblinger-Smith Corporation, 1976.

Capital Improvements Programming

Blair, Lachlan F. "Programming Community Development." *Principles and Practice of Urban Planning*. Edited by W. I. Goodman and E. C. Freund. Washington, DC: International City Managers Association, 1968.

Evans, Richard D. *Guidelines for Municipal Capital Programming*. Boston: Commonwealth of Massachusetts, Department of Community Affairs, 1975.

League of Kansas Municipalities. *A Guide for Capital Improvements Programming and Budgeting in Kansas Cities*. Topeka, KS, 1976.

Minnesota State Planning Agency. Office of Local and Urban Affairs. *Capital Improvement Programs: A Guide for Minnesota Communities*. St. Paul, MN, 1974.

Moak, Lennox L., and Killian, Kathryn W. *A Manual of Suggested Practice for the Preparation and Adoption of Capital Programs and Capital Budgets by Local Governments*. Chicago: Municipal Finance Officers Association of the United States and Canada, 1964.

U.S. Department of Housing and Urban Development. Urban Management Assistance Administration. Office of Metropolitan Development. *Capital Improvements Programming in Local Government*. Washington, DC: Government Printing Office, 1969.

Citizen Participation

Illinois Department of Local Government Affairs. Office of Research and Planning. *Citizens Guide to Subdivision Regulations*. Springfield, IL, April, 1978.

Van Es, John. "Citizen Participation the Planning Process." *Aspects of Planning for Public Services in Rural Areas.* Edited by D. L. Rogers and L. R. Whiting. Ames, Iowa: North Central Regional Center for Rural Development. Iowa State University, 1976.

Voth, Donald E., and Bonner, William S. *Citizen Participation in Rural Development.* Rural Development Bibliography Series No. 6. Mississippi State, MS: Southern Rural Development Center, 1977.

Negotiation

Adamson, John R. "How One Community Provides New Facilities for New Residents." *Illinois Municipal Review*, June 1976.

"Conflict Resolution." *Environmental Comment.* Washington, DC: Urban Land Institute, May 1977. Entire issue.

Jacobson, Larry G. "Coping with Growth in the Modern Boom Town." *Personnel Journal*, June 1976.

National Association of Counties Research Foundation. *Serving the Offshore Oil Industry: Planning for Onshore Growth: Northampton County Virginia.* NACO Case Studies on Energy Impacts. Washington, DC, 1976.

Rivkin, Malcolm D. *Negotiated Development: A Breakthrough in Environmental Controversies.* Washington, DC: Conservation Foundation, 1977.

Sparta, Illinois. *Summary of Agreement with Peabody Coal Company.* Sparta, IL, Jan. 1978. Unpublished.

U.S. Energy Research & Development Administration. Office of Planning, Analysis, & Evaluation. *Assistance from Energy Developers: A Negotiating Guide for Communities.* Washington, DC: U.S. Government Printing Office, 1977.

Chapter III, Using Natural Resources as a Planning Guide.

McHarg, Ian L. *Design with Nature*. Garden City, NY: Doubleday & Company, Inc., 1959.

New Hampshire, Office of Comprehensive Planning. Office of the Governor. *The Land Book: The Challenge of Making Wise Community Development Decisions: A Practical Guide for the Layman*. Concord, NH, April 1976.

Robinson, G. D., and Speiker, M. eds. *"Nature to be Commanded..." Earth-Science Maps Applied to Land and Water Management*. Geological Survey, Professional Paper 950. Washington, DC: U.S. Government Printing Office, 1978.

Sargent, Frederic O. *Rural Environmental Planning*. Available from author, 330 Spear St., South Burlington, VT 05401, 1976.

Searle, Cecila; Everett, Michael; and Doherty, Joanna. *A Rural Land Use Primer for Rhode Island*. Providence, RI: Rhode Island School of Design, 1976.

Soil Conservation Society of America, Land Use Planning Committee. *Planning and Zoning for Better Resource Use*, Ankeny, IA, 1971.

Chapter IV, Zoning and Development Permit Systems

Zoning, General Works

Bair, Fred H., and Bartley, Ernest R. *The Text of a Model Zoning Ordinance*. 3rd ed. Chicago: The American Society of Planning Officials, 1966.

Crawford, Clan. *Handbook of Zoning and Land Use Ordinances – With Forms*. Englewood Cliffs, NJ: Prentice-Hall, 1974.

Delafons, John. *Land-Use Controls in the United States*. 2nd ed. Cambridge, MA: MIT Press, 1969.

Michigan State University. Cooperative Extension Service. *Rural Zoning in a Nutshell*. Extension folder F-272. East Lansing, MI, 1961.

Scott, Robert L. *The Effect of Nonconforming Land-Use Amortization*. Planning Advisory Service Report No. 280. Chicago: American Society of Planning Officials, 1978.

Toner, William. *Saving Farms and Farmlands: A Community Guide*. Planning Advisory Service Report No. 333. Chicago, IL: American Society of Planning Officials, 1978.

University of Oregon. School of Community Service and Public Affairs. Bureau of Governmental Research and Service. *Rural Zoning: A Suggested County Ordinance Format and Illustrative Examples of Use Zone Provisions*. Planning Bulletin No. 4, rev. ed. Eugene, OR, 1971.

U.S. Department of Commerce. Economic Development Administration. *Zoning for Small Towns and Rural Counties*. Washington, DC: U.S. Government Printing Office, 1975.

Sample Zoning Ordinances

Clark County Zoning Resolution. Clark, SD, April 1974.

Codington County Zoning Regulations and Official Zoning Map. Watertown, SD, n.d.

Dunn County Zoning. Manning, ND, n.d.

Town of Ward Zoning Ordinance. Ward, SD, June 1976.

Development Permit Systems

Lefever, Scott. "A New Framework for Rural Planning." *Urban Land*, April 1978.

Longyear, Barry B. "Project Farmington: The Community as Planner." *Small Town*, January 1978.

Thurow, Charles; Toner, William; and Erley, Duncan. *Performance Controls for Sensitive Lands: A Practical Guide for Local Administrators*. Planning Advisory Service Report Nos. 307/308. Chicago, IL: American Society of Planning Officials, 1975.

Wickersham, Kirk. "The Permit System of Managing Land Use and Growth." *Land Use Law and Zoning Digest*, January 1978.

Sample Town Development Codes

Byron Town Development Code. Byron, WY, n.d.

Ten Sleep Town Development Code. Ten Sleep, WY, n.d.

Chapter V, Rural and Small Town Subdivision Regulations

General

Bair, Frederick H., Jr., Regulation of Modular Housing with Special Emphasis on Mobile Homes, Planning Advisory Service Report No. 271, Chicago, IL., American Society of Planning Officials, 1971.

Brooks, Mary. *Mandatory Dedication of Land or Fees-in-Lieu of Land for Parks and Schools*. Planning Advisory Service Report No. 266. Chicago, IL. American Society of Planning Officials, 1971.

Freilich, Robert H., and Levi, Peter S. *Model Subdivision Regulations: Text and Commentary*. Chicago: American Society of Planning Officials, 1975.

Getzels, Judith N. *Zoning and Subdivision Fees: Current Practice*. Planning Advisory Service Report No. 325. Chicago: American Society of Planning Officials, 1977.

Hendler, Bruce. *Caring for the Land: Environmental Principles for Site Design and Review*. Planning Advisory Service Report No. 328. Chicago: American Society of Planning Officials, 1977.

Illinois Department of Local Government Affairs. Office of Research Planning. *Citizen's Guide to Subdivision Regulations*. Springfield, IL, 1977.

Illuminating Engineering Society of North America. *Roadway Lighting*. Publication RP-8. New York, 1977.

Kapelka, Ron, and Reese, Mike. *Model Subdivision Regulations: Community Series #1*. Cheyenne: Wyoming Department of Economic Planning, 1976.

Kusler, Jon A., and Lee, Thomas A. *Regulations for Flood Plains*. Planning Advisory Service Report No. 277. Chicago: American Society of Planning Officials, 1972.

Lamont, William. "Subdivision Regulations." *The Practice of Local Government Planning. Edited by Frank S. So, et al.* Washington, D.C.: International City Managers Association, 1979.

Lynch, Kevin. *Site Planning*. 2nd ed. Cambridge, MA: The Massachusetts Institute of Technology Press, 1971.

Michigan, Department of Treasury. Local Property Services Division, Bureau of Local Government Services. *A Model Guide for an Ordinance Regulating Subdivision of Land Under Authority of the State Subdivision Control Act of 1967, Act 288, Public Acts of 1967*. Lansing, MI, January 1968.

Montana, Department of Community Affairs. *Montana Model Subdivision Regulations*. Helena, MT, 1975.

National Association of Home Builders. *Land Development Manual*. Washington, DC, 1974.

Nebraska, Office of Planning and Programming. *Land Development Regulations*. 3 volumes. Lincoln, NE, 1975.

Rogal, Brian. *Subdivision Improvement Guarantees*. Planning Advisory Service Report No. 298. Chicago: American Society of Planning Officials, 1974.

Rubinstein, Harvey M. *A Guide to Site and Environmental Planning*. New York: John Wiley and Sons, Inc., 1969.

Thurow, Charles; Toner, William; and Erley, Duncan. *Performance Controls for Sensitive Lands: A Practical Guide for Local Administrators*. Planning Advisory Service Report Nos. 307/308. Chicago: American Society of Planning Officials, 1975.

Urban Land Institute. *Residential Development Handbook*. Washington, DC, 1978.

_____. *Residential Storm Waste Management*. Washington, DC, 1975.

_____. *Residential Streets: Objectives, Principles, and Design Considerations*. Washington, DC, 1974.

U.S. Public Health Service, Center for Disease Control. *Environmental Health Guide for Mobile Home Communities*. Atlanta, GA, 1975.

Yearwood, Richard M. *Land Subdivision Regulation: Policy and Legal Considerations for Urban Planning*. New York: Praeger Publishers, 1971.

Local Ordinances Cited

Board of Clallam County Commissioners. *A Subdivision Ordinance for Clallam County, Washington*. Adopted January 27, 1972.

Board of County Commissioners. *Boulder County Subdivision Regulations*. As amended, August 29, 1972. March 27, 1974.

Board of County Commissioners of Missoula County
(Montana). *Missoula County Subdivision Regulations.*
Resolution #76-67, May 4, 1976.

Butler County Board of Commissioners. *Subdivision and Land
Development Ordinance.* Butler County, Pennsylvania
Ordinance No. 24. 1972, 68 pp.

Codington County. *Codington County Subdivision
Regulations,*
n.d, 15pp.

Cumberland County Joint Planning Board. *Cumberland County
Subdivision Ordinance.* Fayetteville, North Carolina.
(Second printing as amended) January 1975.

Dane County, Wisconsin. *Land Division and Subdivision
Regulations,* May 21, 1970.

Frederick County, Maryland Board of Commissioners. *Frederick
County Subdivision Regulations.* Approved and Adopted
May 19, 1975. 75 pp.

Scotts Bluff County, Nebraska. *Subdivision Regulation,* January
1977.

Chapter VI, Infrastructure Planning

Act Systems, Inc. *Residential Collection Systems.* Publication
SW 97C.1. Washington, DC: U.S. Environmental Protection
Agency, 1974.

Binkley, Clark; Collins, Bert; Kanter, Louis; Alford, Michael;
Shapiro, Michael; and Tabors, Richard. *Interceptor Sewers
and Urban Sprawl.* Lexington, MA: D. C. Heath and Co.,
Lexington Books, 1975.

Commonwealth of Massachusetts, Department of Public Works.
Bureau of Solid Waste Disposal. *Solid Waste Management
Study.* Vol. 1. Boston, MA, 1972.

Fair, G. M; Geyer; and Okun. *Water and Wastewater
Engineering.* New York: John Wiley & Sons, 1965.

Greenberg, Michael H., *et al. Solid Waste Planning in Metropolitan Regions*. New Brunswick, NJ: Center for Urban Policy Research, Rutgers University, 1976.

Hardenbergh, William A. S., and Rodie, Edward B. *Water Supply and Waste Disposal*. Scranton, PA: International Text Book Co., 1961.

Ligman, *et al.* "Household Wastewater Characterization." *Journal of the Environmental Engineering Division*, February 1974.

Metcalf, S. Eddy, Inc. *Wastewater Engineering Collection Treatment Disposal*. New York: McGraw-Hill Book Co., 1972.

Real Estate Research Corporation. *The Cost of Sprawl: Environmental and Economic Costs of Alternative Residential Development Patterns at the Urban Fringe*. Prepared for the Council of Environmental Quality and the Department of Housing and Urban Development. Washington, DC: U.S. Government Printing Office, 1975.

SCS Engineers. *Analysis of Source Separate Collection of Recyclable Solid Waste, Separate Studies*. Publication No. SW-95C.1. Washington, DC: U.S. Environmental Protection Agency, 1974.

Select Committee on Natural Resources. U.S. Senate. *Water Resource Activities in the United States*. Washington, DC: U.S. Government Printing Office, 1960.

Tabors, Richard D.; Shapiro, Michael H.; and Rogers, Peter P. *Land Use and the Pipe*. Lexington, MA: D.C. Heath & Co., Lexington Books, 1976.

U.S. Environmental Protection Agency. Office of Solid Waste Management. *Decision Makers Guide to Solid Waste Management*. Washington, DC: U.S. Government Printing Office, 1976.

Chapter VII, Rural Public Transportation— Problems and Possibilities

Barnett, James T. "Securing Support for Rural Transportation." In *Proceedings of the First National Conference on Rural Transportation*. Washington, DC: U.S. Department of Transportation, Office of University Research, 1976.

Burkhardt, Jon. "Estimating Demand for Rural Transportation." In *Proceedings of the First National Conference on Rural Public Transportation*. Washington, DC: U.S. Department of Transportation. Office of University Research, 1976.

Burkhardt, Jon E., and Lago, Armando M. *Evaluation Methodology for the Rural Highway Public Transportation Program*. Bethesda, MD: Ecosometrics, 1976.

—————.*Methods of Predicting Rural Transit Demand.* Bethesda, MD: Ecosometrics, 1976.

Byrne, Bernard F., and Neumann, Edward S. "Low Cost Models for Demand for Rural Transit." In *Proceedings of the First National Conference on Rural Public Transportation*. Washington, DC: U.S. Department of Transportation, Office of University Research, 1976.

Cantilli, Edmund J., and Shmelzer, June L., eds. *Transportation and Aging: Selected Issues*. Washington, DC: U.S. Government Printing Office, 1970.

Coates, Vary. *Revitalization of Small Communities: Transportation Options, First Year Report*. Washington, DC: U.S. Department of Transportation, 1974.

Coates, Vary, and Weiss, Ernest. *Revitalization of Small Communities: Transportation Options; Second Year Report*. Vol. 1. Washington, DC: U.S. Department of Transportation, 1975.

Colangelo, Donald A., and Glaze, Richard S. "Cross-Classification: An Approach to Passenger Estimation in Short-Range Transit Planning." In *Transportation Research Record No. 638: Transportation Planning Techniques for Small Communities*.

Washington, DC: National Research Council, Transportation Research Board, 1977.

Committee on Agriculture and Forestry. Subcommittee on Rural Development. U.S. Senate, 93rd Congress, 2nd Session. *The Transportation of People in Rural Areas: Rural Transit Needs, Operations, and Management.* Washington, DC: U.S. Government Printing Office, 1974.

_____. *"Rural Transit Operations and Management." In The Transportation of People in Rural Areas: Rural Transit Needs, Operations, and Management.* Washington, DC: U.S. Government Printing Office, 1974.

Committee on Agriculture, Nutrition and Forestry. U.S. Senate, 95th Congress, 1st Session. *National Conference on Nonmetropolitan Community Services.* Washington, DC: U.S. Government Printing Office, 1977.

Crain and Associates. "User-Side Subsidy on a Shared-Ride Taxi Service for Handicapped and Elderly: Danville, Illinois Demonstration." Menlo Park, CA: Crain and Associates, 1977.

Flusberg, Martin. "A Tale of Three Cities." Paper presented at the annual meeting of the American Society of Planning Officials, Indianapolis, IN, 1978.

Flusberg, Martin; Kullman, Brian; and Casey, Robert. *Small Transit Vehicle Survey.* Cambridge, MA: U.S. Department of Transportation, Transportation Systems Center, 1975.

Gerald, John O.; Casavant, K. L.; Tosterud, R. J.; and Brown, William, F. eds. *Proceedings of the National Symposium on Transportation for Agriculture and Rural America.* Washington, DC: U.S. Department of Transportation, Office of Rural Transportation Policy, 1977.

Gilbert, Gorman; Garber, Connie A.; and Foerster, James F. *Establishing Innovative Taxicab Services: A Guidebook.* Washington, DC: U.S. Department of Transportation, 1977.

Grecco, W. L.; Wegmann, F. J.; Spencer, J. A.; and Chatterjee, A. *National Cooperative Highway Research Program*

Report 167: Transportation Planning for Small Urban Areas. Washington, DC: National Research Council, Transportation Research Board, 1976.

Hart, Kathy. "Using Taxis to Provide Rural and Small Area Transportation." In *Proceedings of the First National Conference on Rural Public Transportation.* Washington, DC: U.S. Department of Transportation, Office of University Research, 1976.

Kaye, Ira. "Rural Transportation: Problems and Perspectives." In *Proceedings of the First National Conference on Rural Public Transportation.* Washington, DC: U.S. Department of Transportation, Office of University Research, 1976.

Kidder, Alice E. "Economics of Rural Public Transportation Programs." In *Transportation Research Record No. 578: Transportation for Elderly, Disadvantaged and Handicapped People in Rural Areas.* Washington, DC: Transportation Research Board, 1976.

Kidder, Alice E., and Saltzman, Arthur. *Transportation Problems of the Autoless Worker in a Small City.* Greensboro, NC: North Carolina A & T State University, 1972.

Kirby, Ronald F.; Bhatt, Kiran U.; Kemp, Michael A.; McGillivray, Robert G.; and Wohl, Martin. *Para-Transit: Neglected Options for Urban Mobility.* Washington, DC: The Urban Institute, 1974.

Kulka, Francis P., and Sampson, David J. "The Role of Regional Planning in Local Transit Development." Paper presented at the annual meeting of the American Society of Planning Officials, Indianapolis, IN, 1978.

Lerman, Steven, and Wilson, Nigel H. M. "Analytic Models for Predicting Dial-A-Ride System Performance." In *Transportation Research Board Special Report No. 147: Demand Responsive Transportation.* Washington, DC, Transportation Research Board, 1974.

Levine, Arnold L. "Intercity Bus Service to Rural and Small Urban Communities." In *Proceedings of the National*

Symposium on Transportation for Agriculture and Rural America. Washington, DC, U.S. Department of Transportation, Office of Rural Transportation Policy, 1977.

Macy, Bruce W.; Byrd, Robert E.; Bednar, James M.; and Quinlan, Patricia. *Special Transportation Requirements in Small Cities and Towns*. Washington, DC: U.S. Department of Housing and Urban Development, 1968.

McKelvey, Douglas J. *Evaluating Rural Public Transportation*. Washington, DC: U.S. Department of Transportation, Office of University Research, 1977.

_____. *Guidelines and Considerations in Planning and Operating Transportation Systems for Older Americans*, Working Paper No. 15. Iowa City: University of Iowa, Center for Urban Transportation Studies, 1976.

_____. ed. *Proceedings of the First National Conference on Rural Public Transportation*. Washington, DC: U.S. Department of Transportation, Office of University Research, 1976.

Mitre Corporation. *Demand-Responsive Transportation System Planning Guidelines*. McLean, VA: Mitre Corporation, 1974.

National Area Development Institute. *Meeting Rural Transportation Needs, Part II, Prelude to Legislation to Solve the Growing Crisis in Rural Transportation*. Washington, DC: U.S. Government Printing Office, 1975.

National Research Council, Transportation Research Board. *Transportation Research Record No. 164: Paratransit: Proceedings of a conference held November 9-12, 1975*. Washington, DC, 1976.

_____. *Transportation Research Record No. 638: Transportation Planning Techniques for Small Communities*. Washington, DC, 1977.

Patton, Carl V.; Lienesch, William C.; and Anderson, James R. "Busing the Rural Elderly." *Traffic Quarterly*, 29, December 1975.

Pennsylvania Department of Agriculture. Office of Planning and Research. *A Rural Transportation System*. Harrisburg, PA: Pennsylvania Department of Agriculture, 1973.

Peterson, Ernest J., and Smith, Robert L. Jr. "Estimating Demand for Rural Transportation." In *Proceedings of the First National Conference on Rural Public Transportation*. Washington, DC: U.S. Department of Transportation, Office of University Research, 1976.

Resource Management Corporation. *The Transportation Needs of the Rural Poor*. Washington, DC: U.S. Department of Transportation, Office of Research and Development, 1969.

Rupprecht, Erhardt O. "Private Motor Vehicles — Rural America's Pervasive Transportation Mode." In *Proceedings of the National Symposium on Transportation for Agriculture and Rural America*. Washington, DC: U.S. Department of Transportation, Office of Rural Transportation Policy, 1977.

Stocker, Frederick D. "Fiscal Needs and Resources of Nonmetropolitan Communities." In *National Conference on Nonmetropolitan Community Services Research*. Washington, DC: U.S. Government Printing Office, 1977.

Tardiff, Timothy J.; Lam, Tenny N.; and Dana, James P. "Small City and Rural Transportation Planning: A Review." Irvine, CA: University of California, Institute of Transportation Studies, 1977.

U.S. Department of Agriculture. Economic Research Service. *Transportation in Rural America, Part 1, Prelude to Legislation to Solve the Growing Crisis in Rural Transportation*. Washington, DC, U.S. Government Printing Office, 1975.

U.S. Department of Agriculture and the National Council for the Transportation Disadvantaged. *Rural Rides: A Practical Handbook for Starting and Operating a Rural Public Transportation System*. Rio Grande, NJ: Cape May Department of Transportation, 1978 (Preliminary edition).

U.S. Department of Health, Education and Welfare. Administration on Aging. *Transportation for the Elderly: The State-of-the-Art*. Washington, DC, 1975.

_____. *Transportation Services for the Elderly – Planning Handbook*. Washington, DC, 1975.

U.S. Department of Health, Education and Welfare. Office of Human Development Services. "OHDS Transportation Demonstration Program." In *OHD Fact Sheet*. Washington, DC, August 1977.

U.S. Department of Transportation. *A Directory of Vehicles and Related System Components for the Elderly and Handicapped*. Washington, DC: U.S. Government Printing Office, 1975.

U.S. Department of Transportation. Office of the Secretary. Broadcast/Audio Visual Division. "Transit Options for Small Communities." Washington, DC, 1976.

U.S. Department of Transportation. Transportation Systems Center. *Demand-Responsive Transportation: State-of-the-Art Overview*. Washington, DC, 1974.

_____. *Rural Passenger Transportation – State-of-the-Art Overview*. Cambridge, MA, 1976a.

_____. *Small City Transit Characteristics: An Overview*. Washington, DC, 1976b.

_____. *Small City Transit, Merced, California: Dial-A-Ride Transit in an Agricultural Community*. Washington, DC, 1976c.

_____. *Small City Transit, Merrill, Wisconsin: Point Deviation Service in a Rural Community*. Washington, DC, 1976d.

Webb, Charles A. "The Role of Inter-City Transit." In *Proceedings of the First National Conference on Rural Public Transportation*. Washington, DC: U.S. Department of Transportation, Office of University Research, 1976.

Wolfe, Audley, Jr. "TRIP: A Transportation Demonstration Project in West Virginia." In *Proceedings of the First National Conference on Rural Public Transportation.* Washington, DC: U.S. Department of Transportation, Office of University Research, 1976.

Chapter VIII, Housing and Community Services

Adler, Martin R., and Grenell, Peter. "An Interagency Residential Structural Strategy." In *Planners Notebook*, 2. Chicago: American Society of Planning Officials, April 1973, pp. 1-6.

Ahlbrandt, Roger S. *Flexible Code Enforcement: A Key Ingredient in Neighborhood Preservation Programming.* Washington, DC: National Association of Housing and Redevelopment Officials, 1976.

American Friends Service Committee. *Florida Rural Housing Problems and the Farmers Home Administration.* Washington, DC: Rural Housing Alliance, 1971.

American Insurance Association. *Standard Grading Schedule.* New York: American Insurance Association, 1974.

American Society of Planning Officials. *Subdividing Rural America: Impacts of Recreational Lot and Second Home Development.* Washington, DC: Council on Environmental Quality, 1976.

Babbie, Earl R. *Survey Research Methods.* Belmont, CA: Wadsworth, 1973.

Banks, Nancy. "Californians Tackle the Chore of Housing the Rural Poor." In *Planning*, 43. October 1977, pp. 20-23.

Bast, David, ed. *Human Services in the Rural Environment Reader.* Rhinelander, WI: University of Wisconsin—Extension, 1977.

Beale, Calvin L. *The Revival of Population Growth in Nonmetropolitan America.* Washington, DC: U.S. Department of Agriculture, 1975.

Bird, Ronald and Kampe, Ronald. *Twenty-five Years of Housing Progress in Rural America: Agricultural Economic Report No. 373*. Washington, DC: Economic Research Service, USDA, 1977.

Bish, Robert L. "Public Choice Theory: Research Issues for Nonmetropolitan Areas." In *National Conference on Nonmetropolitan Community Services Research*, 1977, pp. 125-140.

Buechner, Robert. *National Park Recreation and Open Space Standards*. Washington, DC: National Recreation and Park Association, 1970.

Bureau of Community Health Services, U.S. Public Health Service. *Building a Rural Health System*. Rockville, MD: U.S. Department of Health, Education and Welfare, 1976.

Bureau of Outdoor Recreation. *How Effective Are Your Community Recreation Services?* Washington, DC: U.S. Government Printing Office, 1973.

Burns, Leland S., and Mittelbach, Frank G. "Efficiency in the Housing Industry." In *Housing and Economics*, 1970, pp. 119-185.

Butler, Stephen; Peck, Susan; and Cavanaugh, Gordon. "Alternative Low Income Housing Delivery Systems." In *Housing in the Seventies: Working Papers, vol. 1, Washington, DC: U.S. Government Printing Office, 1976, pp. 635-690.*

Central Pennsylvania Health Council. *Developing a Rural Primary Health Center*. Lewisburg, PA: Central Pennsylvania Health Council, 1975.

Childs, Dan; Doeksen, Gerald; and Frye, Jack. *Economics of Rural Fire Protection in the Great Plains*. Washington, DC: U.S. Department of Agriculture, 1977.

Cicchetti, Charles. *Forecasting Recreation in the United States* Lexington, MA: Lexington Books, 1973.

Committee on Agriculture and Forestry, U.S. Senate. 94th Congress, 1st Session. *The Economic and Social*

Condition of Nonmetropolitan America in the 1970's.
Washington, DC: U.S. Government Printing Office, 1975.

Committee on Agriculture, Nutrition, and Forestry, U.S. Senate.
95th Congress, 1st Session. *National Conference on
Nonmetropolitan Community Services Research.*
Washington, DC: U.S. Government Printing Office, 1977.

Committee on Banking, Housing, and Urban Affairs, U.S. Senate.
93rd Congress, 2nd Session. *Oversight on Rural Housing
Programs. Hearings Before the Subcommittee on Housing
and Urban Affairs.* Washington, DC: U.S. Government
Printing Office, 1974.

Cordes, Sam M. "Distribution of Physician Manpower." *Rural
Health Services: Organization, Delivery, and Use*, 1976,
pp. 56-80.

_____. "Needs Assessment for Medical Services." In
*National Conference on Nonmetropolitan Community
Services Research*, 1977, pp. 231-242.

Deacon, Robert T. "Review of the Literature on the Demand for
Public Services." In *National Conference on
Nonmetropolitan Community Services Research*, 1977,
pp. 207-229.

DeChiara, Joseph, and Koppelman, Lee. *Planning Design
Criteria*. New York: Van Nostrand Reinhold, 1969.

Dexter, Lewis Anthony. *Elite and Specialized Interviewing.*
Evanston, IL: Northwestern University Press, 1970.

Dillman, Don A. "Preference Surveys and Policy Differences:
Our New Tools Need Not be Used in the Same Old Way."
In *National Conference on Nonmetropolitan Community
Services Research*, 1977, pp. 259-275.

Drury, Margaret. *Mobile Homes: The Unrecognized Revolution
in American Housing*. New York: Praeger Publishers,
1972.

East Tennessee Development District. *Guidebook for
Establishing a Rural Fire Department*. Knoxville, TN,
1976.

Elgin, Duane; Thomas, Tom; Logothetti, Tom; and Cox, Sue. *City Size and the Quality of Life: An Analysis of the Policy Implications of Continued Population Concentration.* Menlo Park, CA: Stanford Research Institute, 1974.

Executive Office of the President and the Office of Management and Budget. *Catalog of Federal Domestic Assistance.* Washington, DC: U.S. Government Printing Office, 1977.

Farber, William O. "Revenue Sharing and Rural Local Government: A New Look at Priorities." In *National Conference on Nonmetropolitan Community Services Research*, 1977, pp. 95-101.

Farmers Home Administration. *Acts of Congress Administered by or Affecting the Farmers Home Administration.* Washington, DC, 1977.

"Four Rural Communities Try A Housing Consortium." In *Practicing Planner*, 7 March, 1977, pp. 6-7.

Fuguitt, Glenn V., and Zuiches, James J. "Residential Preferences and Population Distribution." In *Demography*, 12, August 1975, pp. 491-504.

Glass, Gene V., ed. *Evaluation Studies Review Annual*, vol. 1. Beverly Hills, CA: Sage, 1976.

Gold, Seymour M. *Urban Recreation Planning.* Philadelphia: Lea & Febiger, 1973.

Greendale, Alexander, and Knock, Stanley F., eds. *Housing Costs and Housing Needs.* New York: Praeger, 1976.

Grigsby, William G. *Housing Markets and Public Policy.* Philadelphia: University of Pennsylvania Press, 1963.

Guttentag, Marcia, and Saar, Shalom, eds. *Evaluation Studies Review Annual*, vol. 2. Beverly Hills, CA: Sage, 1977,

Hartling, James E., and Cox, Walter. "Regional Planning for the Delivery of Community Mental Health/Mental Retardation Services in Texas." In *Innovation and Action in Regional Planning*, 1977, pp. 174-198.

Hassinger, Edward W., and Whiting, Larry R., eds. *Rural Health Services: Organization, Delivery and Use*. Ames, IA: Iowa State University Press, 1976.

Hatry, Harry P.; Blair, Louis H.; Fisk, Donald M.; Gresner, John M.; Hall, John R. Jr.; and Schaenman, Philip S. *How Effective Are Your Community Services? Procedures for Monitoring the Effectiveness of Municipal Services*. Washington, DC: Urban Institute, 1977.

Heinz, Charles. "Two Pennsylvania County Authorities Develop New Section 8 Housing Through Innovative Financing." In *Journal of Housing*, 35, April 1978, pp. 167-169.

Hitzhusen, Fred J. "Non-Tax Financing and Support of 'Community' Services: Some Policy Implications for Nonmetropolitan Governments." In *National Conference on Nonmetropolitan Community Services Research*, 1977, pp. 43-53.

Hitzhusen, Fred, and Napier, Ted. "A Rural Public Services Policy Framework and Some Applications." In *Rural Policy Research Alternatives*, 1978, pp. 127-149.

Howard, Dick, and Ashley, David. *Developing Primary Health Care for Rural Areas in North Carolina*. Lexington, KY: Council of State Governments, 1977.

Hyman, Herbert H. *Interviewing in Social Research*. Chicago: University of Chicago Press, 1975.

International City Management Association. *Providing Emergency Medical Services – Management Information Service*. August 1974.

James, George E. *Alternatives for Providing Fire Protection Service to Unincorporated Areas in Tennessee*. Knoxville, TN: Tennessee State Planning Office, Local Planning Division, 1975.

Jones, Lonnie L., and Morgan, Larry C. "Consumer Responses to Rural Public Service Problems in Great Plains States." In *National Conference on Nonmetropolitan Community Services Research*, 1977, pp. 243-257.

Jones, Phil; Hammer, Jean; and Forsyth, Scott. *Addressing the Diverse Needs of Rural Counties: Report on the 1974-1975 Rural Human Resources Program.* New York: National Association of Counties Research Foundation, 1976.

Jubenville, Alan. *Outdoor Recreation Planning.* Philadelphia: W. B. Saunders, 1976.

Mandelker, Daniel R., and Montgomery, Roger. *Housing in America: Problems and Prospects.* Indianapolis: Bobbs-Merrill, 1973.

McDowell, Bruce. *Innovation and Action in Regional Planning.* Urbana, IL: University of Illinois, Bureau of Urban and Regional Planning Research, 1977.

Mishan, Edward J. *Cost-Benefit Analysis*, 2d ed. New York: Praeger, 1976.

Mitchell, Helen. "Section 8, Farmers Home Administration Programs Combined to Provide Rural Housing in Missouri." In *Journal of Housing*, 32. October 1975, pp. 494-498.

Musgrave, Richard A., and Musgrave, Peggy B. *Public Finance in Theory and Practice.* New York: McGraw-Hill Book Company, 1973.

Myer, Joe. *The Sabotage of Freedom Village.* Washington, DC: Rural Housing Alliance, 1974.

National Fertilizer Development Center, Tennessee Valley Authority. *Quality Housing Environment for Rural Low-Income Families.* Muscle Shoals, AL, 1976.

National Fire Protection Association. *Fire Protection Handbook.* Boston: National Fire Protection Association, 1977.

Office of Rural Development. *Getting Human Services to Rural People.* Washington, DC: U.S. Department of Health, Education and Welfare, 1976.

Parrat, Spencer D. *Housing Code Administration and Enforcement.* Washington, DC: U.S. Government Printing Office, 1970.

Pynoos, Jon; Schafer, Robert; and Hartman, Chester W. *Housing Urban America*. Chicago: Aldine, 1973.

Reeb, Donald J., and Kirk, James T. *Housing the Poor*. New York: Praeger, 1973.

Rogers, David L.; and Whiting, Larry R., eds. *Aspects of Planning for Public Services in Rural Areas*. Ames, IA: North Central Regional Center for Rural Development, 1976.

Roth, Irwin; Mullner, Ross; and Goldberg, Jack. *The Delivery of Rural Emergency Services Systems: A Spatial Analysis*. Chicago: Chicago State University, 1977.

Rothenberg, Jerome. "Elimination of Blight and Slums." In *Housing and Economics*, 1970, pp. 90-106.

Sargent, Frederic O. *Rural Environmental Planning*. Available from the author, 330 Spear St., South Burlington, VT. 05401, 1976.

Schreiner, Dean F. "A Planning Framework for Rural Public Sector Analysis." *Aspects of Planning for Public Services in Rural Areas*, 1976, pp. 24-80.

Schretter, Howard A. *Housing Code Enforcement Study Guide*. Athens, GA: Institute of Community and Area Development, 1971.

————. "Making Codes for the Rural Community." *Planning Frontiers in Rural America*, 1975, pp. 158-161.

Simpson, Wood. *Rx: For Small Towns Who Need Doctors*. Lexington, KY: Municipal League, 1977.

Smalling, Webb. "Recruiting Physicians in a Rural Area: The Role of the National Health Service Corps." *Planning Frontiers in Rural America*, 1976, pp. 176-179.

Stabler, Kenneth E., and Patton, Carl V. "Residents of Small Towns Speak Out on Growth." *Planning and Public Policy*, August 1977, pp. 1-4.

Stegman, Michael. *Housing and Economics*. Cambridge, MA:

Massachusetts Institute of Technology Press, 1970.

Stocker, Frederick D. "Fiscal Needs and Resources of Nonmetropolitan Community Services Research, 1977, pp. 25-41.

Subcommittee on Rural Development, Committee on Agriculture and Forestry, U.S. Senate. 94th Congress, 2d Session. *Planning Frontiers in Rural America: Papers and Proceedings of the Boone Conference.* Washington, DC: U.S. Government Printing Office, 1976.

Sumichrast, Michael, and Seldin, Maury. *Housing Markets: The Complete Guide to Analysis and Strategy for Builders, Lenders and Other Investors.* Homewood, IL: Dow Jones-Irwin, 1977.

Surdock, Pete W.; Davis, Gertrude A.; Myllymaki, Jean H.; and Ranta, Roger. *Montana's Rural Social Service Delivery System.* Helena, MT: Montana Department of Social and Rehabilitation Services, 1974.

Tweeten, Luther, and Brinkman, George L. *Micropolitan Development: Theory and Practice of Greater-Rural Economic Development.* Ames, IA: Iowa State University Press, 1976.

U.S. Bureau of the Census. *County Business Patterns.* Washington, DC: U.S. Government Printing Office, 1977.

_____. *Estimates of Population of Counties and Metropolitan Areas: 1975 and 1976.* Washington, DC: U.S. Government Printing Office, Series P-26, Nos. 26, 27, 34, 41, and 50, 1976.

U.S. Department of Agriculture. *Alternative Rural Housing Program Strategies for FY 1976-1980.* Washington, DC: U.S. Department of Agriculture, 1978.

_____. *Rural Development Progress: Fourth Annual Report of the Secretary of Agriculture to the Congress.* Washington, DC: U.S. Government Printing Office, 1977.

U.S. Department of Commerce. *Community Fire Protection*

Master Planning Manual. Washington, DC: U.S. Government Printing Office, 1977.

U.S. Department of Housing and Urban Development. *A Summary of Findings from HUD Research on Rural Housing and Community Development Programs.* Washington, DC, 1978a.

_____. *FHA Techniques of Housing Market Analysis*. Washington, DC: U.S. Government Printing Office, 1970.

U.S. Department of Housing and Urban Development. *Household Survey Manual*. Washington, DC: U.S. Government Printing Office, 1969.

_____. Programs of HUD. Washington, DC: U.S. Government Printing Office, 1978b.

U.S. Office of Business Economics. *Survey of Current Business*. Washington, DC: U.S. Government Printing Office. Monthly publication.

Vlasin, Raymond O. "Linking Research with Planning: Some Implications and Approaches." *Aspects of Planning for Public Services in Rural Areas*, 1976, pp. 367-402.

Weiss, Carol H. *Evaluation Research: Methods for Assessing Program Effectiveness*. Englewood Cliffs, NJ: Prentice-Hall, 1972.

Williams, Ann. "Planning Service Delivery Systems for Rural, Sparsely Populated Areas." *Aspects of Planning for Public Services in Rural Areas*, 1976, pp. 202-234.

List of Contributors

The persons who have contributed to this book are listed below in alphabetical order:

Stephen B. Friedman (Chapter V), Principal Counselor, Real Estate Research Corporation, Chicago.

Judith Getzels (Editor and Chapter II), Principal Research Associate, APA, Chicago.

Carl V. Patton (Chapters VII and VIII), Director, Bureau of Urban and Regional Planning Research, Department of Urban and Regional Planning, University of Illinois at Urbana-Champaign.

Randy L. Suko (Chapter VIII), Graduate Student, Department of Urban and Regional Planning, University of Illinois at Urbana-Champaign.

Richard D. Tabors (Chapter VI), Lecturer, Urban Studies and Planning, Massachusetts Institute of Technology, Cambridge, Massachusetts.

Charles Thurow (Editor and Chapter IV), Assistant Director of Research, APA, Chicago.

William Toner (Chapter I), Planning Consultant and Writer, Chicago.

George C. Turnbull (Chapter III), Research Analyst, Office of Community Development, Olympia, Washington.

Index

Capital improvements program: and role in implementing plan, 36

Citizen participation: as tool for implementing plan, 36; in planning process, 29-30

Codes, building: enforcement of, 269-271; and housing, 269-271; in rural area, 251; as strategy for planner, 59; as tool for implementing plan, 36

Community services: delivery problems, 288; education, 280; estimating need and demand, 281-288; financing, 289-292; fire prevention, 280; health care, 280; problems in, 276-277; resident satisfaction with, 277-280

Data: on existing conditions needed for development of plan, 28-29; housing, methods for obtaining, 256-258; for inventory of natural resources, 40-42

Design: parameters for size of infrastructure facilities, 163-177; requirements in development, 132-134; of sewerage systems, 195-201; of water supply systems, 185-188

Development: consideration of vegetation in, 40,43,51; effect of geology on, 43,51; effect of soil on, 48-50; effect of topography on, 42-45; effect of water on, 45-48; of environmentally sensitive areas, design requirements of, 132-134; natural resources inventory as basis of, 39-40; permits systems and zoning, 89-95

Enabling legislation: and annexation, 9; and authority of county commissions, 7-8; and extraterritorial power of cities, 8; importance of knowledge of, 7-9; in Old West Region, 19-26; role of planning commission under, 8; sources of information on, 8

Financing: concepts in infrastructure planning, 169-177; of rural housing, 263-266, 268-276; of rural transportation, 241

Fire markers: improvement in subdivision regulations, 127

Geology: and importance in site development, 40,43,51

Grading and drainage: improvement in subdivision regulations, 120-122, 134

Grants and subsidies: for community services, 289-292; for housing, 263-266, 272-276; information about sources of, 11-12; transportation, 232-234; water pollution, 165-166,171,177,189,202